SOCIETY AND THE
EDUCATION OF TEACHERS

SOCIETY TODAY AND TOMORROW

General Editor: A. H. Halsey

Fellow of Nuffield College and Head of the Department
of Social and Administrative Studies, Oxford

*

Society and the
Education of Teachers

WILLIAM TAYLOR, 1930–

FABER AND FABER LTD
24 Russell Square
London

First published in 1969
by Faber and Faber Limited
24 Russell Square London WC1
Printed in Great Britain by
Western Printing Services Limited, Bristol

SBN: 571 08734 5

ACKNOWLEDGEMENTS

This book owes much to discussions with colleagues and students in the Colleges and Universities in which I have worked during the past ten years. The Nuffield Foundation generously provided funds for the surveys of staff referred to in Chapter 8, and the Department of Education and Science similarly supported the study of students' origins reported in Chapter 7.

I am indebted to Roger Wilson, Richard Peters, Roy Niblett, W. A. Campbell Stewart and R. A. Becher for helpful critical comments on parts of the material included.

Sections of Chapters 8 and 9 have previously appeared in article form, and I am grateful to the editors of *Comparative Education*, *Education for Teaching*, *The Sociological Review* and *Universities Quarterly* for permission to reprint.

Bristol
April 1968

CONTENTS

9

INTRODUCTION

No comprehensive general survey of the development and work of the colleges and departments of education has been published for over forty years, and this book makes no claim to fill this particular gap in the educational record. Any such survey would have to give a good deal more attention to the universities' role in the training of teachers, to the Institutes and Schools of Education, to in-service training and the activities of the teachers' professional organizations than I have tried to do here.

My concern is with the relations of teacher education to the institutions, forms of social control and patterns of social change of the society in which it functions, and with social relationships within the colleges themselves. If I have omitted to discuss the broader aspects of the work of these colleges, to praise the good and condemn the bad, it is not because such praise and blame are considered unimportant, but merely that this is not that kind of book. A critical examination of teacher education is neither an apologia or an exposé. All it can try to do is to suggest ways of looking at the problems involved that may lend substance to such apologias and exposés as seem all too likely to be forthcoming during the next decade.

Although much of the book is concerned with describing what goes on in the education of teachers, with the history and sociology of institutions and courses, it also seeks to present a case, which can briefly be stated as follows. Despite the obvious heterogeneity of the people, institutions and procedures involved in the education of teachers, there are certain common features in their orientation to their task and in the forms of organization that have developed to perform it, which enable a distinctive subculture to be identified within the broader culture of English society and education. The elements of this subculture can be isolated, examined and described, and an attempt made to account for their particular character in terms of a variety of strands of historical and social change. But of greater importance are the values that permeate the sub-culture of teacher education. These, again, are diverse and shifting; success in capturing them all within the kind of coarse mesh that must necessarily be used for the purpose is virtually impossible. But some such attempt may at least help to organize our perceptions of all the kinds of teaching and learning and living that go on in and around the colleges and departments of education so as to yield some increment of insight and understanding.

I want to argue that the dominant value orientations of teacher education during the first six decades of the present century have been those of social and literary romanticism. A similar movement of ideas has also affected the primary and secondary schools and the universities (especially where the humanities are pre-eminent), but in no case to the extent shown by institutions for the education of teachers. In these institutions, the romantic infra-structure has shown itself as a partial rejection of the pluralism of values associated with conditions of advanced industrialization; a suspicion of the intellect and the intellectual; a lack of interest in political and structural change; a stress upon the intuitive and the intangible, upon spontaneity and creativity; an attempt to find personal autonomy through the arts; a hunger for the satisfactions of inter-personal life within the community and small group, and a flight from rationality.

The romantic infra-structure of teacher education is multi-determined. Contributions have been made by the ambiguous position of the teacher in society, as guardian of elite member-ship without the right of personal entry to the elite; the prob-lem of giving meaning and significance to the education of that majority of individuals who are unlikely to 'succeed' in the terms dictated by a competitive, status-conscious society; the uncertain position of the educator of teachers, poised between the world of the school and that of the university, belonging to neither, vulnerable to criticism from both; the history of social and intellectual inferiority that has dogged the colleges of education; the impact of the progressive movement in education, with its stress upon the individual child rather than the curriculum, its liberation of mind and spirit from the shackles of academic formalism; all these have played some part in shaping the system of values that characterize the way in which teachers are prepared for their task.

This system of values is discussed in some detail in the final sections of the book. In the first two chapters an attempt is made to draw attention to some aspects of contemporary social change that bear upon the way in which teachers are prepared, and to say something about the numbers and kinds of teachers that are needed. The four chapters that comprise Part Two of the book describe the way in which the colleges of education are organized and controlled, the development of the programme of personal and professional education within them, the existing three-year course, and the relationships between the colleges and the schools in which their students rehearse the role that in due course they will be called upon to perform. Part Three is concerned with the people who are involved in teacher education—the staff of the colleges and departments and the students who come to them. The final chapters analyse social relationships within the college of education and the values of teacher education.

PART ONE
THE SOCIAL AND EDUCATIONAL
CONTEXT OF TEACHER EDUCATION

I

ASPECTS OF SOCIAL CHANGE

THE SOCIAL CONTEXT

Industrialization and the nature of skill

The first major factor that we have to reckon with in examining the character of the social framework within which teachers work and are trained is industrialization. Its effects are so pervasive, its influence on our everyday lives so all-encompassing, that it is all too easy to take for granted the characteristics of our world that stem from industrial growth and technology, and to see these as a kind of natural state in terms of which all other undeveloped, rural societies are abnormal. The industrialized pattern of today owes its origins to the power revolution of the late eighteenth and nineteenth centuries; although an urban existence, surrounded by the apparatus of technological invention, is rapidly becoming the norm for the majority of men and women in Western industrialized societies, and constitutes an implicit target for those countries which are still agrarian and underdeveloped, it is still a very new pattern of life in terms of the length of man's span on earth, and one to which, as our traffic problems, crime rates and housing difficulties show, we have not yet become fully adapted. Wrapped up with industrialization is a whole range of associated changes, linked with technological change in complex patterns of cause and effect. Population growth, the decline of mortality, family limitation, changing roles within the family, improved housing and hygiene are only the most obvious of these.

The population of the world in the middle of the seventeenth century has been estimated as approximately five hundred and forty-five million. By the middle of the twentieth century it had reached two thousand six hundred and twenty-six million, and by 1980 will probably have passed the four thousand million mark. Death control and birth control have had fundamental effects upon the expectancy of life and the size of families. The following diagram shows how life expectancy has changed during the past hundred years and the very restricted life expectancies that were characteristic of earlier periods.

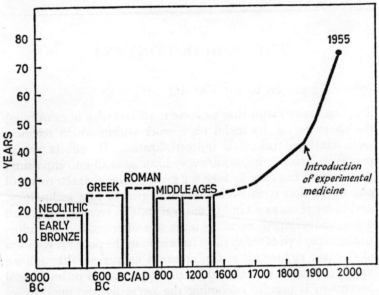

(Based on M. L. Tainter, Bell Telephone Laboratories Inc., quoted Baker, W. O. 'The Dynamism of Technology' in Ginzberg, E. (ed.) *Technology and Social Change*, New York, Columbia University Press, 1964, p. 84.)

These demographic changes are of the greatest importance for the educational system, influencing not only the numbers coming forward for schooling and the number of teachers available to educate them, but also the age structure of the society and the manner in which the family and other institutions perform educational functions.

The task of education in an industrialized society is radically different from that in pre-industrial or non-industrial communities. Taken in its broadest sense, the traditional role of education has been that of 'handing on', of preserving and maintaining culture, of socializing and inducting the young to the patterns of behaviour and belief of the society as a whole or particular groups within it. The family, kin group and neighbourhood are well adapted to provide an education of this kind in an informal, indirect way, without recourse to formal instruction or the setting-up of schools and colleges. In an industrialized society the demand for individual knowledge and skill beyond what can be provided by the family or acquired by informal assimilation requires the creation of specialized educational institutions, which additionally serve to facilitate the social change that accompanies technological development. In the words of Floud and Halsey:

'... modern industrialized societies are distinguished in their structure and development from others of comparable complexity, principally by the institutionalization of innovation – that is to say, by the public and private organization, on an increasingly large scale, of scientific research in the service of economic and military growth. Their occupational structures are characteristically diversified, with relatively high educational qualifications for employment at all levels but the lowest. Education attains unprecedented economic importance as a source of technological innovation, and the educational system is bent increasingly to the service of the labour force, acting as a vast apparatus of occupational recruitment and training. Social selection is added to its traditional function of social differentiation; it must promote new as well as maintain old élites. Furthermore, it must cater to the new educational needs of the mass of population, deriving from the changed status of labour in modern processes of mass production.'[1]

As technology has brought about changes in the structure and organization of industry, so it has altered the pattern and types of skill that are required – always in the direction of more knowledge, more training and additional competence. Technological change has not rendered human skills redundant; it has altered the nature of these skills in the direction of increased complexity and more stringent educational requirements, and the most recent changes have penetrated deeply into those

[1] Halsey, A. H., Floud, J. E. and Anderson, C. A. *Education, Economy and Society.* New York: The Free Press, 1961, p. 2.

19

occupational levels formally classified as unskilled or semi-skilled.[1] In all industrialized countries at the present time there is a shortage of many kinds of skilled labour and an actual or potential surplus of those without qualifications or training–the 'high-school drop-outs' that are so much a problem for the American educationist. In some of these countries –including, to some extent, the British Isles–the school system is still predicated in terms of a demand for hewers of wood and drawers of water that either no longer exists or shortly will not exist. In the early stages of industrialization there were large numbers of unskilled and semi-skilled workers employed in small concerns presided over by individual entrepreneurs, with only a relatively small number of managers and technical staff. Towards the end of the nineteenth and during the early years of the present century the demand for skilled and semi-skilled (production-line) workers began to increase and that for the unskilled labourer to decline. At the same time, with the growing importance of technical knowledge, there was an increase in the numbers of those engaged in supervisory and design functions, and in 'middle management', as a consequence of the growth of the large corporation and trust and the reduction in the numbers of individual owners and entrepreneurs. Today, there is a decreasing demand for unskilled and semi-skilled workers as a consequence of automation. At the same time, there has been a considerable growth of technical, professional, managerial and service levels of employment, and a continuing tendency for the number of individual owners and entrepreneurs to be reduced.

The effect of automation has been to diminish sharply the number of manual workers needed to carry out particular tasks, although its overall effect upon the employment situation is more difficult to assess. Wolfbein has stated:

'. . . we are still at the very beginning of our knowledge of what is happening to the nature of jobs and skill in the new technological age. The little work that has been done in this field seems to indicate a trend towards the need for such forms of higher job competence as diagnostic skill on the part of persons working with machinery, ability to see one's way through

[1] '*15 to 18*'. Report of the Central Advisory Council for Education, England, 1959 (Crowther Report). London: H.M.S.O., 1959.

several strategies in finding machine trouble, ability to organize and interpret information, and ability to take on responsibility and participate in decision-making processes.'[1]

But the measurement of the numbers of people employed in particular industries and on particular processes does not give sufficient emphasis to changes in the nature of skill itself. The nineteenth- and early twentieth-century archetype of the skilled man was the *craftsman*; a whole apparatus of industrial training has been erected around this concept, and may well prove an obstruction to impending changes in the pattern of industrial employment. As an example, we may visualize a skilled workman shaping the leg of a chair on a lathe; with every touch of his chisel or gouge he is exercising his skill, albeit in a manner that is no longer conscious or explicit. Should the tools slip, should he be dissatisfied with his work, he can stop the machine, throw away the raw material and start again; perhaps a few shillings had been wasted. The work of the skilled man of post-industrial society can be visualized in quite different terms. He sits before a bank of dials, supervising the work of a machine; for fifty-nine minutes he appears to do nothing, except check from time to time the readings on particular scales. Then, in the sixtieth minute of his working hour, a particular combination of signals are presented to him, the dials swing round in a particular manner—and if a twenty-thousand-pound process is not to be ruined he must act fast, throw switches, telephone instructions and use a technical skill and understanding that is very different in kind but no less complex and demanding than that of the craftsman at the lathe. Neither of these two figures are typical of their era, but the differences in the concept of skill that they point up are real and significant.

Many of the craftsman's decisions were essentially un-programmed; they could not be made subject to explicit rules, governed by a moment-to-moment and movement-to-move-ment procedure for which explicit training could be provided. What Simon[2] has called the *factual* premises of decision-making could not be laid down beforehand, whilst the *value*

---

[1] Wolfbein, S. L. 'Labor Trends, Manpower and Automation' in Borow, H. *Man in a World of Work.* Boston: Houghton Mifflin, 1964.
[2] Simon, H. A. *Administrative Behaviour.* New York: Free Press, 1945.

premisses could, and were. The craftsman was constrained by his commitment to certain standards, by an internalized sense of responsibility towards the practice of his craft and his fellow practitioners. A similar commitment was required at higher levels, where the range of initiative and degrees of freedom in decision-making were greater; a common educational background and the qualities inherent in the concept of the gentleman and the cultivated man went a good way to control the basic premisses of high-level decision making. Today, however, many of these types of skills are becoming capable of programming; automated production techniques at the one level, and computer analysis at the other, are altering the types of skill and decision-making that the individual is required to exercise.[1] Inter-connected with these changes is a greater pluralism of values, and a tendency for achieved, rather than ascribed statuses to carry a broader mix of value assumptions; these points will require further attention in subsequent chapters in relation to changes in the task of the teacher.

Schools and colleges must necessarily adapt themselves to these changing concepts of skill if they are to contribute to technological development, and the process of doing so is not always an easy one. There is some evidence, for example, that the views we hold regarding the nature of human ability and the limits of individual educability are very much influenced by the particular type of demand that the occupational and social structure is seen as making upon the schools, and these views will clearly have a great deal to do with the way in which we organize our educational system and the pattern of teaching within individual schools.

The Division of Labour

Most of the other characteristics of society to which attention needs to be directed at this stage derive from and in their turn

---

[1] 'As in the military sphere, computers are tending to substitute for "middle management" in the industrial and commercial world, and are thus tending to increase the gulf between the top-level "decision-makers" and the men who still do things on the shop floor. In neither case do we know how the widening gulf is going to be bridged'—Zuckerman, S., 'Hard Facts About the Future', *Sunday Times*, 20 February 1966, p. 27.

influence the phenomena of industrialization and technological change. As society has advanced technically, as, in Durkheim's terms, its volume and density have increased, so it has become necessary for individuals to specialize in their functions and contributions. The division of labour that Adam Smith saw as an element of greater productive efficiency has become characteristic of wider spheres than the economic. It is fashionable to regard this specialization as inimical to the fullest development of the individual personality, although, as Durkheim saw, without it we would lack a good deal of the freedom and opportunities for self-determination that the specialized society provides.

'It is . . . a real illusion which makes us believe that personality was so much more complete when the division of labour had penetrated less. No doubt, in looking from without at the diversity of occupations which the individual then embraces, it may seem that he is developing in a very free and complete manner. But, in reality, this activity which he manifests is not really his. It is society, it is the race acting in and through him; he is only the intermediary through which they realize themselves. His liberty is only apparent and his personality borrowed . . . the progress of individual personality and that of the division of labour depend upon one and the same cause. It is thus impossible to desire one without desiring the other. . . .'[1]

But if specialization is the source of our freedom and prosperity, it can also be the cause of our undoing, as some of the stock figures of contemporary social criticism testify. The scientist who has no awareness of the moral implications of his discoveries and experiments, the teacher who is so concerned with his subject that he lacks all sympathy with the wider educational aims of the school, the worker for whom the daily task has no meaning in the context of an overall product—all these are familiar enough in the literature of popular sociology, in which the concept of alienation has played an important part. What Marx had to say on this subject has a good deal in common with some more recent statements regarding the dangers of a vocational and overspecialized curriculum in the schools.

'In what does the alienation of labour consist? First, that the

[1] Durkheim, E. *The Division of Labour in Society*. New York: Free Press, 1947.

work is *external* to the worker, that it is not a part of his nature, that consequently he does not fulfil himself in his work but denies himself, has a feeling of misery, not of well-being, does not develop freely a physical and mental energy, but is physically exhausted and mentally debased. The worker therefore feels at home only during his leisure, whereas at work he feels homeless. His work is not voluntary but imposed, *forced labour.* It is not the satisfaction of a need, but only a *means* for satisfying other needs ... The alienation of the worker in his product means not only that his labour becomes an object, takes on its own existence, but that it exists outside him, independently and alien to him, and that it stands opposed to him as an autonomous power. The life that he has given to the object sets itself against him as an alien and hostile force. ...'[1]

The achievement of meaning in work, the participation in worthwhile activity for its own sake, is a strong feature of the philosophy of progressive education and has had an especial effect on the work of infant and primary schools and in the education of teachers.

Pluralism and Social Cohesion

The division of labour helped to liberate the individual from the traditional forces characteristic of pre-industrial societies. Freedom has also been enhanced by the greater variety of social settings, by the ability of the individual to leave the family, kinship and neighbourhood group into which he is born and to choose other groups to which he will belong. This freedom is associated with certain costs. 'To be told firmly by tradition just who one is can be experienced as freedom, whereas permission to make original choices can be felt like enslavement to the unknown.'[2] Relationships tend to be *functionally specific* rather than general, diffuse and inclusive; client and customer centred rather than rooted in generalized obligations of mutual

[1] Karl Marx. *Economic and Political Manuscripts.* 1844, Marx-Engels Gesamtausgabe, Vol. I, Pt. 3, pp. 83-4, quoted Bottomore, T. B. and Rubel, M. *Karl Marx: Selected Writings in Sociology and Social Philosophy.* London: C. A. Watts, 1956.
[2] Hunt, E. L. *The Revolt of the College Intellectual.* New York: Aldine Press, 1964, p. 146.

aid and support. For the individual, freedom carries with it the possibilities of loneliness and insecurity; for the society, *pluralism* involves the risk of social cohesion being absent at a time when it is needed to combat outside pressures, of internal dissent undermining the basis of social order. In the plural society there is no single social, philosophical or religious principle to which all subscribe and which serves to constrain individual or group behaviour. A wide diversity of viewpoints flourishes, dissenting groups and associations providing sustenance and support for the dissenting individual.[1] It is a matter of some difficulty to locate the basis of social order and consensus in societies of this kind, to discover what it is that does hold people together, that restrains them from encroaching upon each other's rights and disregarding the interests of other groups on a mass scale, that prevents life from being poor, nasty, solitary and short. One of the sources of cohesiveness is the market, the relationships that people enter into in performing their functions and obtaining the necessities of existence within the overall structure of a political and social system, the obligations and forms of behaviour that the individual must recognize if his own claims are to receive consideration from others. The ultimate constraint of force that is inherent in the law, and tradition and custom also play their part. But in any consideration of the nature of social control and the basis of consensus in a complex and pluralistic society, attention must necessarily be given to the socializing role of the educational system, the means that are used in schools and colleges to impress certain social, political, religious and philosophical beliefs and attitudes upon pupils. This role is one of the most important that the school fulfils; there are almost no examples of educational institutions that do not exert some form of explicit or implicit moral influence upon individuals in addition to the specialized skills and knowledge that they set out to provide. The frequency of references in educational discourse to the need for 'educating the whole man', the attention given to 'character' and the development of good citizenship are all evidence of the importance of this aspect of the work of schools and colleges. The power èlites of a society, however pluralistic

[1] Collier, K. G. *Social Purposes of Education*. London: Routledge and Kegan Paul, 1959.

and free of dogmatic social and religious doctrine the value structure of that society may be, cannot afford to remain indifferent to the nature of the inter-personal relationships that exist in classroom and school and their impact upon the social attitudes and behaviour of pupils. The principal responsibility for shaping such relationships belongs to teachers, and comparatively little direct control can be exercised over how these relationships develop. Hence society is necessarily concerned with the way in which teachers are selected, trained and certified; although responsibility for some part of these processes is sometimes delegated to largely independent bodies, such as the universities and individual colleges, a fairly close oversight is maintained by agencies of political and social control at the national level. It follows that in examining the sociology of teacher education we must pay attention to the procedures that are used to bring influence of this kind to bear, the content of what is communicated and the criteria by means of which colleges select from among the multifarious values and beliefs that are available in the community and society.

Bureaucratic Process

Complexity and the division of labour carry with them other consequences that are of educational significance. Where relationships are no longer simple, unitary and governed by custom and tradition, more has to be written down, formulated into explicit contracts and subjected to legal overview. The variety of specialized groups and organizations, the large number of roles that the individual may fulfil, create complicated patterns of interaction that must be systematized and rationalized if co-operation is to be possible and relationships are not to break down. A specialized corps of administrators comes into existence, and agreed procedures for organizational functioning develop. The term *bureaucracy* is usually employed in a pejorative sense in this country, but for the sociologist it is the key term for a substantial body of research and writing that has followed the classic formulation of Max Weber.[1] The primary components

[1] Weber, M. *Theory of Social and Economic Organization*, edited by Talcott Parsons. New York: Free Press, 1947.

of bureaucratic process are *specialization of function*-the job that each person has to do is defined and he is not normally expected to step outside its limits-*a hierarchy of authority*-who can tell whom to do what is spelled out in formal terms and known to all-*a system of rules*-operating procedures are usually laid down in writing, and careful records are kept of communications both within and outside the organization-and *impersonality*-vacant appointments are advertised for general competition, and it is technical competence rather than social qualifications or being the cousin of the chairman that counts for most. An overall definition of bureaucracy has been attempted by Blau: 'bureaucracy is organization that maximizes efficiency in administration or an institutionalized method of organizing social conduct in the interests of administrative efficiency.'[1]

It will be clear that as a result of the operation of the social factors already discussed in this chapter, the adoption of bureaucratic procedures is tending to become more widespread. A college with a hundred students and eight tutors has little need for any expressly formulated code of administrative conduct; even when it grows to 300 students and 30 tutors it can probably continue to get by with a minimum of paperwork and protocol, although this can sometimes lead to a good deal of administrative muddle and individual frustration. The college with a thousand students and one hundred staff can no longer escape the inevitable; channels of communication start to become important, some formal delegation of authority is necessary, and the duplicating machine runs hot in producing a mass of memoranda, circulars and notices. In some cases the bureaucratic means take over from the educational ends, and the stock book and contributions to committee discussion become more important than the individual student and quality of teaching. But this is the fault of the principal and staff concerned rather than inherent in bureaucracy as such, which is itself neutral, a set of structural forms, procedural rubrics and behavioural norms that is ubiquitous in the functioning of contemporary large-scale organization.

The adoption of bureaucratic principles of open competition and impersonality in appointments has important effects upon the educational system in respect of examinations and the

[1] Blau, P. *Bureaucracy in Modern Society*. New York: Random House, 1956.

acquisition of 'qualifications'. If the competing claims of indi-viduals for particular positions are to be evaluated objectively there must exist some common criterion of competence such as is provided by an examination, and this requirement is an important obstacle in the path of those educational reformers who would like to minimize the part played by examinations and formal teaching in schools.

Social Mobility

Technological growth, specialization, social pluralism and democratic institutions imply that talent must be sought wher-ever it may be found, that there should be 'equality of oppor-tunity' for individuals to obtain secondary and higher education and the chance to receive credit for and employ any qualifica-tions that may be possessed. With the diminution of the power of tradition and the attenuation of the role of family and kin groups, society is more 'open', and there exists the possibility of the individual being socially as well as geographically mobile, of rising or falling in the scale of status evaluations in comparison with the family of birth. Many of our educational procedures are dedicated to the creation of the conditions of a meritocracy, in which social position and reward are formally dependent upon intelligence, effort and performance rather than 'con-tacts', luck and accidents of birth, where status is based upon achievement rather than ascription. Setting aside the desirability or otherwise of such an aim, and the type of social relationships that might characterize a society that had achieved it, it is clear that we are as yet a very long way indeed from fulfilling the task of providing equal opportunity of access to secondary and higher education for all children who have the potential to take advantage of such provision. Although the social claims of the family have been limited by recent social changes, family back-ground still exercises a considerable effect upon individual opportunity. At the one end of the occupational spectrum, well-educated and prosperous parents can provide a variety of direct and indirect advantages for their children; at the other, the deprivations and limitations of development experienced by the under-privileged are strong enough to render ineffec-tive all the procedures designed to equalize opportunity and minimize social disadvantage. A series of official reports and sociological enquiries have spelled out in great detail the lack of success we have had since 1944 in providing genuinely open access to higher education, and a good deal of work is now being done to explain the mechanisms by which the family has succeeded in defeating these objectives.[1] Despite this, however, social mobility still takes place, and on a rather larger scale than during previous periods; teachers and schools act today as the principal agents of this mobility, and in addition to their general task of socialization, have particular tasks of preparing children for the occupancy of social roles at specified social levels.[2] Particular tensions build up round the major watersheds of educational progress—the eleven-plus, 'O' and 'A' level, university entrance and so on—not so much because of their educational importance as due to their significance for the individual's adult social status and the determination of his life chances. The role of the school and college in a society in which status and class differences are still real, important and emotionally salient, yet which is formally devoted to the equalization of educational opportunity, is bound to be a crucial one and to involve elements of conflict and ambiguity.

Social Change

One final social characteristic needs to be mentioned that has been implied by much of what has gone before. Society today is in a process of rapid change, experiencing a pace of development that has no precedent in the history of man. The situation has been admirably stated by Klotsche.

'. . . let us compress the life of man on this planet into a 50-year period. In such an event, 49 years of life would have been spent in a nomadic existence, in search of food and pasture, wandering with no permanent home. As recently as six months ago man would have learned how to read and write. A fortnight ago he would have invented movable printed type and the microscope, and discovered the circulation of blood, the law of falling bodies and the law of gravitation. Less than a week ago

[1] Bernstein, B. 'A Socio-linguistic approach to Social Learning' in *Pelican Survey of the Social Sciences 1965*. London: Penguin Books, 1965.

[2] Stevens, F. *The Living Tradition*. London: Hutchinson, 1960.

he would have discovered the application of electrical energy, the use of ether as an anaesthetic and invented the internal combustion engine, the gyroscope, the modern gun and revolver, the sewing machine, the steam boat, the telegraph, telephone and typewriter. Twenty-four hours ago he would have been introduced to radio and T.V., the air plane, the automobile, motion pictures, radar, insulin, quantum mechanics and vitamins. This morning he would have awakened to learn about jet propulsion, the transistor, aureomycin, penicillin, and anti-polio vaccine. And by tonight a man will have landed on the moon.'[1]

Given the basis for this process of change and the unlikelihood of any diminution in the pace of technological innovation during the foreseeable future, it becomes necessary to face up to a situation in which rapid change is a permanent characteristic of the social environment, with inevitable consequences upon curriculum, methods of teaching and school organization. The problem here is not merely one of adapting buildings, books and equipment to conditions of continuous change, but of enabling teachers and educationists to cope with the personal demands that these conditions will create. A climate must be furnished in which innovation coming from without will be considered positively, if not uncritically, and the responsibility for innovation from within to deal with changed needs and circumstances will be accepted as part of the normal work of the organization. It is in this context that the colleges of education and universities must produce the teachers for tomorrow, and it is against this background that the current work of these institutions must be evaluated.

[1] Klotsche, J. M. American Association of Colleges of Teacher Education *Yearbook*. Chicago: 1964, pp. 77–8.

2

EDUCATIONAL NEEDS AND
TEACHER SUPPLY

The preceding chapter has outlined some of the broad characteristics of the society within which institutions responsible for
the process of teacher education function. It is necessary now to
look at some of the more specifically educational factors that
affect the work of colleges and departments of education.
Among these are, first and foremost, the demand for teachers
by the schools, which has to be examined not only in terms of
overall numbers, but also with reference to the requirements of
particular age-groups, for particular subjects or groups of
subjects, and for special tasks such as those of the teacher/social
worker or teacher/youth leader. An important influence on
demands at each of these levels is the structure of the school
system, the types of primary and secondary schools in being and
the proportion of children who attend them. Thirdly, in common with the schools, the colleges are affected by the prevailing
climate of educational change and innovation in respect of
teaching methods and the organization and content of the curriculum. The manner in which innovations are brought about,
the extent to which the institutions responsible for preparing
teachers are themselves innovating agencies, the existence of an
educational lag between the introduction of new ideas and the
responses of the colleges to them – all these are matters on which
there is an absence of hard information at the present time, and
comment on which must necessarily be somewhat speculative.
Finally, less direct in their influence on the work of the colleges
but nonetheless important, are the conceptions that exist regarding the nature of the teacher's role, its specificity or diffuseness,
the expectations of parents and community regarding what is
essential to 'teacher-like' behaviour, both in and out of school.

The Demand for and Supply of Teachers

Colleges of education and university departments of education are essentially vocational institutions, set up to provide training for certain more or less specific types of teaching. The demand for teachers, which is mainly a function of the birthrate, the age distribution of the population and the stage of technological development attained, exercises an immediate and pressing influence upon the work of the colleges, which tends to take precedence over other educational considerations. During the post-war years, as we shall see, there has been an almost continuous conflict between considerations of the demand for and supply of teachers on the one hand and, on the other, the interests of institutions of teacher education in providing an improved personal and vocational education and in upgrading their own educational and social status. On the whole, supply and demand have led the way, although the interconnectedness of all the factors concerned has enabled the colleges to fulfil a good number of their more strictly educational aims at the same time.

As a result of the overall rise in the birthrate during the two decades after 1944, there has been a considerable increment in the number of children in school; other factors, such as the raising of the statutory leaving age in 1947 to 15 – and in 1973 to 16 – together with the growing tendency to stay on voluntarily beyond 15, have helped to increase the demand for teachers.

Since it takes several years for any decision to increase the supply of teachers to take effect, the scale of the expansion of teacher education has had to be dependent upon estimates regarding birthrates, especially with respect to the provision of teachers for the infants and lower forms of the junior schools. Expectations that the high birthrate during the early post-war years would show a rapid falling off proved to be false, and most of the succeeding estimates have had to be revised upwards. Table I shows the estimates that have been made at various times during the past fifteen years of the school population for even years from 1954 to 1972. The *actual* figures for each of the years from 1954 to 1964 are shown in brackets. It can be seen that most of the earlier figures for the school population

TABLE I

Estimates of school population (maintained primary and secondary schools), 1954–72 (000's)

Date of Estimate	1954	1956	1958	1960	1962	1964	1966	1968	1970	1972
1951	6222	6445	6585	6550	6432	—	—	—	—	—
1956	(6376)	(6649)	6843	6905	6910	6757	6697	6691	—	—
1958	—	—	(6839)	6898	6909	6861	6910	7016	—	—
1960	—	—	—	(6924)	6981	6927	7085	7338	7525	—
1962	—	—	—	—	(6965)	7030	7148	7444	7736	8033
1963	—	—	—	—	—	7086	7211	7543	7947	8703
1964	—	—	—	—	—	(7033)	7153	7460	7871	8668

Sources: Reports of the Ministry of Education, 1956–60; Statistics of Education, 1962 and 1963; Ninth Report of the National Advisory Council on the Supply and Training of Teachers (1965).

of the 1960s were underestimates; only during the last few years has there been any tendency to overestimate the numbers coming forward for schooling.

In addition to the overall numbers of children in school, the effects of rises and falls in the birthrate on the distribution between infants, junior and secondary stages need to be taken into account in assessing the demand for teachers, and re-appraisals of these distributions have had a considerable influence upon the work of the colleges of education. In 1960 the National Advisory Council on the Supply and Training of Teachers and the Ministry of Education calculated between them that the following decade would see an increase of some $12\frac{1}{2}$ per cent in the number of children of primary school age, but only a small increase in those at secondary school. In the light of these figures, and taking into account the larger number of graduate teachers likely to be available for work in Arts subjects with under 15-year-olds by 1970, the Ministry felt that the 1959–60 figure of 37 per cent of all students in general colleges following courses normally taken by intending secondary teachers was inappropriate, and recommended a reduction to 15 per cent, these students to be mainly in the shortage subjects such as Mathematics and Science. At the same time it was suggested that the proportion of women students in the colleges should be increased above the 1960 figure of 70 per cent in order to help to offset the effects of wastage due to earlier marriage and childbearing.

The Ministry of Education memorandum setting out this policy caused an uproar in the colleges. It was feared that the long-term effects would be to divide the teaching profession into two strata – the three-year trained college teachers of infants and juniors and the graduate teachers in the secondary schools.[1] Resolutions flowed in to the Association of Teachers in Colleges and Departments of Education (A.T.C.D.E.) from constituent branches and college groups; the report of a discussion at the Association's Principals' Panel in 1960 makes clear how closely the colleges felt their broader educational tasks and status to be linked with questions of teacher supply.

[1] Although the circular made clear that, even by 1970, it could not be expected that more than one teacher in four in secondary schools would be a graduate.

'. . . the afternoon session was addressed by Mr. Odgers, of the Ministry, whose amplification of the letters was an expression of reluctant necessity. The contribution to the discussion by members could have left him in no doubt that the panel considered the immediate and long-term effect of the letters to be profoundly grave and disturbing, and that both staff and students of the colleges felt that the professional standing of the colleges and the appropriate staffing of schools was being sacrificed to expediency. The recruitment to the secondary schools of untrained graduates of inferior quality was regarded as disastrous in its effect on secondary education. Without compulsory training of graduates and a substantial share of this work being undertaken in the colleges, it was argued that both the colleges and the teaching profession as a whole would suffer, and that the movement of the colleges towards a closer university connection would suffer a blow from which it would take years to recover.'[1]

In the event, the balance of training policy has not had the disastrous effect initially attributed to it. Many colleges adopted the expedient of providing junior/secondary courses for work with the nine-to-thirteen age range in either the secondary or primary schools;[2] a large number of college of education students continued to find employment in secondary schools, including, it now appears, most of those who had followed junior/secondary courses; the Minister of Education reaffirmed his policy of making graduate training compulsory as soon as this became practicable; and the recommendation of the Newsom Committee regarding the value of a concurrent college training for teachers of the majority of pupils in secondary modern schools, and of the Robbins Committee regarding the future status of the colleges, took the sting out of the implied threat to the unity of the teaching profession.

During the four years between the balance of training circular and the publication of the Ninth Report of the National Advisory Council on the Supply and Training of Teachers in 1965 there was continued pressure for an expansion of teacher training

[1] A.T.C.D.E. *News Sheet 30*, December 1960, p. 12.
[2] *A Compendium of Teacher Training Courses in England and Wales*. London: H.M.S.O., 1966.

facilities, both by the provision of extra college places via a large-scale building programme, and by the crowding up of existing plant and an increase in the output of the colleges. The colleges themselves were wary of the second type of proposal and produced considerable resistance to some of the schemes that were suggested, such as 'box and cox' arrangements, whereby a substantial section of students are at any one time out on teaching practice, and the introduction of a four-term year. Although at one time it appeared that the latter–supported by a minority addendum to the Ninth Report of the N.A.C.–might become the policy of the Department of Education and Science, resistance to the proposal led to an undertaking from the Secretary of State that no such scheme would be imposed upon the colleges against their will. The responsibility for co-ordinating schemes for the fuller use of training facilities was handed over to the Institutes of Education, who were more likely to take cognizance of the point of view of those actually involved in teacher education than some of the local authorities that administered the colleges. Some of the pressure for the introduction of new patterns of training was in fact removed by the colleges' efforts to take a larger number of students for the normal three-year and shortened courses without the provision of extra buildings and facilities; by crowding up, opening outposts in existing premises, and the recruitment of larger numbers of day and mature students, the colleges managed between 1965 and 1968 to exceed considerably the estimates of the Robbins Committee and the National Advisory Council regarding the numbers of students in training. The Robbins Committee had recommended an intake for 1967 of 26,400, and the N.A.C. suggested that this be increased to 27,500. The actual number of acceptances for the year was just under 37,000.[1] During this same period about 58 per cent of those nominally qualified for university entry actually obtained university places. Lord Robbins has commented that 'an increasing proportion of those who would have been regarded as eligible for university education will have to content themselves with alternatives which, despite all the fanfares about the

[1] *Ninth Report* of the National Advisory Council, *op. cit.*, table 2, p. 26; *Report on Entry to Colleges of Education 1967–8*, Central Register and Clearing House, London, 1968.

creation of a second system equal in status to the universities, they will continue to regard as inferior.'[1]

Few of the official reports that helped to shape the development of education between the wars gave much attention to the implications of their findings and recommendations for teacher training: the Hadow Report of 1926, the Report on the Primary School of 1931, the Spens Report of 1938 and the Norwood Committee in 1943 devoted no more than a few pages to the preparation of teachers. The Spens Committee clearly felt that professional training was hardly a necessity for the grammar school teacher.

'. . . we have not suggested a break with the tradition of requiring specific training in the art of teaching for posts in a Modern school. On the other hand, we have not suggested that such a requirement should be made universal in Grammar schools. While we would not be held to depreciate the importance of specific training, we recognize that teachers who are required to do specially advanced work in Grammar schools may often spend their fourth university year more profitably in increasing their mastery of their special subjects than in following a course in the university training department. . . .'[2]

The Report of the McNair Committee, which was explicitly concerned with teacher training, will be discussed in a subsequent chapter. The two major post-war reports of the Central Advisory Council for Education—*15 to 18* (Crowther Report) in 1960 and *Half our future* (Newsom Report) in 1963—gave rather more attention to teacher education than most of their predecessors. In relation to the needs of the schools educating pupils beyond the age of 15 the Crowther Report stresses the wider range of subject demands that will be made upon teachers in the future, and the need for a higher proportion of specialist teachers than has previously been available. Suggestions are also made regarding the use of ancillary staff to undertake some of the non-teaching tasks of craft shop and classroom, art room and library. The use of unqualified auxiliary teachers is rejected.

[1] Lord Robbins, 'The Achievements and Setbacks since 1963', *Financial Times*, 11 March 1968, p. 14.

[2] *Secondary Education*. Report of the Consultative Committee on Education, 1938 (Spens Report). London: H.M.S.O., 1938, p. 300.

'Unless the teacher knows the individual mistakes that particular pupils make, unless (at the top of the school) he can study the whole "form" of his pupils, he cannot teach well. Teachers' assistants are not really a possibility.'[1]

The Crowther Report had little to say in detail regarding the demands of the schools on teacher education, a subject on which the Newsom Report is much more explicit. In February 1963, six months before the full report was submitted, the Chairman of the Central Advisory Council wrote to the Secretary of State urging the value of the concurrent training college course in preparing teachers for the 'average and below-average' children in modern schools and elsewhere who were the particular concern of the Council. It was suggested that the balance of training policy, whereby the colleges were to produce only a small number of teachers for the secondary schools, should be regarded as a temporary expedient rather than a basis for the preparation of long-term policies for teacher education.

Whilst accepting the form-teacher principle, whereby one member of staff is responsible for all the non-specialist subjects taken by a particular class group of pupils, the Newsom Council felt that there was a need to reconsider the basis on which form teachers were assigned. All too frequently it was assumed that the form teacher should be responsible for English, Mathematics and Religious Instruction, whatever his degree of competence in these subjects, often with unfortunate effects upon the student's attainment. The Council saw a need for semi-specialist teachers, who 'in addition to offering one major subject which they are competent to teach at all levels in the school, [would] be able to contribute to the teaching of at least one and preferably two other subjects over a more restricted range whether of age or ability'.[2] Following from this it was felt that the colleges could well offer students opportunities to undertake work in Housecraft, Handicraft, Science, Art, Music, or Physical Education in addition to their main subjects, but at a level appropriate for semi-specialist teaching.

Among the other recommendations of the Council was that

[1] '*15 to 18*'. Report of the Central Advisory Council for Education (Crowther Report). H.M.S.O., 1959, p. 441.

[2] *Half our Future*. Report of the Central Advisory Council for Education, 1962. London: H.M.S.O., 1962, p. 101.

some appointments to schools should be of the teacher/youth leader type, with employment, especially in difficult areas, of specially trained teacher/social workers. Provision for training for both these special roles exists at present in a number of colleges of education, and there is a small but growing output of qualified staff finding their way into the schools.[1]

The compulsory training of graduate teachers has been official policy since 1944, but successive Ministers of Education have felt that the teacher supply position did not 'yet' permit implementation of this policy. By the beginning of the sixties roughly the same proportions of graduate teachers were entering the schools with and without training, but a substantial proportion of the latter taught for only a short time. The Newsom Report re-emphasized the views of the N.A.C. in its Eighth Report regarding the importance of graduate training; the prospects of the modern schools staffed to an increasing extent by untrained graduates was 'intolerable'. The N.A.C. advised the Minister of Education in 1965 that compulsory graduate training should be introduced by 1970, but at the time of writing no official announcement has been made.

In 1966 there were 334,868 full-time teachers employed in all kinds of maintained, direct-grant and independent schools in England and Wales; the distribution between types of school is indicated in Table II overleaf.

As we have seen, the proportion of teachers engaged in different types of school is affected by changes in the birthrate over time, and also by alterations in the length of schooling (whether statutory or the result of voluntarily staying on) and in the structure of the educational system. All these changes will have their effect upon the demand for teachers and thus upon the work of the colleges and departments of education; some of these effects may well be indirect—for example, the tendency of secondary schools to become larger and for graduate teachers to be preferred for headships in them has diminished the promotion prospects of a three-year-trained man teacher. Many men students realize this, and also that the rapid wastage of women in primary education is tending to increase the opportunities for men to obtain senior appointments in

[1] Craft, M. (ed.) *et al. Linking Home and School.* London: Longmans Green, 1967.

primary schools, thus enhancing the attractiveness of work in such schools.[1]

TABLE II

Full-time Teachers in Schools in England and Wales, 1966

		%
Primary Schools (inc. Nursery and Special)	147,373	46·0
Secondary Modern	73,490	21·9
Secondary Grammar	40,009	12·0
Secondary Technical	4,192	1·2
Comprehensive	16,280	4·8
All Other Secondary	9,656	2·9
All Maintained Schools	297,503	—
Direct-grant Grammar	7,562	2·3
Independent Schools Recognized as Efficient	21,540	6·4
Independent Secondary	8,263	2·5
Total	344,868	100·0

Source: Statistics of Education 1966.

Educational Change and the Teacher

Just as technological growth, the higher value attached to achieved rather than ascribed status, and rising numbers of pupils have brought about structural changes in the schools and in their relations with institutions of further and higher education, so they have helped to create a climate of innovation and change in the curriculum and in teaching methods. The pace of curriculum change has hitherto been slow in this country, especially in secondary education. The absence of a viable tradition of post-primary education outside the academic programmes of a grammar school vitiated the early post-war attempts to create a 'separate but equal' system of non-examined secondary work in the modern schools.[2] Although primary schools–especially at the infant stage–have been very much affected by the ideas of educational reformers and by the progressive educa-

[1] *Ninth Report* of the National Advisory Council on the Supply and Training of Teachers. London: H.M.S.O., 1965, p. 18.
[2] Taylor, W. *The Secondary Modern School*. London: Faber and Faber, 1963.

tional movement in the United States, the backwash effect of the eleven-plus allocation examination has tended to slow down the changes that these influences might have brought about in the upper forms of the junior school.[1]

As Young has stated, 'it is as common to say that all reforms in the school must begin in the training college as it is that all fundamental reforms in society must begin in the schools. Neither is true.'[2] Colleges of education have not been well placed in the past as agents of specific innovation in curriculum content and teaching method; their research role has been minimal; their staff have not possessed the type of qualification and experience that inspires an innovating role; during the early years of teaching their students have usually been too busy establishing themselves to be able to go against the existing mainstream of pedagogical practice. But to speak of 'innovation' as a unitary concept in this way is misleading, since there are clearly several stages involved in the process; the problem is to locate the points at which institutions of teacher education make their contributions. There are now a number of models available for the analysis of innovation processes in education. These range from the simple '(1) unfreeze (2) move (3) refreeze' formulation of Lewin,[3] through fuller conceptualizations such as those of Farmsworth—'recognize and articulate the need; propose a solution; create interest in the suggested solution; demonstrate usefulness; invite group and public interest; obtain official approval and financing, and remove legal restrictions'[4]— to the type of complex schema proposed by Guba and Clark and illustrated on pages 42–43.

Using Guba and Clark's categories, it is clear that colleges and departments of education have played very little part in the research and development stages—although there have been exceptions to this such as the work done in the field of closed-circuit television. The colleges have been in a position to do a good deal more at the diffusion stage, although their activity

[1] Cremin, L. *The Transformation of the School.* New York: Vintage Books, 1964.

[2] Young, M. *Innovation and Research in Education.* London: Routledge and Kegan Paul, 1965, p. 110.

[3] Miles, M. B. (ed.). *Innovation in Education.* New York: Teachers' College, Columbia University, Bureau of Publications, 1964. [4] *Ibid.*

A CLASSIFICATION SCHEMA OF PROCESSES RELATED TO AND NECESSARY FOR CHANGE IN EDUCATION*

OBJECTIVE	Research	Development		Diffusion		Adoption		
		Invention	Design	Dissemination	Demonstration	Trial	Installation	Institutionalization
	To advance knowledge	To formulate a new solution to an operating problem or to a class of operating problems, i.e. *to innovate*	To order and to systematize the components of the invented solution; to construct an innovation package for institutional use, i.e. *to engineer*	To create widespread awareness of the invention among practitioners, i.e. *to inform*	To afford an opportunity to examine and assess operating qualities of the invention, i.e. *to build conviction*	To build familiarity with the invention and provide a basis for assessing the quality, value, fit, and utility of the invention in a particular institution, i.e. *to test*	To fit the characteristics of the invention to the characteristics of the adopting institution, i.e. *to operationalize*	To assimilate the invention as an integral and accepted component of the system, i.e. *to establish*

42

	Validity (internal and external)	Face Validity (appropriateness)	Institutional feasibility	Intelligibility	Credibility	Adaptability	Effectiveness	Continuity
CRITERIA		Estimated Viability	Generalizability	Fidelity	Convenience	Feasibility	Efficiency	Valuation
		Impact (relative contribution)	Performance	Pervasiveness	Evidential Assessment	Action		Support
				Impact (extent to which it affects key targets)				
RELATION TO CHANGE	Provides basis for invention	Produces the invention	Engineers and packages the invention	Informs about the invention	Builds conviction about the invention	Tries out the invention in the context of a particular situation	Operationalizes the invention for use in a specific institution	Establishes the invention as a part of an ongoing programme; converts it to a 'non-innovation'

Source: Guba, E., and Clark, D. L. 'An Examination of Potential Change Roles in Education', National Education Association –Committee for Study of Instruction Symposium–Innovation in Planning School Curricula, Airielhouse, Va., Oct. 2–4, 1965, quoted in *Strategies for Educational Change Newsletter No. 2*, Ohio State University, October 1965.

has tended to be directed to intending and beginning teachers rather than the more senior people in the schools themselves. Individual members of college staff have been able to reach some members of the latter groups through the short courses and special lectures provided by the in-service programmes of Institutes of education and local authorities. Some testing of new innovations has been possible in conjunction with schools, although there is little evidence that college staff have attempted to evaluate, say, one method of teaching against another in any systematic way or on a large scale. Although curriculum evaluation is a difficult and complex business, requiring substantial resources and specialized skills to yield worthwhile results, there is something to be said for small-scale efforts such as the colleges might undertake because of the way in which institutionalization of innovations tends sometimes to be very much quicker than the evaluation itself.

By virtue of their position within the educational system, the colleges have been unable to do much to influence the installation and institutionalization of innovations – although installing a certain piece of apparatus in the college itself for daily use may be effective in accustoming future teachers to regard this as a normal and useful item of teaching hardware.

All this does not mean that the colleges and departments have been resistant to innovation; such impressionistic evidence as exists indicates that they have been more than ready to adopt new techniques in their own work and to try to persuade their students to respond positively to innovation and change. But it is possible that this readiness can sometimes have the paradoxical effect of diminishing the actual influence of the colleges upon the work of the schools; beginning teachers, as we have seen, are not in the best position to try out and evaluate new techniques, and the inevitable failure and difficulties of the early stages of a teaching career may be attributed by them more to the method than the manner of its use. If the colleges lack contact with the schools in those areas in which their students practise and are employed, are insensitive to the element of threat that is present in many innovations, or underestimate the practical difficulties of introducing particular techniques or ideas into the classroom, their efforts are likely to be dismissed in terms of the familiar and derogatory division between theory and practice.

Studies of educational innovation during the early decades of the century show that a period of some fifteen years elapsed between the introduction of a new technique or idea and the 'tipping point', defined as when 3 per cent of school systems had installed the innovation. Adoption of the innovation increased rapidly after this point, but it could still be many years before it became institutionalized. Miles suggests that during recent years the innovating process has become much more rapid. Skinners' teaching machine was first made available in 1954; by 1962 over 17 per cent of American schools had installed and were using machines of this kind. Team teaching was introduced in the United States in 1952; by 1955-6 some 5 per cent of schools were using the procedure, a proportion that had increased to 12 per cent by 1960 and an expected 31 per cent by 1965.[1] Similarly rapid rates of change could be reported in this country for the employment of structured arithmetic apparatus, the adoption of the 'new mathematics', and the taking into use of curriculum and methods of teaching derived from foundation-supported research and development work, particularly in science. The colleges of education have done a good deal to diffuse innovations of this kind, and it seems possible that the increasing pace of educational change and a recognition of a formal research function for the colleges may expand the area within which influence may be exerted in the direction of innovation and change. At the broadest level, the internal organization of the college courses will affect the range of teaching content that students are able to handle and thus, in an indirect manner, the structure of the school timetable and employment of the teaching force. If, for example, main courses in History and Geography in the colleges gave way on a very substantial scale to integrated programmes in social studies, this would almost inevitably have an effect upon the teaching of these subjects in the schools; there are examples of where this has already occurred in certain fields, such as the place of modern dance in programmes of Physical Education.

The lack of hard evidence that makes it difficult to assess the role of the colleges and departments in curriculum innovation and teaching techniques is even more marked in the important

[1] *Ibid.*, p. 7.

area of the influence of teacher training on the teacher's attitudes and values—upon the sentiments from which his response to the specific changes and problems will be derived. The importance of this issue justifies separate consideration being given to it in a later chapter. It remains here to consider the effect that recent and forthcoming changes in the schools may have for the definition of the teachers' role, and the implications of these for the process of teacher education.

The Teachers' Role

A number of quantitative and qualitative aspects of the two-way relationship between the schools and the institutions responsible for training teachers have already been considered. The work of the latter is affected by, and in its turn affects, demands for particular type of competency among teachers with respect both to instruction and the broader aspects of socialization. At a specific level this shows itself in a demand for more men and women qualified in Mathematics or Science, or with a better understanding of the needs of pupils of average and below-average ability, or with the capability of organizing particular kinds of extra-curricular activity. On a broader plane, these demands are related to existing conceptions of the role of the teacher in school and society, and the types of behaviour and attitude that legitimize his status.

There is an extensive literature about teachers' roles, most of which is based upon impression and observation rather than empirical study and systematic analysis. Several classifications have been proposed. Havighurst suggests those of participant in community affairs, sociological stranger, social reformer, public servant, surrogate of middle-class morality, mediator of learning, disciplinarian, parent substitute, judge and confidant.[1] Blyth mentions instructor, parent substitute, organizer, value bearer, classifier and welfare worker.[2] Floud has drawn attention to the differences between the *teacher-missionary* role of the nineteenth century, where the task was primarily that of engi-

[1] Havighurst, R. and Neugarten, B. *Society and Education*. Boston: Allyn and Bacon, 1962.
[2] Blyth, W. A. *English Primary Education*. London: Routledge and Kegan Paul, 1965.

neering a minimum degree of literacy and social cohesion in an industrializing society, and the *teacher-counsellor* role of the twentieth, dedicated to raising the standards of culture and taste that are threatened by the massification inherent in conditions of advanced industrialized and technological revolution.[1] Parsons stresses the role of the teacher as an agent of both socialization and selection.[2] Kob extends his discussions of teachers' roles to a typology of professional self-images—teacher *type A* stresses pedagogy rather than academic standing, the task rather than the subject, whilst *type B* has a self-image based upon academic qualifications and knowledge of specialized subjects.[3] Musgrove and Taylor have studied the expectations of pupils and teachers regarding different elements of role performance and considered the diffuseness or specificity of the teachers' role; their findings suggest that the grammar school teacher conforms very closely to Kob's type B, the primary school teacher, whose role is much more diffuse, to type A.[4] Merton examined the role conflicts inherent in the teachers' task and provided a conceptualization of the role set of community and individual expectations regarding the teachers' behaviour.[5] Gross, Mason and McEachern, in considering the role of the school superintendent, suggest a language for role analysis designed to limit the ambiguities and inconsistencies that have crept into the discussion of social roles.[6]

Few of the studies so far cited focus attention on the relation of the teachers' role to his professional education and preparation, or take into account the likelihood that a substantial redefinition of this role may be brought about by contemporary

[1] Floud, J. E. 'Teaching in the Affluent Society'. *British Journal of Sociology* XIII: 4. 1962, December.

[2] Parsons, T. 'The School Class as a Social System' in *Education, Economy and Society, op. cit.*

[3] Kob, J. 'Definition of the Teacher's Role' in Halsey, Floud and Anderson, *Education, Economy and Society, op. cit.*

[4] Musgrove, F. and Taylor, P. H. 'Teachers' and Parents' Conception of the Teacher's Role', *British Journal of Educational Psychology* XXXV: 1965.

[5] Merton, R. K. 'The Role-Set: Problems in Sociological Theory', *British Journal of Sociology* VIII: 2, 1957.

[6] Gross, N., Mason, W. S. and McEachern, A. W. *Explorations in Role Analysis: Studies in the School Superintendency Role.* New York: Wiley, 1958.

changes in society and in the schools. In considering this problem it may be useful to move away from the familiar concept of *role*, the utility of which has been diminished by unsystematic usage and habitual accretions,[1] and to adopt instead the *decision premise* as proposed by Simon.[2] This is a wider concept than that of role, the latter being a 'specification of some, but not all, of the premises that enter into an individual's decisions'.[3] In addition to the socially patterned role expectations, many other premisses may influence the individual's decisions, including 'informational premisses and idiosyncratic premisses that are expressive of personality'.[4] The analysis of the teacher's behaviour then shifts from a consideration of his roles to the statement, analysis and classification of the types of decision that he is required to make, and the character and source of the premisses on which these decisions are based. This is essentially an empirical problem that can be tackled by objective methods, such as the observation and recording of group and individual behaviour, study of written and conventional rules and procedures and the degree to which observed behaviour is in accordance with these, and the extent to which the internal organizational needs of educational institutions contribute to the content and orientation of the value and factual premisses of the individual. Comparatively little work has yet been undertaken on any of these topics.

For present purposes attention can be concentrated upon the decisions that the teacher is called upon to make in connection with his activity in classroom and school. Analysis of such decisions can be made at a number of different levels, from at the one extreme the moment-to-moment restructuring of a reading or a work assignment in terms of class feedback, or the action taken to silence an interrupter, to the overall determination of a syllabus for the year's work or the laying down of long-term goals and norms of class conduct at the other. Decisions at the first level are difficult to programme; the decision-premisses differ from situation to situation and speed is often the essence of the matter. In a study of elementary school teachers who were considered by their Principals or Superintendents to be outstanding, Jackson and Belford found that it was immediate response and classroom feedback, rather than the observation

---

[1] Simon, *op. cit.*, p. xxx.   [2] *Ibid.*   [3] *Ibid.*   [4] *Ibid.*

or growth of achievement or pupil performance in tests and examinations, that provided these teachers with their chief source of evaluation of effectiveness.[1] The experienced teacher responds to the feedback and to the interrupter in a practised manner; there is little search or conscious problem-solving involved in discovering a solution to a difficulty. The ability to respond in this way is the product of previous experience in dealing with similar or related situations; instructions as to how to do it or detailed analyses of how it is done do little to help the student or beginning teacher to cope. What is done and the manner in which it is done are presumably cognate with certain values to which the individual subscribes, such as the desirability of children understanding what is being read to them and profiting from it, the positive long-term effects of polite behaviour and a willingness to listen, the need to avoid punitiveness and to relate severity of sanctions to the magnitude of the misdemeanour and so on. Since the operational decision-making of the teacher at this level cannot be programmed by means of instructions, rules or direct supervision, it is necessary to try to obtain a commitment from him to certain standards and values which will act as referents in dealing with such immediate problems. Institutions responsible for the training of teachers have always stressed this value element, and it is the dominant theme of much of the contemporary literature of teacher education.[2]

Although decisions at the level of syllabusses and long-term goals are in principle a good deal easier to programme than those relevant to class management, in this country the tendency has been to permit the individual teacher a very substantial measure of freedom in these respects, relying upon his overall identification with certain of the values promulgated by church, state and university to guarantee acceptable decision premisses. The range of decisions that the English teacher had been asked to make in the area of the curriculum has been larger than is characteristic of his French or American counterpart, whilst his identification with national rather than local values and insulation from the local community have minimized the influence of neighbourhood and parents on his decision-making.

[1] Jackson, P. W. and Belford, E. 'Educational Objectives and the Joys of Teaching', *School Review* 73:3, Autumn 1965.   [2] See Chapter 10.

Until recently, the individual teacher's decision-making has played a relatively minor part in the processes by means of which the educational system exercises its selective and differentiating functions. These have been carried on by the system rather than by the individual teacher, structurally rather than personally. The effect of streaming on the basis of objective tests and across a range of subject performances, of selecting for particular types of secondary education on a county-wide basis, of final assessment by external examinations, and of secondary education being provided within separate institutions of different types, has all been to relieve the teacher of many of the decisions that he might otherwise have needed to take regarding the content of education and the fields of further study and occupation that might best suit individual children. With the abolition of the eleven-plus and the coming of comprehensive schools, the selective and differentiating functions move from the system to inside the school, and impose new demands upon the teacher. Although specialist guidance and assessment personnel may come to play a larger part, every teacher will require something of their outlook, the seeds of which will need to be provided during initial training in the colleges and departments. The importance of this kind of decision-making underlines the dangers inherent in the teacher overestimating the validity of his prognoses, or being dependent upon out-dated and inappropriate conceptions of ability acquired during training.

In the early years of the twentieth century a minimum level of education and professional competence and an appropriate value commitment on the part of teachers could be assumed, the structure of the curriculum was still basically simple, the technology of teaching undeveloped, and social and economic life chances little affected by the content of the education that the majority of children received. In these circumstances, it made sense to give teachers a substantial degree of freedom to determine their own syllabuses and the content of their teaching. Within a few years the effects of the progressive movement in the United States began to spread to this country, with an emphasis upon the spontaneous interaction of teacher and pupil, the value of giving individual attention to the needs of the child and the dangers of rigid syllabuses and programmes of work;

these views had a considerable liberating effect upon the schools, especially at the primary stage, and did nothing to modify the pattern of individual and school initiative in curriculum matters.[1] *De facto* control over output was maintained, however, by the growing use and importance of external criteria such as G.C.E. passes and eleven-plus successes. During the last few years the programming of teachers' behaviour has begun to be affected by the growing availability of forms of programmed instruction, greater use of film and television, the introduction of team teaching, and the development, after considerable research and trial, of sets of instructional materials that imply their own syllabuses and patterns of classroom work. All these influences are also tending to break down the traditional concept of the lesson as a confrontation between teacher and pupil.

Pidgeon has described some of the possible characteristics of the secondary school of the future:

'Students (not children) entering the secondary school would join existing groups containing about twenty-five others whose age range spanned the whole age range of the school (for example 11–18+). Entry to a particular group would depend largely upon the students' wishes. . . .

'Such a group would *not* be for instructional purposes. It would meet in a room which would have facilities for individual learning, possibly in the form of carrels. . . . Physically these "home" rooms would be grouped around the library, and the rest of the school would branch off from this central area. Each basic group of subjects would occupy a wing of the building. . . .

'A student's time in school would be shared between individual learning and group activities, the time devoted to each varying with the age and specific needs of the student. About a third to a half of his time would be spent in the home room in individual study, and for the remaining time he would be engaged in large group activities such as games, music and drama.'[2]

Within such a school it is clear that the role of the teacher would be quite different from that of today – 'The teacher's task is not to instruct but to help and advise, and ensure that each

[1] Cremin, L. *The Transformation of the School.* New York: Alfred Knopf, 1961.   [2] *New Society.* 10 June 1965, p. 16.

child is placed in the particular environment that is appropriate to the stage which his learning has reached.'[1] Such a role demands decision-making of a different order from that required at present. The freedom to determine the syllabuses and methods of teaching on a personal basis—which sometimes means that they are suitable for the teacher, less so for the children—would largely disappear. So at the same time would many of the decisions needed for class control in the formal lesson situation. Responsibility for a good deal of the routine preparation and organization of materials could be undertaken by ancillary staff. The effect of programming a good deal of the decision-making at present engaged in by the teacher would be to free him to attend to the individual learning of children; the overall degree of freedom in the learning situation would be enhanced rather than reduced.

It is unlikely that the organization of teaching will change as dramatically as the extracts referred to above suggest; traditional modes of instruction are likely to remain dominant in most schools for many years to come. But with the introduction of new teaching media modifications are already occurring in the way in which teachers perform their task, and the growth in the size of schools is likely to bring about further change. Cole remarks how some newly appointed members of staff of large comprehensive schools have found it surprising that 'a head of department is expected to consider the teaching of the staff in his department to the extent of sitting in on lessons';[2] some of the departments in such schools already function as teams, with more interchange of information and mutual self-help than used to be characteristic of secondary schools, if not the full team-teaching pattern that is growing in the United States.[3] Teacher turn-over is also increasing in this country, with the inevitable bureaucratic tendency to emphasize the post rather than the individual, to define more closely the nature of the responsibilities that applicants will be required to undertake as a means of assuring some degree of continuity.

If in matters of curriculum and teaching method more of the

---

[1] *Ibid.*

[2] Cole, R. *Comprehensive Schools in Action.* London: Oldbourne, 1965.

[3] Shaplin, E. and Olds, T. *Team Teaching.* New York: Harper and Row, 1957.

teachers' decision-making is becoming programmed and therefore less subject to the influence of underlying value premises, in the case of relationships with parents and the community the teacher is being asked to deal with new types of problems. The traditional alienation of school and home in this country has already been referred to, and the effect that this has upon the relationships of parents, teachers and pupils has been the subject of a number of recent studies.[1] Full recognition on the part of many parents of the role that the school can play in determining their children's life chances and a rising standard of education in the community as a whole have encouraged a groundswell of family and community concern that is beginning to be felt in administrative office, headmaster's study and classroom.

What all this may amount to is that the same forces that in the economy as a whole are creating redundancy among the unskilled and semi-skilled and emphasizing the need for higher-order understanding and knowledge are also at work in the complex of behaviours that constitute the process of teaching. Many of the more routine levels of instruction and teaching can now be more effectively performed with the aid of audio-visual and mechanical teaching devices. These machines can be controlled and serviced by personnel who do not need to be fully qualified teachers in the old sense. But it goes without saying that, despite the wilder dreams of some of the 'cyber-culturalists' the most important tasks that have to be performed within the school will be interpersonal:

'Only the human being can provide a sense of what a lived culture can be. This he does, not only by example but also by bringing to the fore the importance of the dimensions of feeling and sensitivity for the human condition. Knowledge is not enough. One must distinguish, as Archibald MacLeish once put it, between a fact and the feel of a fact.'[2]

There is thus a need for a substantial proportion of teachers to be drawn from those groups in the population who are most capable of achieving the high-order understanding that will

---

[1] Jackson, B. and Marsden, D. *Education and the Working Class*. London: Routledge and Kegan Paul, 1962; Craft, M., *et al* (eds.). *Linking Home and School*. London: Longmans, 1967.

[2] Winthrop, H. 'What can we expect from the Unprogrammed Teacher?', *Teachers' College Record* 67:5. 1966, p. 325.

increasingly be required in the schools, and for such teachers to be given the kind of education and training that will best develop these capacities and enable them to be successfully employed in the pursuit of the goals of learning. Evidence from both this country and the United States indicates that it is at present by no means true that teaching is chosen as a career by the most able school and college graduates.[1] There are indications that colleges of education here will have to accept more school-leavers with minimum qualifications for entry if they are to fill the places available during the next few years of rapid expansion. It may well be that if education can be provided for several future generations on the basis of more flexible assumptions about the upper limits of attainment and performance than have been common, there will ultimately be enough talented people available to supply the half million or so teachers who will by then be required, all of them capable of superior cognitive and intellectual functioning and with an adequate sensitivity to the needs and problems of children and adolescents. But at the present time the supply of such people for work in the schools is limited, and little improvement can be expected for some time to come. The problem thus remains of making the best use of the scarce resources of teaching potential that we have, resources which hitherto have been distributed mainly by the institutionalized separation of secondary schools, and by market forces both within the profession and among the families that constitute the teachers' clients. Among the solutions of the problem that have been suggested has been a revision of our ideas regarding the structure of the teaching force, and a consideration of such a scheme will provide an opportunity to sum up some of the points that have been made earlier in this chapter.

The Structure of the Teaching Force

The future structure of the teaching force can be looked at from both a long-term and a short-term perspective. In the short term, we are faced with the problem of using limited financial

[1] Koerner, J. *The Miseducation of American Teachers*. Boston: Houghton Mifflin, 1963; *Higher Education*, Appendices 2A and 2B. London: H.M.S.O., 1964.

resources to obtain enough men and women to cope with steadily increasing numbers of children in already existing types of schools and in largely familiar types of teaching situation. In these conditions it makes sense to look for ways of increasing the productivity of the colleges, to study how teachers' aides have been and might be used, and to base discussion of teacher supply – as did the National Advisory Council in their Ninth Report – on assumptions about the desirability of class sizes of thirty. In the long run, there are other issues to be taken into account.

Firstly, the impact of research on our understanding of learning processes, of curriculum development work, the introduction of a wide range of new teaching media, and concomitant changes in the internal organization of schools will all have an effect upon the types of decision that the teacher will be called upon to make.

Secondly, there are at present substantial social and economic costs involved in absorbing back into the schools a continuing large proportion of the best-qualified school leavers; the time lag in the economic returns from the growth of the knowledge industry reinforce this point.[1]

Thirdly, although rapidly increasing numbers of teachers will initially create substantial opportunities for professional advancement, promotion prospects within the much enlarged teaching force of the eighties, which on present projections will have increased by 127 per cent over the figure for 1963, will be much more limited.

Fourthly, the present pattern of status, salaries and rewards, which reflects tradition and piecemeal reform rather than any systematic relationship of qualifications, training and skills to performance and output, is already unsatisfactory and will become increasingly so as the colleges of education begin to produce teachers with B.Ed. degrees. The average male teacher reaches his salary maximum at about thirty-five. From then until sixty-five he has no increase to look forward to other than what may come from additional responsibility allowances, across-the-board rises, and appointment to a headship. But as schools become larger, the prospects of promotion to a headship are becoming more limited. Secondary reorganization is creating the problem of the redundant head.

[1] *Trends in Education 1,* January 1966. London: H.M.S.O.

Fifthly, with the increase in the number of part-time teachers, married women returners and classroom helpers, there is a need to protect the status and position of the 'career teacher', who is willing and able to make a life-long commitment to the job. Curriculum change and reorganization within the school is creating the image of the teacher as an organizer of learning resources, rather than as a distributor of information and exhortation by means of forty-minute confrontations with pupils. In this role, he may need to guide the work of a number of qualified and unqualified helpers, library assistants, audio-visual technicians and secretarial staff, a task quite different from that which acts as a model for present-day salary arrangements.

Sixth, there will soon be getting on for half a million teachers; to regard these as all of equal status and requiring similar training is to remove for ever the hope of a genuinely professional and self-governing body. The range of tasks to be done in the schools is much greater than in the past; some of these could be done by people with less training than most teachers have at present, many of them should be done by those with a better education and training than is now general. What is needed is a more functional relationship between desired educational outcomes and particular types of teaching skill and competence.

In the light of these considerations, there have been suggestions about the desirability of a more structurally differentiated teaching force, between the various levels of which movement would be possible by means of further study and training of various kinds. A possible framework for such a force is set out as follows:[1]

1. Master Teachers/Directors of Studies. Experienced teachers with a minimum length and type of experience, and certain further qualifications (among which the conventional higher degree in education would be only one of the possibilities). Staff of this grade would be employed, for example, as heads of departments and house masters in comprehensive

[1] This is an adaptation to the English setting of a scheme suggested by Trump, J. L., *Images of the Future*. New York: Commission in the Experimental Study of the Utilization of the Staff in the Secondary School, 1959.

schools and in charge of diagnostic and remedial work at the primary level. They would co-ordinate the work of teachers and teaching assistants and provide consultative services within the school in their special field of interest. Their responsibilities would include supervision of practice teaching by college students and teaching assistants, in which they would play a much larger role than that of the present-day supervising teacher. The salary attaching to this grade would be substantially greater than the present Burnham scale, approximating to that of a good honours graduate head of a large department in a secondary school. The establishment of this and each of the following grades in each school would be determined in accordance with both educational and social needs.

2. Teachers. The basic general grade occupied by all those with a three-year college training, B.Ed., or a degree plus postgraduate training. A broad range of specialist and semi-specialist skills covering the whole field from infant work to sixth-form studies. The proportion of staff in this grade would be a good deal smaller than at present, and the intake of the colleges of education would be adjusted accordingly. Any surplus capacity would be used to provide facilities for the in-service work and further professional study that is an essential feature of a scheme such as this. On the National Advisory Council's assumptions regarding the numbers of school leavers coming forward with 'A' level passes, all the entrants to colleges of education could be expected to be so qualified, and a substantial proportion would work for a B.Ed. degree.

3. Teaching Assistants. The work of this grade would be mainly with individual pupils and small groups, and could also include the preparation and organization of teaching materials, certain types of routine testing and assessment, and clerical, administrative and supervisory duties. Training would be provided by means of non-residential, two-year sandwich courses in colleges of technology, combining academic and professional instruction with practical experience under the supervision of master teachers in schools. Entry to these courses might normally be at the age of 17 or 18, but suitable preliminary courses of general education could be provided for those who had left school at 16. Mature entrants would be encouraged. The minimum qualification for this grade could be flexible,

and include passes in the Certificate of Secondary Education as well as at 'O' level.

4. School Aides. At this level would be many of the unqualified part-time helpers who are at present employed in infant and junior schools, although there might also be scope for some kind of more specialized work, such as part-time library assistant in secondary schools. This would not be thought of as a career grade, but short courses concerned with various aspects of service providing by aides could be provided by local authorities and institutes of education.

Among the less radical ideas that have been proposed to achieve some of the same ends is a 'stepped' salary scale, with teachers moving from one grade to another as they undertake further study and gained experience. The beginning teacher would start off on scale I, and receive increments for each of his first six years of service. If by the end of this period he had undertaken a specified amount of further professional study and had satisfied certain minimum criteria of teaching efficiency, he would move to scale II. Without this further study, he would remain on scale I, without further incremental additions. The same process would apply to each of the other steps from scale II to V, each stage being of six years' duration. It would be possible for those who wished to do so to accelerate their progress by undertaking more intensive study and training, although certain minima of experience might need to be laid down before a teacher could move on to the higher scales. Not all teachers would attain scale IV and V, but for those who did there would be incremental additions extending to the age of 50 or 55. It might be possible to restrict some kinds of promotion to teachers who had already attained certain levels on the scale, and for some kinds of experience—in slum schools, for example—to count extra in terms of satisfying time requirements at each stage. Various formulae would also need to be computed to deal with cases of broken or split service.

The drawbacks and difficulties associated with schemes of this kind are obvious enough to any teacher or administrator. We are unable to agree as to what constitutes a 'good teacher', or how his quality can be evaluated. There are a whole series of vested interests which need to be taken into account. The additional resources available for teachers' salaries are limited—

although studies in the United States suggest that the overall cost of a differentiated structure may be little more than at present.[1]

It is not the purpose of this chapter to recommend these or similar schemes, but merely to indicate that, since changes in the types of decision-making that the teacher is called upon to perform are occurring, and that teacher education cannot remain unaffected by these, it is likely that the type of provision for the training of teachers that exists at present may need some radical alteration during the next few decades. Despite the conservatism of the teachers' organizations, and the opposition that there has been to the idea of unqualified staff being employed in the school, there are already signs of change. In a speech to the National Union of Teachers' Annual Conference in 1966, the Secretary of State for Education likened the teacher of the future to a personnel manager, equipped with the ability to use effectively the techniques and devices available to him and responsible for focusing these–and his own talents–on a given learning situation. The notion of the 'learning-centred' rather than the subject-centred or child-centred school is an effective compromise slogan which takes into account the growth and importance of the knowledge industry as well as the enduring contribution of the progressive movement in concentrating attention upon the needs and interests of the individual child. Several thousand unqualified helpers are already at work in the schools, many of them in direct contact with the pupil in the classroom, for which type of work the professional associations see qualified teacher status as a *sine qua non*. The effort on the part of the Department of Education and Science to establish training departments in technical colleges and polytechnics can be seen as an attempt not merely to increase the capacity of the system, but also to change some of the prevailing assumptions about the process that are embodied in existing institutions. But such efforts also have important implications for the organization and control of teacher education, and this is a subject which requires a separate chapter.

[1] Trump, *op. cit.*

PART TWO
STRUCTURE AND CONTENT

3

THE ORGANIZATION AND
CONTROL OF TEACHER EDUCATION

Up to the Act of 1944

Just as during the last thirty years of the nineteenth century the
state took over from the churches and private bodies much of the
provision of mass elementary education in this country, so
during the first three decades of this century it assumed the
major share in the education and training of teachers. But public
involvement in these areas did not become a reality overnight,
and nor was it complete. The training of teachers might have
been a matter for the state from the beginning, if the Minute of
the Committee of the Privy Council on Education of April 1839
suggesting the setting up of a state normal school had not encountered such strenuous denominational opposition. In his
evidence to the Newcastle Commission, Kay-Shuttleworth,
then secretary of the committee, stated that the intention had
been to take a 'first step towards the establishment of a common
school upon the basis of religious equality', in which the 'teachers
of all the several classes of schools connected with the religious
communions of England were to be educated together.'[1] The
proposal gave rise to what Rich has called an 'outburst of sec-
tarian protest.'[2] In Kay-Shuttleworth's words, 'very warm
debates occurred in both Houses of Parliament, and a deputa-
tion of bishops and peers waited upon the Queen with an address
against the proposed constitution of the normal school.'[3] The

[1] *Education Commission: Minutes of Evidence taken before the Commissioners*,
Vol. VI. London: H.M.S.O., 1861, p. 301.
[2] Rich, R. W. *The Training of Teachers in the Nineteenth Century*. Cambridge
University Press, 1933, p. 52.
[3] *Education Commision: Minutes of Evidence, op. cit.*, p. 301.

proposal was abandoned. For the next few years state aid was confined to building grants for the denominational colleges that were being established in various parts of the country. In 1846, with the introduction of the pupil-teacher system, the basis was laid for the private and denominational control of teacher education that was to hold sway for the next fifty years.[1] But the state did not lack influence on the work of the colleges. From the beginning it was responsible for conferring qualified teacher status, and colleges were inspected and reported upon regularly by Her Majesty's Inspectors. The finances of the system were controlled via the grant regulations and the pupil-teacher scheme.

What was new in the period after 1902 was not the intervention of the state in teacher training, but the direct provision of facilities for such training in the form of local authority colleges. Until 1889 the only institutions available to train teachers were private and residential, and the vast majority were denominational. The creation of the day training colleges in conjunction with the universities and university colleges after 1890, and the setting up of local authority colleges from 1904, furnished a much larger number of places not subject to denominational restrictions. In 1880 only 500 such places existed, but by 1913 their number had grown to nearly 11,000.[2] Faced with direct state intervention in the provision of elementary education after 1870, the churches had for a time tried to keep up; between 1870 and 1880 the number of voluntary schools increased by 75 per cent, from 8,000 to 14,000, and it was not until 1900 that the number of children in Board schools approached those attending the voluntary schools.[3] No such effort was made in relation to the setting up of new training colleges, partly due to the fact that there was only a slow growth in the number of local authority institutions between the 1902 Act and the second world war, voluntary colleges remaining in a majority throughout this period. By the time the big increase in the number of publicly provided colleges came, during the twenty years after 1944, it was too late for the churches to compete; only the Roman Catholics have made a real effort to increase their stake in teacher training.

[1] *Ibid.*, p. 307.   [2] *Report of the Board of Education, 1913*, p. 6.
[3] McClure, S. *Educational Documents*. London: 1965, p. 7.

CONTROL OF TEACHER EDUCATION

Between 1902 and 1921 twenty-one local education authority training colleges were set up, against no increase in the number of those controlled by the Church of England or the Free Churches (32), five new colleges provided by the Roman Catholics and one by an undenominational body. By 1938 only two additional council colleges had been created, but within the next ten years their number had increased to forty and by 1968 there were one hundred and thirteen colleges of this kind. In contrast, the number of Church of England institutions remained practically the same throughout this period, as can be seen in Table III.

TABLE III

Number of Colleges and Providing Bodies, 1921–66[1]

Year	Local Authority	Church of England	Roman Catholic	Other	Total
1921	22	30	8	12	72
1928	22	29	8	13	72
1938	21	29	8	15	73
1948	40	25	11	14	90
1968	113	27	17	9	166

Until the turn of the century the control of the Education Department over instruction and examination had been complete, but with the creation of the day colleges came the recognition of examinations in the general (as distinct from the professional) subjects conducted by a university or by the staff of a college itself under the supervision of the department.[2] But by 1921 the great majority of candidates for certification—3,877 out of 5,419—were still being entered for the examinations conducted by the Board of Education, a further 1,237 being examined in their colleges and 305 by a university.[3] The Report of the Departmental Committee on the training of teachers for elementary schools of 1925 recommended substantial changes

[1] Calculated from Board of Education *Reports* for 1921 to 1928, *Report and Statistics*, Ministry of Education, 1948, and *A Compendium of Teacher Training Courses in England and Wales* (List 172). London: H.M.S.O., 1967.
[2] Jones, L. *The Training of Teachers.* Oxford: Clarendon Press, 1924.
[3] *Ibid.,* p. 87.

in the system of examinations, including the handing over of responsibility for their conduct to joint boards or delegacies acting under the aegis of universities; central control was still to be exercised over syllabuses and schemes of work and the Inspectorate to continue to play a part in the assessment of practical teaching.

The Joint Board scheme did not succeed in linking the colleges with the universities to the extent that had been hoped; in the words of those members of the 1944 McNair Committee on the supply and training of teachers who supported a substantial revision of the system,[1] the Joint Boards had not (a) 'brought into being any constitutional relationships between the training colleges and the universities as such or (b) resulted in the university training departments and the training colleges, though engaged in a common task, sharing any work or influencing each other's activities, or (c) promoted among the training colleges themselves any more intimate relationship than they had twenty years [before] as far as the pooling of staff and sharing of facilities are concerned.'[2] Part of the blame for this may have been due to the indecent haste with which the examination link with the universities had to be forged in the face of the Board of Education's reluctance to accept responsibility for examining after 1928. Humphreys has suggested that 'a high price was paid for the speed with which the operation was carried out. In order to get the new examination going as quickly as possible scant attention was paid to the wider aspects of co-operation between the universities and the training colleges.'[3]

The Influence of the McNair Report

In March 1942 the then President of the Board of Education, R. A. Butler, appointed a committee to 'investigate the present sources of supply and the methods of recruitment and training of

[1] *Teachers and Youth Leaders.* Report of the Committee appointed by the President of the Board of Education to consider the supply, recruitment and training of teachers and youth leaders (McNair Committee). London: H.M.S.O., 1943.

[2] *Ibid.*, p. 49.

[3] Humphreys, D. W. *The relationships between the training colleges and the universities before McNair.* Lyndale House Papers, University of Bristol Institute of Education, 1965, p. 22.

teachers and youth leaders and to report what principles should guide the Board in these matters in the future.'[1] The chairman was Sir Arnold McNair, Vice-Chancellor of the University of Liverpool, and the recommendations of the report that now bears his name did much to shape the post-war development of teacher education.

With respect to the future organization and control of the institutions responsible for training teachers the McNair Committee made two sets of recommendations, each supported by five of its ten members. Neither group favoured the setting up of a centralized, integrated training service; the members responsible for the criticisms of the Joint Board scheme already quoted felt that it should be replaced by the creation of university schools of education, responsible for the pattern of training in their areas and governed by a delegacy representing the university, the federated training colleges and the local education authorities. The other five members favoured the continuance of the Joint Board scheme, fearing that too close an association between the universities and teacher training might at one and the same time give an excessively academic orientation to the work of the colleges and swamp the universities with a large number of students preparing themselves for a single profession. It was felt that '. . . the training colleges value the connection with the universities established by these Joint Boards and the attendant Boards of Studies and that they would welcome closer contact with the universities, provided that it takes the form of a partnership between equals and does not lead to the universities having a predominant influence in the training of the students in training colleges.'[2]

This question of the relationship of institutions of post-secondary education to the universities was not a new one in 1944 and is still very much alive today. It had come up at the time of the establishment of the day training colleges at the end of the nineteenth century, and, in the event, the universities had gone some way towards absorbing these institutions into their overall structure as graduate training departments. The issue was prominent in the discussions of the future of teacher education that followed the publication of the report of the Committee on Higher Education in 1964, and again the suggestion has

[1] McNair Report, *op. cit.*   [2] *Ibid.*, p. 56.

been made that the relationship between the universities and the colleges of education should be 'separate but equal'. One of the reasons why the matter was still at issue was that although after 1944 it was the university school of education group rather than the supporters of the extended Joint Board scheme who prevailed, neither the letter nor the spirit of this scheme was implemented on a general basis by the universities. Most established not schools of education, in which the graduate training department and the training colleges could be partners, but Institutes of Education. The latter fulfilled many of the functions that had been forecast by the McNair Committee. They were governed by delegacies along the lines proposed; many–but not all–of their directors were accorded professorial status and took part in the policy-making deliberations of the university; they were provided with a physical plant within which boards of studies could meet and other co-ordinating work could be carried on, and which could be used for in-service work with practising teachers. But in many respects the hopes that Sir Fred Clarke and his McNair colleagues had shared regarding the future relationship of teacher training and the universities, and between the colleges themselves, were not fulfilled. The university department of education, although nominally part of the area training organization on the same basis as the colleges, in some cases stood aside from the work of the Institute. Even where relationships were close and Institute and department staff shared the same buildings, the fact that the department had the largest number of full-time staff and students had its effect upon the status of the Institute and its activities, which sometimes came to be associated with committee work and the provision of short courses for serving teachers. As far as the attitude of the remainder of the university was concerned, this 'may be said to range from warm welcome, through tolerance to apathy; even open hostility has not been unknown.'[1] The close co-operation and pooling of resources between colleges that the McNair group saw as essential to the success of the school of education idea in no sense became general in the twenty years after 1944. Contact between the colleges was often limited to common membership of boards of studies and other Institute committees.

[1] 'Institutes of Education', *Times Educational Supplement*, 30 July 1954.

CONTROL OF TEACHER EDUCATION

There are several other respects in which the purposes of the dominant McNair group failed to be implemented. It had recommended that the schools of education should offer a common professional qualification to graduate and non-graduate students alike; to this end many universities replaced their post-graduate diploma in education by a post-graduate certificate, reserving the title of diploma for advanced qualifications. The change has not been universal, however, and there are still some university departments of education that offer a diploma rather than a certificate as the initial qualification for their post-graduate students. These distinctions are in some ways unimportant, but they are symptomatic of the confusion of attitudes that attended the implementation of the major proposals of the McNair Report.

The university school of education proposal envisaged that the affiliated colleges should be financed by direct grant from the (then) Board of Education, but the possibility of a block grant to the school to cover all the institutions affiliated to it should not be ruled out as the ultimate solution. In the event, the majority of colleges continued to be administered and financed through the local education authorities, only those provided by the churches and other voluntary bodies receiving direct grants. The proposal for direct financing of the colleges through the school of education was resurrected by the Robbins Committee and decisively rejected by the government.

The suggestion that the title of recognized teacher in the university should be conferred upon certain members of the staff of the affiliated colleges has again not been taken up generally, although it is now being adopted by some universities in connection with teaching for the Bachelor of Education degree. The possibility of certain of the courses undertaken in the training colleges being recognized as satisfying part of the requirements of a first degree course (apart from a B.Ed.) has in most cases remained only a possibility; in some cases where a university accepted a student for degree work who had already completed one or two years of the college course it refused to recognize any part of this course as contributing credit towards undergraduate study.

The University Department of Education

A word needs to be said at this stage about the university departments of education, reference to which has already been made at several points. Many of these departments first came into existence between 1890 and 1900 as day training colleges for the preparation of teachers for elementary schools, sometimes providing added facilities for degree studies within the university itself. As such they played a most important part in the development of the modern universities of this country. Armytage has stated that 'it is not too much to say that these Education departments saved the younger universities from remaining glorified technical colleges. For they gave grant-aided students to the struggling faculties of arts and pure science for practically fifty years, at a time when other grants were meagre.'[1] They assumed their post-graduate training functions after the 1902 Act created an additional demand for trained secondary teachers, and the 1906 report of the Board of Education had intimated that it might be required for a certain proportion of newly appointed staff in such schools to have pursued appropriate courses of training.[2] By 1912, eighteen institutions had been approved for this purpose, including nine university departments—Birmingham, Durham, Leeds, Liverpool, London, Manchester, Oxford, Reading and Aberystwyth—and eight training colleges. Four other university institutions were at that date providing secondary training—Bristol, Sheffield, Bangor and Cardiff—but were as yet not 'recognized or certificated as efficient under the regulations of the Board of Education for the training of teachers for secondary schools.' In 1911 the possession of a university degree had become a prerequisite for attendance at one of these departments, but the numbers involved were small—205 in 1914.[3] The majority of secondary teachers obtained teaching posts immediately after graduation; between 1908 and 1921 a total of only 2,761 undertook post-graduate training courses, and out of this total no fewer than

[1] Armytage, W. H. G. *The Role of an Education Department in a Modern University*. Sheffield: 1954, p. 6.
[2] For a full account of the creation of these departments see Rich, *op. cit.*, especially Chapters VIII and IX, Jones, *op. cit.*, and the *Report of the Board of Education for 1913*.   [3] Jones, L., *op. cit.*, p. 32.

2,179 were women. Analysing the figures of trained and untrained teachers in secondary schools in 1923, Jones comments:

'. . . in 1913 only 180 out of 5,246 men teachers in the 1,010 secondary schools to which the figures apply had followed a course of professional training specifically for secondary teaching. The great majority of the trained men teachers in these schools (1,790 out of a total of 1,970) had passed through an institution for elementary teachers and had transferred after training or after a few years' service, into secondary schools. Compare with these figures for women teachers and it becomes evident in which part of the field the battle for training is still to be won. Were figures available for other than grant-earning secondary schools there is little doubt that in the boys' schools the number of trained teachers would be negligible.'[1]

By the beginning of the second world war the number of graduate students undertaking one-year professional courses in departments of education and elsewhere had grown to nearly two thousand, men being in the majority. Some 63 per cent of these students were completing a four-year programme of three years' undergraduate study plus one year of professional training for teaching to which they had committed themselves on leaving school. In order to obtain grant aid for such a course students had to sign a declaration known as 'the pledge', stating their intention on completion of the course of following the profession of teaching, acknowledging that advantage had been taken of public funds to qualify themselves for this profession and none other. The McNair Report stated that 'it is common knowledge . . . that many students in receipt of ear-marked grants for the recognized four-year course at universities are not there because they have freely chosen to be teachers but because the Declaration and its attendant grants offer them a chance which would otherwise be denied to them of obtaining a university education and particularly a university degree. . . .'[2]

With the creation of separate schools for the post-primary years during the twenties and thirties and the up-grading of all post-primary education to secondary status after 1944, the distinction between institutions providing training for elementary and secondary teaching respectively began to disappear.

[1] *Ibid.*, p. 123.   [2] McNair Report, *op. cit.*, p. 90.

A substantial proportion of the teachers prepared in training colleges have found work in secondary schools; and there is a regular traffic of teachers between schools catering for different age ranges. With the shortage of teachers at the primary stage during the post-war period, however, there has been official pressure upon the training colleges to concentrate upon preparing teachers for the younger children, culminating in the Minister's 'Balance of Training' circular of 1960, with its proposal that 80 per cent of the output of the colleges should be channelled into the primary sector. There are today many graduate teachers who are interested in working in junior schools – for men, in particular, the opportunities for promotion in this sphere are a good deal better than elsewhere. A number of the university departments of education offer courses of training for work in junior schools, four of these also providing for potential teachers of infants. One-year post-graduate training is also available in twenty-two general colleges of education, and one-year secondary courses in nine other colleges offering specialist work in domestic science, agriculture, handicraft, physical education and drama.[1]

At the present time all the universities established up to 1950 have departments of education, one or two of which offer a course that runs concurrently with the undergraduates' degree studies. Of the newer universities – York, Sussex, Essex, East Anglia, Lancaster, Warwick and Kent – not all have yet established such departments.[2] Lancaster and Warwick have entered into special relationships with near-by colleges, whereby these undertake the graduate training that elsewhere takes place in the university itself. Several of the technological universities (formerly colleges of advanced technology) have appointed professors of education and are in process of establishing post-graduate courses.

---

[1] *Compendium, op. cit.*

[2] For a description of the organization of the School of Education and Social Work in the University of Sussex, see Ford, B., 'The School of Education and Social Work', in *The Idea of a New University*, edited by David Daiches, London: André Deutsch, 1964. For an account of the work of a more conventional department see Wagner, F. W. and Douch, R., 'The Education of Graduate Teachers', *Education for Teaching*, May 1965, p. 24.

CONTROL OF TEACHER EDUCATION

Robbins and after

On 8 February 1961 a committee was set up under the chairmanship of Professor Lord Robbins to 'review the pattern of full-time higher education in Great Britain and in the light of national needs and resources to advise Her Majesty's government on which principles its long-term development should be based.'[1] The only member of the committee directly involved in teacher education was H. L. Elvin, Director of the University of London Institute of Education, and at first it was feared that the absence of any member with active training college experience might lead to the interests of the colleges being neglected. Deputations from the Association of Teachers in College and Departments of Education, representing a substantial proportion of the college staffs, waited upon the Minister of Education and questions were asked in the House of Commons; since it appeared that there was little hope of obtaining direct representation the Association decided to concentrate its attention upon the effective presentation of its views on the future of the colleges in the form of written and oral evidence.

During the next two years all the bodies involved in any way with teacher education prepared statements of written evidence and in many cases made further oral submissions. In addition, teacher education was referred to directly and indirectly in a number of statements from other bodies and private individuals, and these have been subsequently published in the six volumes of evidence issued for the committee. In a memorandum submitted in July 1961 the A.T.C.D.E. affirmed its faith in the concurrent college course in which professional and subject courses proceed side by side; suggested the possibility of interprofessional colleges in which probation officers, social workers and so on might be educated alongside teachers;[2] called for the provision of degree courses in colleges and the strengthening of links with the universities, and proposed a new structure for the administration of the colleges, involving a system of direct

---

[1] *Higher Education: Report.* London: H.M.S.O., 1963, p. (iii).
[2] This suggestion also received support from other bodies—see, for example, the written evidence submitted by the Association of Chief Education Officers *Evidence: Part One, Section D*, p. 1287, and the Conference of Institute Directors, *ibid., Section E*, p. 1584.

grants distributed by a sub-committee of the university grants committee.

Several of these recommendations were echoed by other bodies; in particular, there were many common points in the evidence of the Association, the Conference of Directors of Institutes of Education (C.I.D.) and the Conference of Heads of University Departments of Education (C.H.U.D.E.).[1] As might be expected, the local authorities' representations were less sympathetic to the granting of a larger measure of administrative and financial autonomy to the colleges. The chief officers not only wanted to retain control of their own institutions, but also to have a share in the government of those in receipt of direct grant.[2]

In the event, the training colleges need not have worried about the possible neglect of their interests. The Report of the Robbins Committee placed teacher education firmly within the orbit of higher education, and made a series of recommendations regarding the future of the colleges that were closely related to the wishes of the bodies most directly concerned. The most important of these from the point of view of many of those engaged in training teachers related to the creation of a new degree, the Bachelor of Education, for those college students capable of work of degree level, and the organization of the colleges, departments and Institutes of education into university schools of education, with financial responsibility being shifted from the local authorities to the university, ear-marked grants being made to the latter for this purpose. The committee supported the continuance of concurrent training in the colleges, the new degree course to occupy four years, in line with the existing course of three years of undergraduate study plus a one-year professional course followed by trained graduate teachers. Suggestions were also made for a considerable expansion of the colleges, from the 42,000 students of 1962–3 to a total of 111,000 by 1973–4, utilizing existing foundations as far as possible in such a way as to ensure that by the latter date the majority of colleges should have at least 750 students.[3]

The Robbins Committee proposals were greeted by the

[1] Now merged as the Universities Council for the Education of Teachers (U.C.E.T.).   [2] *Section D*, *op. cit.*, p. 1287.

[3] *Higher Education: Report*, *op. cit.*

colleges with 'general rejoicing'.[1] The A.T.C.D.E. particularly welcomed the strengthening of links with the universities, the provision of degree courses and the emphasis that had been laid upon the value of the concurrent course.[2] In a further statement issued a month later the Association re-emphasized in greater detail the advantages that would accrue from linking the administration and finance of the colleges to the universities rather than continuing under the local authorities.[3] The latter were already gathering their forces, and it was clear that they were not prepared to surrender control of the colleges without a fight. In December 1963 the chairmen of the A.T.C.D.E., C.I.D. and C.H.U.D.E. sent a joint letter to *The Times* reiterating the need for the colleges to come wholly within the university framework,[4] and during the next three months a lively correspondence took place in the national press regarding the future position of the colleges. It was clear that the government had not yet made up its mind. In February 1964 Mr. Quintin Hogg was reported as having expressed the view that he 'was less inclined than the vice-chancellors to hurry in establishing teacher training colleges as parts of universities', and that he saw them 'as much more like liberal arts colleges than anything we have at present.'[5] This statement ran directly counter to the policies of the A.T.C.D.E., C.I.D. and C.H.U.D.E. and to the expressed views of the Robbins Committee, and strengthened the opinion of many of those in the colleges that substantial pressures were being brought to bear upon the government to preserve the *status quo* in the administration and control of the colleges. The response to the Robbins proposals on teacher education on the part of the universities had been a good deal more favourable than had been expected in some quarters, and informal groups were already beginning work in some places on the preparation of syllabuses and regulations for the B.Ed. The teachers' associations and the Association of University Teachers were also sympathetic to the new status of the colleges. The debate with the local authorities—not all of whom opposed the Robbins proposals for transfer of control—continued during the first nine months of 1964, and with the calling of a general

---

[1] A.T.C.D.E. *News Sheet* No. 43, December 1963, p. 1.
[2] 26 October 1963.   [3] Quoted in A.T.C.D.E. *News Sheet* No. 42, p. 3.
[4] 16 December 1963.   [5] *Times Educational Supplement*, 14 February 1964.

election for October of that year any hope for an early decision
by the government was abandoned. The issue was not mentioned by any of the political parties in their election manifestos,
and it was not until 11 December that an announcement was
made by the newly appointed Secretary of State for Education
in the incoming Labour government, Mr. Michael Stewart.[1]

The statement supported the Robbins proposals that there
should be closer links between the colleges and the universities,
and expressed the hope that the latter would proceed to work
out with the colleges the form that B.Ed. degree courses might
take. But the government did not feel able to agree to fundamental changes in their administration and finance. The Director of
Education for Sheffield echoed the l.e.a. view in a conference
address early in 1966:

'. . . I confess that I have, at various times and as occasion
offered, spoken and lobbied against this particular proposal of
the Robbins Report [for university control of the colleges] and I
make this admission without either penitence or shame. What
indeed have I to be ashamed of?–doing all I could to ensure
that the children in the schools had teachers to teach them?
My authority maintains three colleges of education which in
1960 had 700 students; today they have 1,400, and by 1968 they
will have over 2,100. We represent one-hundredth of the
country and we are producing teachers for one-fiftieth. In
exerting ourselves to this end we have not been motivated by
any ideology or lust for power, but simply by enlightened self-
interest combined apparently by about the same amount of
sheer altruism towards our neighbours.'[2]

This feeling can be likened to that of the ill-fated school
boards towards their higher-grade schools during the last
decade of the nineteenth century.[3] A similar attitude had also
been shown in 1925, when the Departmental Committee on the
Training of Teachers for Elementary Schools recommended that
the responsibility for examining college students should pass
from the Board of Education to a system of Joint Boards under
the aegis of universities. In stating their views on this proposal

[1] *Hansard*, 11 December 1965.
[2] Tunn, T. H. 'The Significance of 1970', *Education*, 4 February 1966.
[3] Eaglesham, E. *From School Board to Local Authority*. London: Routledge
and Kegan Paul, 1956.

76

the local authorities made clear that they 'were concerned, not so much with the mechanism of training college examinations as with the training and supply of teachers as a whole and they regarded the two-year colleges as an essential part of the system. They were not willing that control of their own colleges should pass from the hands of the l.e.a's either to a university or any other body.'[1]

A second and no less important reason for the failure of the government to agree to the measure of autonomy for the colleges that the Robbins Committee had recommended arose from their concern, at a time of chronic teacher shortage, to retain through the local education authorities and the arrangements for finance, a close supervision over the number of student places and the supply of teachers. The chief officer of a local authority, representative of the employing body, has greater opportunities to persuade a college principal and staff to accept 'box and cox', 'crowding up' and other schemes designed to secure greater productivity than he would have as the leader of a one-third minority on a largely autonomous governing body.

A third factor was that the decision regarding the future of the colleges came to be made during a period of acute financial stringency, when the government was considering every possible way of getting value for money from the educational system. The universities were an extremely expensive item in the educonomy, and to allow the colleges to pass within their orbit would be likely to increase the overall cost of teacher education.

Government Policy and the Colleges

There are many respects in which, from the beginning, the training colleges have been national, rather than local, institutions. They provide a qualification of universal currency throughout England and Wales, and receive large numbers of students, if not the majority in the case of certain colleges,[2] from distant areas. But at no time have they been subject to direct central control. The possibility of the latter has come up at several points in their history. As we have seen, if denominational opposition had not been so strong there would have been a national college as early as 1839. Nearly a hundred years

---

[1] Humphreys, *op. cit.*   [2] Chapter 5, *passim.*

later, when the departmental committee of 1925 was considering future arrangements for the finance and control of the colleges, a leading article in *The Times Educational Supplement* suggested that if the colleges were in fact engaged upon national work they should not be administered by local authorities–'[Local] control is inconsistent with a national service.'[1] This suggestion found no echo in the recommendations of the committee, although the financial arrangements proposed, whereby all local authorities, including those without colleges in their own area, contribute to the support of whole system in proportion to their school population, once again emphasized the national character of teacher education. It has been suggested that 'this pooling of expenditure is the most important single fact in the administration of the college today . . . it is a nice point whether the Department [of Education and Science] controls the expenditure of local authorities on their own colleges. Its effective control is *ex poste facto*–a drawing of the attention of the governors and hence of finance and establishment committees to headings under which a college has exceeded average expenditure.'[2]

At the beginning of academic year 1968–9 there were 166 colleges of education in England and Wales, and twenty-eight university departments of education. One hundred and thirteen colleges were provided by local education authorities, twenty-seven by the Church of England and the Church in Wales, seventeen by the Roman Catholic Church, and nine by the Methodists, Free Churches and undenominational bodies. During the post-war period the most notable change in the pattern of organization and control of teacher education has been the increase in the number of local authority colleges, which now constitute 68 per cent of the total, as compared with 29 per cent in 1938. The share of the Church of England has fallen from 40 per cent to 17 per cent, that of the Roman Catholics from 11 per cent to 10 per cent. Twenty-seven of the county authorities in England and Wales and twenty-eight county boroughs maintain colleges; the Inner London Education Authority is responsible for nine, the West Riding

[1] Quoted Humphreys, *op. cit.*
[2] Baird, K. 'The Status of the Teacher', *Aspects of Education 3*, December 1965, p. 60. Hull: University of Hull Institute of Education.

has six, Lancashire and Manchester five, Leeds and Liverpool four, Sheffield and Buckinghamshire have three apiece and the remaining forty-four authorities one or two each.[1]

In practice, a local authority college of education has to deal with three masters—the local authority, the university and the Department of Education and Science. It has been said that 'a Secretary of State who proclaims that the increase in the numbers of teachers in training is urgent top priority would have to think hard to work out a more cumbersome machinery to secure it.'[2]

Official and lay influence on the work of the colleges at the local level has varied a good deal from one area to another. Despite the recommendations of the Minister of Education in 1960 that governing bodies should reflect the national character of the colleges, representing interests wider than those of a single maintaining authority, the governing body in some areas continued to be made up very largely of elected councillors and aldermen, with a membership that shifted with the changing fortunes of the political parties in local elections. The committee structure within which the governing body operated was often very complex, and there was great variety in the freedom given to principals and staff in such matters as expenditure, staffing and leave of absence. Two examples of how local authority procedures affected the work of the colleges have been provided by college principals.

'Standing orders define the number of committees through which resolutions of the governors must pass before becoming effective. Here, the governors are a sub-committee of the Further Education Committee, and the minutes go to that Committee. From there they go to the Education Committee, and from there to the County Council. . . . In addition to this wearisome journey, all ancillary staff, even maids, are referred to the Establishments Committee. Matters of policy, especially in comparison with other colleges, are often referred to the Policy committee, and, above all, *all* purchases have to go to the Purchasing Committee of the County Supplies Department. You can imagine what happens in this complicated situation.'

And in another case:

'The college is not allowed to get in touch directly with any

---

[1] Calculated from *Compendium, op. cit.*   [2] Baird, *op. cit.*

other department of the local education authority, other than the Education Department. Nor must it get in touch with the Department of Education and Science with the exception of the college H.M.I. This causes interminable delays, and interferes with the confidential relationship between principal and students. The application forms and references of all grades of staff are kept in the Town Hall, so that it is not easy to refer to them. All the interviewing procedure is in the hands of a largish staffing sub-committee'.[1]

The direct grant colleges have been largely free from such control over their affairs. The providing body is represented among the governors, among whom are also numbered university and local authority members, but the principal is often free to decide such matters as the expenditure of money, the choice of staff and the general determination of development policy within a very wide range of discretion.

In his statement on the future of the colleges of 11 December 1964, the Secretary of State had stated his intention that the existing arrangements for the internal government of colleges should be reviewed 'forthwith'. The local authorities at once approached the A.T.C.D.E. with a request that the association should meet their own study group on this matter, an invitation that was a first rejected by the colleges on the grounds that the Department of Education and Science had already been asked by them to set up such a group. Later a single informal meeting with local authority representatives was held, but this was not followed by any further talks. The Secretary of State's formal approach in January 1965, suggested that the group should include ten local authority members, four from the voluntary providing bodies, and four from the A.T.C.D.E., it being left to the group itself to decide, once constituted, 'whether, and if so, how, they could best bring university or other experience to throw light on the subject of this discussion'. This was unacceptable to the Association, which made clear that it would find it impossible to accept an invitation to join the study group if university representatives were excluded from it.[2] In at least one area it appears that the matter became linked to the establishment of the B.Ed.–at a meeting of the North Eastern branch of the A.T.C.D.E. at Darlington in February 1965 it

[1] A.T.C.D.E. *News Sheet* No. 48, April 1965.   [2] *Ibid.*

was reported that the Director of the University of Leeds Institute of Education had informed his professional committee that the university was delaying action on the proposed B.Ed. degree until it became clearer whether or not universities would be invited to participate in discussions on the government of colleges.[1]

In consort with the Association of University Teachers it was decided that questions on the matter of university representation on the study group would be asked in the House of Commons and the House of Lords. In the latter, Lord Bowden made it clear that whilst the government felt that '. . . in the first instance', the study group should include only representatives of 'those people directly concerned with the government of colleges' – the providing bodies and the staff association – it was envisaged that 'the other parties concerned should be brought in urgently and quickly'. On this basis the Association agreed to participate in a first meeting of the group, suggesting that one of the subjects for discussion might be the inclusion of universities in the study group. A few weeks later, however, the Parliamentary Secretary for Education stated at the end of a debate on higher education in the House of Commons that 'The university's view will be welcome and they will be asked to come in and talk with the study group, but it was felt on balance that the universities should not actually be members of the study group itself. That was the view both of the local authorities and the government.'[2] This appeared to be a reversal of the position previously stated by Lord Bowden, and the Association once again requested clarification. The Secretary of State, having already agreed to increase the Association's representation to six, then 'urgently' requested them to join the study group, which they agreed to do. At the first meetings there was a good deal of opposition to university representation, but at the fourth meeting, in July 1965 four vice-chancellors, the chairman of the Conference of Institute Directors and two heads of university departments of education attended.

During the course of the study group's work a report appeared in *The Times* outlining the position that had been taken up by the colleges and the local authorities, and emphasizing the strength of the differences of opinion that existed between the

---

[1] *Ibid.*   [2] *Ibid.*

college and local authority representatives.[1] The fact that this statement accurately reflected the position at the time was made clear by the A.C.T.D.E.'s protest to the Minister at its appearance. The article 'could not have been written without full knowledge of the discussions that have been taking place within the study group . . . the article anticipates the findings of the Study Group, and, further, we find its general tone objectionable in the interpretation it puts on the colleges and their viewpoint.'[2] In a footnote to his letter of reply the Secretary of State said 'I detest these inaccurate (or accurate!) Press leaks as much as you do—they do nothing but harm.'[3]

The report of the study group was eventually published in March 1966 and soon became known as the Weaver Report, after the name of the chairman. It recommended a considerable liberalization of the arrangements for the government of colleges, including the setting up of separate governing bodies in areas where they did not exist, the inclusion on the governing body of university and teacher representatives and, on an *ex officio* basis, the college principal and a 'small number' of lecturers nominated by the staff academic board. The report strongly supported the continuing development of academic boards within the colleges, this having been a major plank of A.T.C.D.E. policy for some years. It was suggested that these boards should include the principal and deputy principal, all those principal lecturers with responsibilities for a department, members of such other departments as did not have a principal lecturer at their head, and a third group of members elected by the teaching staff as a whole.[4]

Perhaps the most surprising feature of the report was the measure of agreement that appeared to have been secured between the representatives of the various interests. Little trace of the earlier differences remained. In the words of the report itself:

'We hope that we have managed to import into our report some overtones of the consensus we have established and that

[1] 19 October 1965.

[2] A.T.C.D.E. *News Sheet* No. 50, December 1965, p. 18.

[3] *Ibid.*

[4] *Report of the Study Group on the Government of Colleges of Education.* London: H.M.S.O., 1966.

CONTROL OF TEACHER EDUCATION

these will find an echo in the minds of those who read it. We know from our intensive study of these issues that some of them can be productive of tensions, and we recognize that these may well be magnified in the larger world of action. But we are convinced, again by our experience round the table, that all of them can be relaxed and most of them can be removed by patient and frank discussion and the exercise of goodwill.'[1]

Vickers has pointed out how in any such discussions as those in which the study group was involved, the state of mind of those taking part is gradually modified as a product of their participation; using as an example the Report of the Royal Commission on Capital Punishment of 1953 (The Gowers Report), he shows how the commissioners' views on the subject, once they had made their appreciation, were different from when they began their work, 'and this change, communicated through the Report, provoked change, similar or dissimilar, in greater or lesser degree, in all it reached, from serious students to casual readers of newspaper paragraphs, and thus released into the stream of event and into the stream of ideas an addition to the countless forces by which both are moulded.'[2]

The Executive of the A.T.C.D.E. welcomed the Report of the Study Group on the Government of the Colleges, feeling that it represented 'the best compromise solution in the present situation' and, providing that it gained acceptance by all concerned, 'an important step forward in the liberalizing of college government.'[3] In a parliamentary reply during November 1966 the Secretary of State informed the House that 'the organizations concerned have endorsed the [study group's] general conclusions', and that the local authority associations concerned 'have endorsed and welcome the general spirit and purpose of the report, although making recommendations on points of detail.'[4]

Early in February 1967 the Secretary of State issued Circular 2/67, which required local authorities and voluntary colleges to prepare draft articles of government in accordance with the recommendations of the Weaver Report. Legislation was introduced in November 1967 to enable local authorities to

[1] Ibid., p. 24.
[2] Vickers, G. The Art of Judgement. London: Chapman and Hall, 1965, p. 24.   [3] A.T.C.D.E. Press Statement, 20 June 1966.
[4] Hansard, 10 November 1966.

establish governing bodies for the colleges that are not sub-committees of the authority, and to require college government to be carried on in accordance with articles of government which 'determine the functions to be exercised respectively, in relation to the institution, by the local education authority, the body of governors, the principal, and the academic board, if any'.

Official pressures on the colleges during recent years have been of two kinds – those directed to increasing the supply of teachers and those involving changes in the structure of teacher education. Efforts directed towards the first of these two aims have sometimes been seen as having implications for the second – the suggestion that the colleges might increase their output by means of a four-term year, for example, was opposed by some on the grounds that this would still further divide the practice of the colleges from that of other institutions of higher education. The official statement of 11 December 1964 that rejected the Robbins proposals for the colleges to be more closely associated with the universities in administrative and financial affairs had included the words 'for the present'. But in April 1965, in a speech at the Woolwich Polytechnic, the Secretary of State outlined a new policy for higher education, in which there would be a clear separation between the 'auto-nomous sector' of the universities and the 'public sector', the latter to include the technical colleges, colleges of education and other non-university institutions of higher education. All subsequent official proposals affecting teacher education have tended to be regarded with a good deal of suspicion by the universities, the colleges and the professional bodies concerned, on the presumption that they are directed towards reaffirming the place of the colleges in the 'public sector' and further attenuating their relationships with the universities. An example of this was the announcement in March 1966 that teacher train-ing departments would be established in five major technical colleges. These new departments would be free to seek validation for their certificates from either the University Institutes of Education or the Council for National Academic Awards, which had been set up as a degree-granting body for non-chartered institutions in the public sector. This proposal was greeted with 'astonishment' and dismay by the A.T.C.D.E., who feared the effects of splitting teacher training between university and non-university bodies. It is clear that there were strong hopes in some quarters that the technical colleges concerned would choose to work within the C.N.A.A. structure, but in the event four at once went in with the local Institutes of Education and the fifth followed them soon afterwards. There was no official reaction to these moves, but in a speech to the Central London Fabian Society in July 1966, the Chairman of the Parliamentary Labour Party Education Group, Mr. E. Armstrong, expressed views that undoubtedly reflected a good deal of non-university opinion.

'I believe that the strong links that exist between technical colleges and industry and commerce present a unique opportunity for teachers in training to study and live in a community undertaking varied disciplines. I was very disappointed, therefore, when I learned that the selected colleges had succumbed to the fears of the Universities and Colleges of Education and decided to work with the Institutes of Education rather than the Council for National Academic Awards.

'Teachers need closer contacts with the workaday world and I am certain that a departure from the traditional approach to teacher training by working under the auspices of C.N.A.A. would have brought a much needed breath of fresh air to the new venture. . . . If the new training departments are to be exact replicas of existing colleges of education then it is extremely doubtful whether the expense and effort can be justified. If the present timid, cautious approach persists a great opportunity will be missed and I wonder how long the Secretary of State can stand aside and leave the decisions to local opinion.'[1]

The Colleges and the Universities

The college's third master, the Institute of Education that constitutes the area training organization, is principally interested in academic matters, but in certain respects has responsibilities that overlap those of the central authority and providing body. The colleges are organized into twenty area

[1] Reported in *Education*, 1 July 1966, p. 14.

training organizations, nineteen of which are associated with universities. The distribution of colleges between these organizations is by no means uniform; the range is from two to thirty. The full figures are shown in Table IV.[1]

TABLE IV

Numbers of Colleges of Education in each Area Training Organization (1968)

Birmingham	17	London	30
Bristol	8	Manchester	12
Cambridge	11	Newcastle	6
Durham	7	Nottingham	8
Exeter	2	Oxford	4
Hull	2	Reading	3
Keele	3	Sheffield	7
Leeds	15	Southampton	5
Leicester	2	Sussex	5
Liverpool	10	Wales	9

One of the main lines of A.T.C.D.E. policy in recent years has been to ensure that decisions regarding such matters as increasing the output of the colleges should be decided through the area training organizations rather than by the local authorities and the Department of Education and Science, and this policy seems largely to have succeeded. The discussions that took place regarding the Ninth Report of the National Advisory Council for the Supply and Training of Teachers, especially with respect to the possible setting up of a four-term year in the colleges, seem to have resulted in a victory for the college representatives, the Secretary of State making clear that he had no intention of imposing such schemes on the colleges against their will and inviting local Institutes to prepare 'productivity' plans suitable for the situation and needs of their colleges. Although there are variations in the extent to which the college membership of the various boards and committees of the Area Training Organizations permit full consultation and participa-

[1] Calculated from *Compendium, op. cit.*

tion, the colleges have little to fear from the Institutes, and co-operation between them in relation to the university is nearly always amicable and relatively uncomplicated. Diversity is the keynote of this relationship. The extent to which, for example, common examination papers are required for certain subjects in all the colleges in a single Institute area varies not only between areas but also between subjects within the same Institute. On the whole there is a large measure of freedom for colleges to experiment and devise new courses on an individual basis; in the boards of studies the principle that dog does not eat dog helps to ensure more autonomy than might otherwise be the case.

During the period after the publication of the Robbins Report boards of studies and other Institute committees were active in planning the structure of the B.Ed. degree in their areas, and negotiating with the faculty boards, senate and other university bodies concerned. There was very little consultation between universities at this stage, and in consequence a great variety of arrangements have been made. In some colleges students need normal university entrance qualifications (two passes at 'A' level in subjects approved by the university concerned) before they can register for the degree, but provision is made for exceptional registration of those without such qualifications but who perform exceptionally well during the college course. Registration for the degree is effective in some colleges from the end of the first year, and B.Ed. and Certificate courses begin to diverge at this stage. Elsewhere this divergence begins at the end of the second year, whilst in some universities the certificate course is common for all students, with an additional year of study for those going on to the B.Ed. These patterns are commonly referred to as 'one plus three', 'two plus two' and 'three plus one'. There is no uniformity in the levels at which the B.Ed. can be awarded, and the grades in terms of which it is classified. At Bristol, Leeds, Leicester, Reading, Sussex and Warwick it is a classified honours degree. At other universities it is a pass or general degree, although in some it may be awarded with honours (classified or unclassified) to particularly outstanding candidates. These differences are important in terms of the payments for good honours degrees that form part of the Burnham scale of teachers' salaries, and may have some effect on the recruitment of students to colleges.[1] These issues are further considered in Chapter 5.

Although only one university (Cambridge) initially rejected the B.Ed., some negotiations have been difficult and involved. Jeffreys has commented adversely upon the attitudes shown by some university men outside the Institutes.

'Unfortunately the Institutes worked so well that the universities forgot that they were carrying a burden of responsibility which had originally been accepted under protest. In most cases they were thankful to let their Institutes get on with the job, and the university senates contentedly rubber-stamped the papers that came up from the Institute Delagacies. When controversy broke out over the Robbins recommendations, senates and faculties had to be told that they had been doing, for many years, what they now protested was unthinkable, i.e. trusting their Institutes of Education to oversee the work of the colleges and award qualifications in the name of the university. For the most part their response to this information was that of the incorruptible when told that they are unwittingly living in sin.'[2]

Despite disappointment regarding the rejection of the Robbins Committee recommendations for the closer administrative link with the universities, the colleges appear to have been reasonably well satisfied with the way in which B.Ed. plans have developed. It is therefore interesting to notice Jeffrey's comments that it is the administrative recommendations of Robbins that are the vital ones, 'much more important than the proposals for a B.Ed. degree', and that, if these are not implemented, sooner or later 'the present structure of Institutes of Education will disintegrate.'[3]

The planning and implementation of the B.Ed. degree has in some respects brought the colleges and the universities closer together, but in others it has left scars that may take some time to heal. Especially in those areas where an Honours B.Ed. is being offered, the universities have taken great care to ensure that the quality of the staffing, libraries and other facilities in

[1] For a discussion of some of these points see Taylor, W. 'Commentary on the Education Section's Report on Education in the B.Ed.' in *Report of a Conference on the Education and Training of Teachers*. London: Department of Education and Science, March 1967 (mimeographed).

[2] Jeffreys, M. V. C. 'Institutes of Education from McNair to . . . Robbins?', *Aspects of Education 3*, December 1965, p. 68.   [3] *Ibid.*

the colleges are adequate for this purpose, and this has entailed a measure of university oversight of what the colleges do that is new and unfamiliar. In some cases, individual members of college staffs have had to apply for recognition as teachers for the B.Ed., and not all these applications have been granted. There has been some anxiety in the colleges lest the needs of the 10 per cent or so of students who are likely to take the B.Ed. will come to overshadow those of the much larger Certificate group. There are organizational problems that arise from the fact that the college teacher who is preparing students for the B.Ed. is responsible to the head of the relevant university department and the B.Ed. Board of Studies, as well as to his or her own college head of department and Academic Board. It will be some years before it is clear what impact the existence of the B.Ed. is going to have upon the colleges and, more particularly in terms of the theme of this chapter, upon their relationships with the university.

The relationship of the colleges to the universities cannot be examined outside the whole context of the future structure of higher education. The tradition of academic freedom and administrative self-determination in the university sphere is very strong; such autonomy has been less a consequence of full recognition as a university institution than a condition for such recognition. Given the growth of the universities in recent years, and the larger part that they now play in economic, scientific and social development, the cost of maintaining the 'autonomous sector' of higher education has risen sharply. At the same time other institutions of post-school education have striven to emulate the achievements of the university, have placed greater emphasis upon advanced work, sought to develop research functions, to reduce the size of their classes and acquire a larger proportion of residential accommodation for their students.[1] In his speech at the Woolwich Polytechnic in April 1965, the Secretary of State for Education sought to call a halt to this process; 'if the universities have a class monopoly as degree-giving bodies and if every college which achieves high standards moves into the university club, then the residual public sector becomes a permanent poor relation', and an unhealthy rat race mentality is allowed to develop. He felt that it was essential

[1] Silberson, D. *Residence and Technical Education*. London: Deutsch, 1960.

89

that 'a substantial part of the higher education system should be under social control, directly responsible to social needs.'[1]

This statement sparked off an acrimonious debate, in which political allegiance played little part in determining the positions taken up. From the right the policy was attacked as threatening the growth of genuinely higher education and the traditions of the universities; from the left it was seen as an attempt to impose upon post-school education the same kind of 'separate but equal' bipartite policy that had failed in the secondary sphere. Some defenders saw it as part of an apparently deep-laid plot to introduce a genuinely comprehensive pattern in higher education – in a letter to the press a former member of the National Advisory Council referred to the fact that 'comprehensive reform in the secondary field will mean the end of the grammar schools . . . comprehensive reform in tertiary education will obviously mean the end of the universities. . . . To get a reasonable deal for the majority of students . . . we need a strict limitation of the universities and material standards to which they are accustomed. . . .'[2]

The position of the universities in modern society is based partly upon certain ascriptive and affective considerations regarding the likely behaviour of staff and administrators. It is assumed that they have internalized certain norms and values that effectively constrain 'irresponsible' conduct, and that their commitment to academic values carries with it a parallel set of moral sanctions against behaviour that might be judged as an abuse of what, in contemporary society, must inevitably be regarded as a privileged status. The professional code of the academic man takes the place of committee surveillance and close financial control; behaviour is programmed in accordance with internalized commitments to goals, rather than by means of rules and direct supervision.[3] Accountability and observability are minimal.[4] These conditions are in part a survival from

[1] Administrative Memorandum 7/65, Department of Education and Science, 1965.

[2] Letter from E. Robinson, *New Statesman*, 8 April 1966, p. 501.

[3] Strauss, G. 'Some Notes on Power Equalization' in Leavitt, J. J. (ed.), *The Social Science of Organizations*. Englewood Cliffs, New Jersey: Prentice Hall, Inc., 1963.

[4] Merton, R. K. *Social Theory and Social Structure*. New York: The Free Press, 1957.

an earlier, traditional, non-bureaucratic, ascriptive society, and are in some respects incongruent with the more open, achievement oriented social structure of today. The occupation of privileged statuses in contemporary society requires much more by way of formal and overt legitimization than used to be the case. Part of this legitimacy is provided by the apologists of the system, who make every effort to underline the sense of social responsibility of those concerned in its functioning. Part is also furnished by the existence of lay governing bodies, university councils and the like, and by the machinery of public control through committees of local authorities.

Sixty years ago, Graham Wallas, referring to the 'distinction between the comparative independence of a university professor or a public school headmaster and the real subordination of the teacher in a public elementary school or even in a municipal school or college of whatever grade', suggested that 'greater freedom will have to be given to the teachers in the new institutions, and some of those in the old institutions will have to lose part of their existing freedom.'[1] He went on to speculate on lines that have particular relevance today:

'This tendency towards a more equal distribution both of discipline and self-respect among the teachers in different types of schools is not likely to stop at the exact stage which it has now reached. A generation hence the heads of Oxford and Cambridge colleges may be lamenting the fact that they are liable to dismissal unless they perform a definite list of duties to the satisfaction of someone else, while the youngest teacher in an elementary girls' school may feel that she belongs to a profession which will not only ensure her fair treatment, but will stimulate her work by a conscious connection with the traditions of a great and progressive art.'[2]

It may be surmised that some such thinking lies behind recent attitudes to higher education on the part of governments in this country. It is by no means sure, however, that a limitation of freedoms at the one end of the scale will necessarily increase those available at the other. The Robbins Committee was clear that 'a system that aims at the maximum of independence compatible with the necessary degree of public control is good in itself, as

[1] Wallas, H. 'The Future of English Education in the Light of the Past' in *Men and Ideas*. London: Allen and Unwin, 1940, p. 171.　　[2] *Ibid.*

reflecting the ultimate values of a free society.'[1] The Committee went on to specify the constituents of academic freedom—freedom of appointments, to determine curricula and standards, of admissions, to determine the balance between teaching and research, and to determine the shape of development. But however legitimate these may be, there is little doubt that to a government concerned with using the educational system as an instrument of social policy, committed to the achievement of certain standards of social justice, and desirous of adopting a substantial volume of centralized educational planning, the extension of such freedoms to a wider area of post-school education can only serve to diminish the effectiveness with which such goals can be pursued. Because of the nature of these goals, and because of the non-revolutionary social and political climate in which they are embedded, there is little apparent risk at present to the essential freedoms of expression and operations that the universities prize. Furthermore, as has been shown in this chapter, organized professional opinion has shown itself capable of successfully resisting certain aspects of government policy, and it is by no means true that the centre of power in matters affecting higher education has decisively moved into the area of central government control. But some shift in this direction has taken place. As yet this has had little direct effect upon teacher education, but it does seem possible that a situations has been created in which stronger pressures could be exercised in the future.

For the present, if colleges of education are to secure the degree of self-determination in material, academic and financial affairs that has been agreed upon as desirable, then ways will have to be found to debureaucratize the relationships between the colleges and the providing bodies, without sacrificing the necessary accountability and responsibility that an open system requires. But formal statements of intent with respect to the machinery of college government are less important than the attitudes and traditions that influence the position taken up by providing bodies and college staffs, and the relationships between them. As has already been indicated, during the period since 1944 there has been a considerable variety in the way in which colleges have fared under local authority control; in

1 *Higher Education*, 1964, p. 230.

some areas they have had virtually no autonomy, the important aspects of their administration being handled outside the colleges and the less important being subjected to detailed and time-consuming scrutiny; elsewhere a degree of independence has been permitted that differs little from that accorded to a university institution. These large differences have existed within the framework of a single set of statutory regulations, sometimes in adjoining local authority areas; it seems perfectly possible that they will continue to exist within a reformed pattern of college government. Although the articles and instruments of government prepared by local authorities and voluntary bodies in response to Circular 2/67 are subject to approval by the Secretary of State, there can be little direct control of the spirit in which these are administered, and it is this, rather than the formal provisions themselves, that will determine the nature of the relationships that exist.

It would be premature to arrive at any conclusions about the viability of the existing pattern of central government, university and local authority control of colleges of education in terms of the social and educational needs that have been suggested in the first two chapters of this book. The present arrangements are in many respects typical of the way in which education has come to be administered in this country, and, as many college principals have discovered, the interstices of control often permit a larger range of discretion and opportunity for manoeuvre than would be possible under a single authority. Among the trends that seem likely particularly to affect the existing pattern are the reform of local government, the introduction of a greater measure of accountability in respect of the universities and the spread of teacher preparation to institutions other than colleges of education and universities.

4

THE DEVELOPMENT OF THE
COLLEGE COURSE

Early Days

The fact that only a tiny minority of children attended secondary schools during the first half of the nineteenth century meant that many students entering the training colleges during the first years of their existence had no more education than they would have obtained in a public elementary school up to the age of 13, and had already been employed in a variety of other occupations. The average age of the students resident in 1845 at the Pioneer Battersea Training School, for example, was 21½ years. Of the sixty-four students in 1846, four had been schoolmasters, eleven assistants in schools, eight clerks, six shopkeepers and shopmen and four had come straight from school. Others had been printers, shoemakers, tailors, gardeners, agricultural labourers and companions or 'had followed various laborious occupations connected with the manufactures'.[1] One quarter of the total had 'belonged to the class of workmen'. Some of the early colleges took their students straight from school – at St. Mark's, Chelsea, boys were admitted from the age of fifteen and remained three years, against eighteen months at Battersea. There were other and important differences between the assumptions on which Kay-Shuttleworth based his course at Battersea and those of the Reverend Derwent Coleridge, just across the river at St. Mark's. Kay-Shuttleworth, the founder of the Battersea College and later Secretary of the Committee of Council on Education, thought it essential for the teachers of the poor to accept for themselves a

[1] Moseley's report on St. Mark's College, Chelsea. *Minutes of the Committee of Council on Education*, 1846, Vol. II, p. 337.

way of life little different from that of their charges; it was not the intention at Battersea to encourage students to acquire increased social status or respectability from the training undergone. Coleridge held rather different views, and did not despise 'that keen sense and appreciation of social respectability, together with that energetic desire of social advancement, which unite at once the moving spring, the self-acting safety valve and self-adjusting regulator, of that great machine which we all call the British community.'[1] He took the view that the 'better the schoolmaster is bred, the more highly is he trained, and the more he is socially respected, the more ready will he be to combat the difficulties, to submit to the monotony, and to move with quiet dignity in the humbleness of his vocation'.[2] St. Mark's set out more directly than did Battersea to provide something by way of a secondary education for its students, in addition to classroom competence. The recognition of this raised difficulties for the Inspectors during the early years. The Reverend Moseley felt the need to define the scope of his inspection of St. Mark's in his report of 1844.

'The estimate which I am called upon to form of its efficiency for the purpose of its foundation must evidently be limited to its uses as a school intended to create an efficient body of schoolmasters for the instruction of the children of the labouring classes in connection with the established church; and I am bound to eliminate from my view of it all those objects of its friends which would make of the schoolmasters a "clerkly office" and unite it with holy orders and the function of a deacon.'[3]

Coleridge admitted to taking his models, not from the pedagogical seminaries of Switzerland and Germany that Kay-Shuttleworth so much admired, but from the 'older educational institutions of [this] country, originally intended, even those of the higher class, with their noble courts, solemn chapels, and serious cloisters, for clerks to the full as humble as those I had to train.'[4]

[1] Derwent Coleridge. *The Teachers of the People*, London, 1862, p. 36, quoted Rich, R. W. *The Training of Teachers in England and Wales during the Nineteenth Century*. London: Cambridge University Press, 1933, p. 88.

[2] *Ibid.*

[3] Moseley's report on St. Mark's College. *Minutes of the Committee of Council*, 1844, Vol. II, p. 599.

[4] Coleridge, *op. cit.*

The social position of the teacher was in many respects ambiguous; a former associate of the same 'lower orders' that he was called upon to teach, he lacked the authority traditionally associated with membership of the upper social strata. As one of the inspectors put in his report for 1846:

'*We must have educated men* to educate the *uneducated*. We cannot have them ... unless we place them in such a position that they will be respected, as superiors, by those whom they may have to teach, and not look down upon as inferiors, by those of the upper classes, with whom they ought to associate. Their position, I believe, my Lords, should be such that they should not *reasonably* desire any other, no, not even entrance into the holy order of our Church. The object of our training colleges is to train schoolmasters, not clergymen – to form a class of men who will worthily fill the most honourable and responsible station in the world, a station in honour of which, but not its responsibility, depends upon themselves, and who will not waste their thoughts and expend their energies in seeking other offices than those to which they have been called.'[1]

The inspectors had hard things to say about the tendency for the alumni of some colleges to renounce teaching and utilize their newly acquired education as a means of gaining entry to the ministry. Coleridge claimed that of the 659 students completing their courses of training at St. Mark's between 1841 and 1834, 391 were working in elementary schools at the later date; a further ninety-nine were employed as teachers in 'grammar, middle class and private schools or [as] private tutors', a further thirteen were in holy orders, thirty-five were laymen not engaged in education, nine were unemployed ('chiefly from ill health'), fifty-one were engaged in missionary, educational or other work in the colonies, and the occupations of twenty-nine were unknown. These figures were challenged by H. M. I. Cowie, who claimed that less than half of the output of St. Mark's during this period were working in inspected elementary schools.[2]

In a letter to the principal of the Chester diocesan college, Kay-Shuttleworth, as secretary of the Committee of Council,

[1] Frederick Watson's report on the Northern District. *Minutes of the Committee of Council on Education*, 1845, Vol. II, p. 181.

[2] Rich, *op. cit.*, pp. 107–8.

emphasized the need for the whole of the student's work to be directed towards his future vocation.

'It has been too generally assumed that almost the only preparation necessary for a schoolmaster is the acquirement of the knowledge which he is to impart, and it cannot be denied that the methodic instruction of students in Normal schools may and ought in itself to become one of the means of improving them in method. With this in view, not merely the subjects of instruction, but also the methods of teaching the candidates, should be so ordered as to be in itself a preparation for their future vocation as teachers. On this account the oral instruction of classes in a Normal school is greatly to be preferred to any other mode.'[1]

Some of the inspectors, however, felt that a narrow concentration upon method was equally dangerous. In his report on the training school at Battersea, Moseley was not enthusiastic about the oral method that Kay-Shuttleworth had encouraged. If it made teachers, it did not make students, giving neither the habit of self-instruction, nor the taste for it. In a passage that is not irrelevant to some of today's concerns, Moseley fears 'lest, when the college course is over, the student, now become a schoolmaster—deprived in great measure of that motive to the acquisition of knowledge which his desire for advancement had supplied, and with no other help than the books which he has been unaccustomed to use—should *cease* to be a *student* at all. This step once taken he will cease to be a good schoolmaster. His lessons will echo, day by day, more faintly the knowledge which with so many pains he had once acquired and nothing but a name will in a few years remain to distinguish him from the class of teachers to whom the same advantages have never been afforded.'[2]

The syllabuses of study in the early colleges covered an enormous range of subject matter in what would now be regarded as a shallow and superficial manner. At the Chester college, for example, during each week of the course students devoted twelve hours to education, eight hours to scriptural knowledge, five hours ten minutes to arithmetic, four and a half hours to the preparation of lessons, three and a half hours to English

[1] Appendix to *Minutes of the Committee of Council*, 1847–8, Vol. II, p. 486.
[2] *Minutes, op. cit.*, 1845, Vol. II, p. 583.

grammar, three hours to vocal music, two hours forty minutes to English literature, and a further thirteen hours to subjects such as 'evidence of Christianity, Church history, English history, algebra, Euclid, mensuration, natural and experimental philosophy [40 minutes only], writing, geography and linear drawing'—a total of fifty-one hours ten minutes timetabled work.[1] At St. Mark's the daily schedule provided for eight hours five minutes study, three and a quarter hours of industrial occupation—and thirty minutes leisure.[2]

From 1846 to the Twentieth Century

The content of the course provided in training colleges after 1846 was dominated by the introduction of the pupil-teacher system, which furnished a means whereby boys and girls might obtain something better than the ordinary elementary education prior to entering upon a course of training for teaching, and also gave the necessary financial support for such training in the shape of 'Queen's Scholarships'. For the first nine years of the operation of the pupil-teacher system the colleges were examined individually, and there was no fixed syllabus of instruction. Even so, the fact that the examination existed, and that the inspectors responsible for determining its structure shared many common assumptions about the content of teacher training, meant that there was an increasing uniformity in the work that the colleges did. By 1854 the committee of council 'after great consultation with every principal and every body of managers of a training institution . . . at last brought out a syllabus'.[3]

But the syllabus did little to bring the course of training given to students closer in touch with the needs of the schools and the communities that they served. Part of the trouble was that the college principals and many of the inspectors were Oxford and Cambridge graduates, clergymen who had little personal knowledge and awareness of the conditions of the social classes that their students were being trained to serve and the limitations that these conditions would impose upon their work. Not only

[1] Calculated from Rich, *op. cit.*, p. 105.
[2] *Minutes, op. cit.*, 1845, Vol. II, p. 583.
[3] *Education Commission, 1861, Minutes of Evidence.* Oral evidence given by Rev. H. Baker, Principal of Whitelands College, p. 235.

THE COLLEGE COURSE

was there no popular control over the schools and the training of teachers for them, but there existed no means at the time whereby popular pressures might be brought to bear. Referring to the proposal for a state Normal school in his evidence to the Newcastle Commission of 1858, Kay-Shuttleworth stated a view that bears closely upon the whole development of education in England, and which distinguishes the pattern of this development from that of other countries, particularly the United States, where local and popular interest have played, and to a degree, continue to play, a large part in educational decision making.

'The Constitution of the Battersea Training College, therefore, was one of the fruits of experience, and I define that experience to have resulted, first, in a deeper appreciation of the exceeding strength of the religious principle in this country, which devotes so large a portion of charity to the school as part of the religious social organization—as a nursery for the Church and congregation. Secondly I was led to admit what was reluctantly forced upon my mind, mainly, the weakness of any other principle; as for example the patriotic or civil principle—upon which the government could in any degree rely for the support of such an institution. I believe that no civil body in this country, apart from the Central Government, has done anything worth speaking of for public education. I believe that all that has been done for education hitherto, excepting what has been done by the Central Government, has been derived from religious zeal. . . .'[1]

The views expressed here can be compared with the history of the origins of the public school in the United States. The early schools were essentially built for the community, and were usually the first buildings to be erected after immediate housing needs had been met. The American communities hired their own teachers and later on helped to support the facilities that were necessary to train them. If this resulted in certain losses in the freedom of the teacher, it also helped to create a genuine popular base for the provision of public education, a base that was largely missing in this country at the time when industrial, technological and political developments began to generate the need for a larger measure of mass

[1] *Ibid.*, evidence by Sir James Kay-Shuttleworth, p. 305.

99

literacy and numeracy than the Church and private sources could provide.

In most of the colleges during the period after 1846 the course was of two years' duration, but in some institutions a proportion of the students left after only a year's residence; a unique situation was presented by Homerton College, Cambridge, established by the Congregationalists and other evangelical denominations, where an attempt was made between 1845 and 1867 to operate without benefit of Queen's Scholarships and government grant. The course was of a year to sixteen months' duration, and comprised a 'study of the Bible, the first part of Butler's anthology, arithmetic, writing, English grammar, orthography and etymology, geography, English history, the elements of astronomy, and natural science; free-hand drawing from the flat, the theory and practice of vocal music, the outline of mental philosophy, and the art of teaching'. The college admitted both men and women students, and in addition to the foregoing subjects, the men studied 'algebra as far as quadratic equations, proportion and variation, arithmetical and geometrical progression, the elements of Euclid . . . bookkeeping, mensuration, and land surveying, Latin (as a means of mental discipline, and to give an insight into the general structure of language) drawing from models and chemistry.' The male students also, 'as a voluntary exercise', obtained instruction in French and Greek, the former because it was beginning to form part of the elementary curriculum in the large towns, the latter 'with a view to matriculation'.[1]

Such a curriculum is easily attacked, especially with the advantage of hindsight that we now possess. But, for all its faults, it was at least within the same cultural tradition as the education provided at Oxford and Cambridge and regarded as characteristic of the educated man of the time, and as such provided at least the smatterings of the social and educational skills that would eventually enable larger numbers of the less privileged to secure access to this tradition and, in doing so, to change it. To base the syllabus for the training college firmly upon the subjects appropriate to the elementary school, as Moseley had desired, might conceivably have produced more

[1] Education Commission, 1861, *op. cit.*, evidence by Rev. W. J. Unwin, p. 277.

THE COLLEGE COURSE

teachers able to cope with school conditions as they found them, and to rest content with the salaries and status that they were offered. But in doing this it might have still further delayed the process by which elementary education began to pull itself up by its own boot-straps—a process that was sharply interrupted by the enactment of Lowe's revised code in 1862.

The new code followed the voluminous report of the Newcastle Commission, appointed in 1858 'to enquire into the present state of popular education in England, and to consider and report what measures, if any, are required for the extension of sound and cheap elementary instruction to all classes of people'. The recommendations of the Commission regarding the supplementation of state capitation grants by rate aid (the only type of grant to which the Commission suggested the infamous 'payment by results' should be applied) and the creation of a new class of examiners to assist Her Majesty's Inspectorate, organized in country and borough education boards, were ignored. The revised code laid down that grants could only be paid to schools if their scholars were successful in the annual examinations; a similar rule was to apply to the colleges, the sum paid being determined by the grade of pass attained by the student— between £13 and £20 for first-year and £16 and £24 for second-year candidates. The range of subjects forming the certificate examination was modified; physical science, mechanics, higher mathematics, English literature and Latin were all dropped from the second year's work—changes that amounted to the 'excision of the more ambitious parts of the original scheme' and a greater attention to the subjects of the elementary school curriculum. The new conditions for grant and the abolition of the Queen's Scholarships announced in 1863 hit the colleges particularly hard, and for the next ten years, until the effects of the Education Act of 1870 began to make themselves felt on the demand for teachers, many of them had considerable difficulty in keeping going.[1]

[1] Rich (*op. cit.*) quotes a number of interesting suggestions of the time regarding the uses to which the colleges might be put, including one from Derwent Coleridge that indicates something remarkably like a system of 'liberal arts' colleges on the American pattern.

THE DEVELOPMENT OF

Twentieth-century Developments

The Education Act of 1870 had comparatively little effect upon
the college courses; during the next 30 years there was a slow but
perceptible liberalization of the curriculum, and standards in
the colleges gradually rose as the quality of preparation of those
entering them improved. Shortly after the turn of the century
permission was given for colleges to produce their own syllabuses
for approval by the Board of Education, but only a small number took advantage of this proviso. The day training colleges,
set up under university auspices during the nineties, in which
some of the lectures were given by university professors and the
final examination set by the university and recognized by the
Board, had some influence on the system as a whole, but hardly
affected the content of the Board's syllabus for the grant-aided
residential colleges. The fact that some of the teaching in the
day colleges was found to be too academic for the tastes and
abilities of some of their students, and the difficulties, where
degree studies were undertaken, of combining these with the
professional content of the course, again emphasized the conflict
between academic and classroom-centred studies that is still
with us today.[1] The work of psychologists was beginning to be
felt in the professional courses; Sully's *Teachers' Handbook of
Psychology* went through five editions between 1886 and 1909,
and the researches of Thorndyke, Terman and Spearman began
to affect what was taught about learning and mental development in children.[2] By the beginning of the twenties the syllabus
for the two-year course included a number of obligatory professional subjects—principles and practice of teaching, hygiene
and physical training—and two groups of other subjects, in each
of which were both ordinary and advanced courses. In the first
group (A) were English, History, Geography, Mathematics,
Elementary Science and Welsh; at the advanced level Physics,
Chemistry and Biology took the place of Elementary Science,
and French was added. Group (B) included singing and music,

[1] *Report* of the Board of Education, 1912–13, pp. 32 ff.

[2] Tibble, J. W. 'Psychological Theories and Teacher Training' in the
Yearbook of Education for 1963, *The Education and Training of Teachers*,
edited by G. Z. F. Bereday and J. A. Lauwerys. London: Evans Brothers,
1963.

102

drawing, needlework and handwork (for women only and known as 'housecraft' at the advanced level) and, at the advanced level only, special handwork and gardening.[1]

Students preparing for work in elementary schools were required to take English and one other subject from group A, two from group B, and a fifth from either group. Students intending to teach in post-primary schools had to choose two subjects from group A (one to an advanced stage), one from group B and a fourth from either group; prior to 1920 students were sometimes required to take as many as six or seven separate subject courses. The establishment of the Joint Board scheme in 1926 threw the responsibility for examining students on to Boards organized under the aegis of universities, on which local colleges were represented; the Board of Education still had to approve the syllabuses and examinations in each area, and His Majesty's Inspectors had the responsibility of inspecting the practical teaching of a sample of candidates from each college. But although this pattern of organization laid a foundation of co-operation with the universities that was to be more formally developed during the post-war period, in itself it did little to bring the colleges closer together or to make the university link a real influence on their work; the relationship was almost entirely limited to the examining of students, and in the view of the McNair Committee was no more influential on the work of individual colleges than when they were all under the direct control of the Board of Education.[2] Nor did the Joint Board scheme have much effect upon the structure and content of the course of training; any changes proposed in the syllabuses outlined above had to be submitted to the Central Advisory Committee for the Certification of Teachers, and such changes took the form of the reduction in the number of subjects and their integration into single courses rather than any more fundamental revision.

[1] Jones, L. *The Training of Teachers*. Oxford: The University Press, 1924, p. 84. (I had the advantage of using Mr. Jones's annotated copy of this book, which is the most recent detailed study of the provision for teacher education at present available.)

[2] *Teachers and Youth Leaders*. London: H.M.S.O., 1943 (McNair Report), p. 16.

Towards the Three-year Course

During the twenties and thirties there were frequent complaints that the college timetable was overcrowded, and in recommending that the training college course should be lengthened to three years the McNair Committee made clear that they did not contemplate the longer period being used for 'any general increase in the number of subjects which students are called upon to study'.[1] The Committee made few suggestions regarding how the additional year might be used; they saw it as being justified by the need for better-educated men and women in schools, by the lack of maturity of the average 20-year-old at the end of the college course, and by the need for more time being spent in practical teaching than had previously been possible. The recommendation that the university school of education or re-organized Joint Board should accept full responsibility for determining and approving the structure and content of the courses meant that the Committee could hardly lay down what it was or was not desirable to include. Some broad recommendations were made about the content of the professional courses; Physiology and Physical education should be compulsory subjects for all students, as should Psychology – but with the reservation that such studies should not be pursued as if students were reading them for a degree. The Committee had 'reason to believe that in some university training departments, and perhaps in some training colleges, specialist lecturers in psychology, in particular, exact[ed] too large a proportion of the time available and expect[ed] too much of their students'.[2]

Although the Minister of Education accepted in principle in 1946 that the course of training for non-graduate teachers should be of three years' duration, implementation of this proposal was delayed owing to the post-war shortages of teachers and the need to provide for the larger number of older children remaining in school consequent upon the raising of the school-leaving age in 1947. During the first five post-war years many thousands of teachers were trained in the emergency training colleges, where the course was of fourteen months' duration, plus a period of guided reading and study after qualification.[3]

[1] *Ibid.*   [2] *Ibid.*, p. 68.
[3] *Challenge and Response*. London: H.M.S.O., 1954.

The effect of the emergency scheme upon the overall pattern of teacher education is not easy to assess. Its main influence seems to have been in liberalizing the institutional life of students; war veterans could not be expected to submit easily to the type of personal restriction that had all too often been the mode in the pre-war two-year college; the larger number of male lecturers recruited also did something to influence the institutional image. But the shortness of the course, the need to cram a great deal of both subject content and teaching method into just over one year, the heterogeneity of student qualifications, and the lack of specialized expertise on the part of many of the staff, together with the temporary nature of the whole enterprise, meant that the emergency colleges were hardly able to exercise a permanent influence on the scope and nature of the training course.

With the gradual closing down of the emergency training scheme, the Association of Teachers in Colleges and Departments of Education began to re-emphasize its support for the lengthening of the course to three years–a proposal that had originally been made by the Committee of Principals in Training Colleges as long ago as 1919. In view of the need for more teachers to be made available, the association recommended a phased development with three-year training being introduced for secondary teachers in 1952, for infants' teachers in 1955 and for teachers of juniors in 1958. The National Advisory Council for the Supply and Training of Teachers set up a sub-committee to consider how the transition from a two-year to a three-year course might be effected, but did not at the time feel able to recommend any immediate moves in this direction. The Sub-Committee reported in 1952 to the effect that a phased introduction was undesirable, but that the earliest date for introducing a full three-year course would be 1960, 'with additional provision in the preceding two years for voluntary entry in certain circumstances upon extending training'.[1] In a footnote to the last statement the National Advisory Council explained, in a manner that seems somewhat quaint in terms of the chronic teacher shortage that now exists, that this recommendation was added:

[1] *Three Year Training for Teachers*, Fifth Report of the National Advisory Council for the Supply and Training of Teachers. London: H.M.S.O., 1956, p. 3.

'. . . because with the experience of 1949–51 in mind, the Council thought that with the falling school population of the 1960's, newly trained teachers might find it difficult to get posts, notwithstanding that staffing standards might still leave much to be desired.'[1]

In 1955, with continuing pressure on the teachers' associations for the implementation of the McNair Report, the Minister of Education asked the National Advisory Council for a statement on the educational advantages of a three-year course for all non-graduate teachers, and the report of a sub-committee of the Council made in response to this request is included in the Council's Fifth Report. This contains little that had not already been stated by the McNair Committee twelve years earlier. The Council did give some attention, however, to the possibility of substituting for the third year of training a compulsory 'refresher' year after a period of teaching service; the idea was rejected, both on practical grounds of the expense and domestic difficulties that it might occasion for many teachers, and because, given the facts that only limited resources were available, it was felt that the advantages of a three-year initial training were greater.[2] The weaknesses of the existing two-year system were clearly regarded as such as to limit the gains that experienced teachers might obtain from later study; before such study could be thought of as a universal requirement a better base must be provided through an improved initial training.[3]

The N.A.C. agreed with the view of its earlier sub-committee that 1960 would be the best date for the introduction of the three-year course, since at that time the expected decline in the school population would enable a reduction in the output of the colleges to be made without adversely affecting the

[1] *Ibid.*

[2] This idea has been revived from time to time during the decade or so since the publication of the National Advisory Council's Fifth Report. At the Conference of the Association of Education Committees held at Brighton in June 1967 (reported in *Education*, 30 June 1967) a resolution was moved urging the Secretary of State to examine the possibility 'of the period of teacher training being divided into two parts, comprising a first period, say, of two years at college, followed by five years' service, followed by a further full-time deriod of one year in college to complete final recognition'.

[3] *Ibid.*, p. 6.

teacher/pupil ratio. The Council went on to state, in a paragraph that merits full quotation:

'To the reader in the mid-1950's it may seem surprising that the possible difficulty of absorbing into employment all the trained teachers available is a factor of which account need to be taken in considering the introduction of a three-year course in the early 1960's. There is, however, a limit to the number of additional teachers which the schools can absorb and the country afford in a period of declining school population. Without introduction of a three-year course or some other equivalent restriction of recruitment (and without some major new source of demand for teachers), it is not impossible but there may be some difficulty in the early 1960's, as there has never been in the 1950's, in maintaining full employment in the teaching profession. In such circumstances it seems wise not to bank up too many teachers for employment so soon, but rather to adjust the flow of training in good time by the introduction of the three-year course.'[1]

The Minister received the Council's Fifth Report in September 1956. It is clear that, whatever the strength of the educational case in favour of the three-year course, it was implemented mainly as a consequence of the forecasts of school population and teacher wastage that were made in the mid-fifties. If the trends that soon created a shortage of teachers in nearly every branch of educational activity had been perceived in 1956, it seems unlikely that the National Advisory Council would have felt able to recommend to the Minister the extension of the college course; once committed to its introduction, and to the building programme that an additional year in college entailed, it was found impracticable to go back to the previous position. Prior to announcing his decision the Minister asked a group of H.M.I.s to provide advice about the content of the three-year course, and at the same time the National Advisory Council sought the views of the area training organizations, whose replies formed the basis of the Council's Sixth Report, issued in July 1957. The Inspectors' advice to the Minister was also published during 1957 in Pamphlet No. 34, *The Training of Teachers; suggestions for a three-year training college course.*

There is virtual consensus between these statements and the

[1] *Ibid.*, para 37.

107

views of the A.T.C.D.E., which had been expressed in a number of memoranda issued between 1955 and 1958.[1] The necessity to avoid overloading the course is a common theme; the Inspectors drew attention to the way in which 'professional studies are particularly open to the addition of more and more topics as the years go by' and adopted the view that 'the most substantial changes following from the extension of the course from two years to three should be in the academic work of the colleges'.[2] The A.T.C.D.E. felt that the extended course would enable the students to work in a 'more spacious way than has been possible in the [previous] hurry and pressure'.[3] Pamphlet No. 34 spelled out how this might be accomplished, including the limitation of lectures to the number previously given in two years and an increase in tutorial and seminar work. The National Advisory Council felt that problems might arise in relating the subjects taught in the colleges and the numbers taking them to the needs of the schools and in achieving a balance between full academic freedom on the one hand and too rigid imbalance on vocational training on the other.[4] The Inspectors saw the vocational element in the pursuit of academic studies as a positive advantage.

'A training college should certainly accept all reasonable demands for the full development of its students through hard thinking and sustained study, but these aims are attainable, even more probably attainable, with training college students when vocational relevance adds motive power to otherwise dis-interested study. Such a policy, far from diminishing the quality of work in specific courses of academic study, would rather enhance their significance. . . .'[5]

Another common theme was the undesirability of the college

[1] For example, *Memorandum on the Three Year Course*, A.T.C.D.E., June 1955, *Memorandum on the Three Year Course*, A.T.C.D.E., 1957 (mimeographed), and *Memorandum on the Three Year Course of Training with special reference to the size of colleges and the range of studies*, A.T.C.D.E., 1958.

[2] *The Training of Teachers*: suggestions for a three-year training college course. H.M.S.O., 1957 (Pamphlet No. 34), p. 2.

[3] *Memorandum on the Three Year Course*, 1955, *op. cit.*, p. 2.

[4] *Sixth Report* of the National Advisory Council on the Supply and Training of Teachers. London: H.M.S.O., 1957, p. 3.

[5] Pamphlet No. 34, *op. cit.*, p. 6.

course being assimilated in structure and emphases to the university programme for a degree.

'The curriculum appropriate to a training college student has a different range from that for the university undergraduate. In some respects many subjects in a training college can be related to subjects in universities, but in the subjects for which there are counterparts in the universities the nature of the training college course may be very different. In the aesthetic and practical subjects there are tried, educative and creative disciplines which are of no less merit and worth than a recognized course of a university.'[1]

The long-standing conflict between academicism and the needs of the classroom teacher, which has been a perennial theme in the development of teacher education, had by no means been settled by the gradual improvement in the calibre of students, the qualifications of the staff and the facilities and status of the colleges. Such improvements had in certain respects made for additional difficulties, since most of the students entering the colleges during the post-war period had experienced the same type of secondary education as their university counterparts and many of them possessed the necessary qualifications for university study. At one and the same time the colleges wished to establish a certain parity of status with the universities – the salary policy of the A.T.C.D.E. is particularly noteworthy in this respect – and also to relate their work to the vocational interest of their students and the needs of the schools. To do this effectively would amount to the creation of an independent tradition of higher education outside the universities, and the colleges have never been in a position to bring this about by their own efforts. One reason for this has been the effect upon the work of the individual colleges of membership of the area training organization, which, whilst providing a valuable check upon standards and a means whereby the colleges have been able to manage their own academic affairs, has also tended to damp down the type of outstanding individual and pioneer work on the part of particular colleges that might have acted as a more general model. In many respects, the colleges have been passing through a similar phase to that of higher education in the United States during earlier years of this century, when

[1] *Memorandum on the Three Year Course*, A.T.C.D.E., 1958, *op. cit.*

certain outstanding college presidents, such as Aydelotte and Hutchins, were able to initiate developments which have had a considerable effect upon the system of higher education in the country as a whole. But here outstanding individual work has not had a chance to develop. The immediate needs of the schools for teachers, the restrictions imposed by democratic local control on the local authority colleges, which is essentially unsympathetic to idiosyncratic ideas, the absence of links with the technical colleges and other institutions providing post-secondary education, the failure of teacher education as a field of activity or study to attract first-class minds—all these factors have worked against the type of creative nonconformity that might have enabled the colleges to advance significantly in the quality of their work and its effect upon the educational system in general. The decision of the government in 1965 to retain the colleges of education under local authority control and to try to create a 'separate but equal' system of higher education outside the universities represents a belated and perhaps inadequate response to this problem. Whether it will succeed will depend as much as anything else on the degree of genuine independence that the colleges can achieve in governing their own affairs.

5

THE THREE-YEAR COURSE
IN THE COLLEGES OF EDUCATION

The Main Subject Courses

The three-year course of training provided in most colleges of education today comprises three main elements. First and foremost are the *main courses*, which include the full range of academic subjects – English, History, Geography, Mathematics and so on – and a variety of practical and aesthetic subjects. There is considerable variation between the number of main subjects that students are required to take, as the following examples from the 1966–7 *'Compendium of teacher training courses in England and Wales'* shows:

A.T.O. 1   One or two main subjects.

A.T.O. 2   Either two principal courses or one principal and one subsidiary subject course.

A.T.O. 3   At least one main course.

A.T.O. 4   One main course. Selected students may do work at advanced level in one subject only. They may take up two optional subjects of which one can be another main course.

A.T.O. 5   Either: two subjects at advanced main level; or: two subjects, one at advanced main and one at main level; or: one subject at advanced main level; or: two subjects at main level.[1]

If we exclude the specialist colleges of housecraft, physical education and handicraft, which generally provide only for intending secondary school teachers in these particular subjects,

[1] *A Compendium of Teacher Training Courses in England and Wales, 1966–7.* London: H.M.S.O., 1966, p. 2.

main courses in Divinity, English, History, Geography, Mathematics, light crafts and Music are available nearly everywhere. The sciences are less well provided for–main courses in Physics, for example, are not available in over two-thirds of the colleges.[1]

The chief purpose of the main course was seen by the National Advisory Council as 'carrying further the personal education of the student', and its standard is claimed by the A.T.C.D.E., in so far as direct comparisons can be made, as approximately that of a university pass degree. In the twenties Jones suggested that 'training college syllabuses for ordinary courses in general subjects appear to correspond approximately to higher local examinations or to matriculation examinations in the newer universities, those in advanced subjects to the intermediate subjects for degrees'.[2] Taking these assessments at their face value it is clear that today there are higher expectations regarding the quality and extent of the work in main subjects than in the past, which the considerably improved academic standards of those entering the colleges today would seem to justify. But in addition to providing for the personal education of students, the main course is also intended to provide the future teacher's principal classroom subject, especially for the minority who will be employed in secondary schools. The Sixth Report of the National Advisory Council states unequivocally:

'It follows that the needs of the schools must influence the training he is given. Taking the country as a whole, the spread of subjects in the colleges must be related to the subjects taught in the schools, and, within wide limits, the number of students taking a subject must be governed by the number of teachers of that subject the schools need.'[3]

This dual function of the main subject is echoed by the requirements of the area training organizations; intellectual development and vocational relevance are both aimed at, although it is admitted that the latter will have less significance for the teacher of the younger children.

'... students will select as a main course for examination by the institute one field of study for their own personal development.

[1] *Op. cit.*

[2] Jones, L. *The Training of Teachers*. Oxford: Clarendon Press, 1924, p. 86.

[3] *Sixth Report* of the National Advisory Council on the Supply and Training of Teachers. London: H.M.S.O., 1957, p. 4.

In the case of students training for work at the secondary school stage, and normally for those training for work at the junior/secondary stage, the main course must be appropriate to the curriculum of the secondary school and the college must provide a professional course in relation to it.'[1]

This last sentence emphasizes the second main element in most college courses—curriculum or professional studies. It is clear that the study of one or two main subjects does not provide adequate preparation for the junior school teacher, who is expected by most headteachers to be able to work within the whole range of the junior curriculum. Nor is it suitable for the semi-specialist teacher in the lower forms of secondary schools, who may be expected to take certain basic subjects with his own class. The purpose of curriculum courses is to give students a general grounding in the range of subjects which they are likely to have to teach; the demands made upon such courses are heavy.

'The curriculum courses must give students at least some appreciation of the value of the subject to children, some understanding of what is involved in teaching it, some insight into the difficulties that children are likely to meet and how these may be handled, and some knowledge of the organization of the work in school and the materials required for it. . . .'[2]

There is very considerable variety in the way in which curriculum courses are organized within and between area training organizations. It is common for English to be a compulsory course for all students for the first two years of the course; at the end of this time students are sometimes assessed internally, the college certifying to the Institute of Education that the required standards have been reached, and sometimes by the Institute itself by means of papers common to all the colleges within its area. Obligatory work in Mathematics is also found in some colleges, although the group of Inspectors who produced Pamphlet 34 felt that there was a certain risk in making this a requirement for all students.

'There could well be a case for accepting a student whose music, for example, was exceptionally good but whose arithmetic

[1] *Regulations and Syllabuses for the Teachers' Certificate, 1965–6.* London: University of London Institute of Education, p. 10.
[2] Pamphlet No. 34, *op. cit.*, p. 8.

was almost non-existent; but there should not be a requirement that such a student should be taught just so much arithmetic as will enable him to appear to children not to be a failure
in the subject or to appear to an appointing authority to be able
to teach it when in fact he cannot. Such a student should, when
accepted, be given a programme suited to his abilities, and he
should seek an appointment suitable to his training.'[1]

In some places the courses that we have referred to as 'professional' or 'curriculum' are known as 'college courses'. In the
voluntary colleges these usually include compulsory work in
Religious Education or Divinity, the examination of which as a
college course is usually internal. A report on the work of one
mixed training college mentions a range of from five to eight
timetable periods a week being devoted to curriculum work,
with variations according to the year of the course and the type
of work for which students are being trained. The following table
indicates the range of work concerned.

TABLE V[2]

Curriculum Courses in a College of Education

	Number of 45 minute periods per week						Special Co.
	First Year			Second Year			
College Courses	Sec.	Jun.	Inf.	Sec.	Jun.	Inf.	Jun. & Inf.
Art and Craft	0	4	4	0	0	0	0
Geography	0	0	0	0	2	0	0
History	0	0	0	0	0	0	0
Mathematics	2	2	1	1	1	0	0
Music	3	3	3	2	3	3	3
Natural History	2	2	2	0	0	0	0
Religious Knowledge	1	1	1	2	2	2	2
Totals	8	12	11	5	8	5	5

Given the range that curriculum work must cover, and the
fact that it sometimes ends after the first two years of the

[1] *Ibid.*, p. 8.

[2] 'Staff Report on Timetables: Kenton Lodge College', *Education for
Teaching* 60, February 1963, p. 43.

course, the third year being devoted to a more intensive consideration of the main subject(s) and Education, there is frequently an element of superficiality in teaching that leaves both staff and students dissatisfied and fails to provide the future teacher with the necessary equipment that he needs for work in a junior school and elsewhere. Lecturers sometimes find curriculum courses less rewarding then teaching their main-subject students, and the large size of the groups with which they have to work contributes to this. Despite such feelings, however, many tutors have strong views on the desirability of all students having some acquaintance with their particular subject, and the pressure on the timetable is correspondingly great. Efforts have been made in a number of colleges to integrate curriculum studies and to concentrate upon the common features of a number of school subjects rather than provide content teaching of a specific kind.

We have seen that the fragmentation and overcrowded nature of the college programme has been a problem for many decades, and the fact that colleges have still to make considerable efforts to minimize the effects of these characteristics is testimony to the strong forces that they represent. The 'pull' between the needs of the polymath classroom teacher, who, despite recent changes, is still the required norm in most primary schools, and the desire of the college to provide opportunities for studies in depth—partly out of a proper sense of the intellectual obligation, partly for considerations of academic status, partly in response to the students' own specialized backgrounds of study—is a perennial problem that derives from certain of the fundamental characteristics of the role of the teacher. Waller indicates some of these in the following passage.

'The teacher, from the very nature of his work, must spend much of his time in the classroom in drilling his students upon those subjects which may later open to them the doors that lead to wisdom. Other men, when they have reached maturity, may themselves use these tools to unlock the doors of the palace and enter within. But the teacher, unfortunately, must always sit upon the front steps and talk about the means of opening the door. . . .'[1]

[1] Waller, W. *The Sociology of Teaching*. New York: John Wiley, 1965.

Kenneth Richmond applied a test of general cultural knowledge to various groups of graduate and non-graduate teachers, students and sixth-formers, and found that even among an atypical group of non-graduate teachers who were undertaking further study for advanced qualifications, the overall score declined with years of teaching experience. Commenting upon these figures, he observes:

'Perhaps only those who know what it is like to spend a lifetime teaching five-year-olds or backward readers in a C-stream class who will perceive the human tragedy that lies behind the bare figures. Always taking care not to talk above the children's heads, sharing the company of others who do the same, rarely or never meeting new learning situations which demands the exercise of intellectual powers. . . .'[1]

The problem of upholding the status of general subjects and elementary level teaching is more of a problem for the college and its staff, who function within the universe of post-primary education, with its emphases upon standards, depth, academic excellence and so on, than it is for the individual student and teacher, whose post-college contact with this universe is likely to be very limited. One of the solutions that educators of teachers have tried is to elevate the importance of Educational studies as such, to stress those courses of study that contribute to the professionalization of the teacher's role, to put children and teaching first and the particular subject content a good way behind.[2] Work in Education, the third major aspect of the college course, has been seen by some as the means whereby these attitudes might be fostered and a child-centred rather than a subject-centred orientation created. It is to this aspect of the college's work that we must now turn.

---

[1] Richmond, K. *Culture and General Education*. London: Methuen, 1963, p. 172.

[2] '. . . the main intellectual discipline of the course should be the Psychology, Sociology and Philosophy of Education. If this idea were to be followed we should find in our colleges that the emphasis was in the right place—we should avoid the present danger of students saying "I want to teach History", "I want to teach English", etc. . . . The first statement would then be "I want to teach children" and then only would we be justified in asking through which field of knowledge the student would like to teach children.' Daniel, M. V. 'The Challenge of the Three Year Course', *Education for Teaching*, May 1959, p. 54.

The Education Course

The study of Education in the colleges has three main roots. The first is the method work that has always formed part of the formal preparation of teachers; the 'Master of method' is the precursor of the present-day Principal Lecturer in Education.[1] The second is the study of the history of education and educational ideas that was often featured in the early colleges, usually based on lectures given by the Principal or Vice-Principal. The third root, which now tends to dominate the other two, derives from the growth of psychological studies of the learning process and the development of children, to which has more recently been added the systematic exploration of the social factors that influence educability and the work of teachers and schools.[2] Since the introduction of the three-year college course in 1960, a substantial change has taken place in the organization and content of Education courses. The former tutorially-based programmes, with students divided into 'infants', 'junior' and 'secondary' groups, and undertaking all their work in Education with a single tutor over one, two or three years, are giving way to a more systematic treatment of educational issues along philosophical, psychological, historical and sociological lines.

There are several reasons why a unitary approach was formerly so common. The shortness of time available for Education and the need to introduce some principle of limitation in an ever enlarging range of studies, encouraged the dignifying of compression and abbreviation by such titles as 'synthesis' and 'integration'. Until very recently, shortness of time was coupled with a relatively low level of academic attainment and intellectual motivation on the part of students, which again put pressure on the tutor to make educational studies seem relevant to the practical affairs of the classroom; the 'pragmatic barrier' had to be overcome.[3] Tutors themselves often lacked the necessary

[1] There are two members of staff in the Department of Education at University College, Swansea, who hold the titles of Master and Mistress of Method.

[2] Tibble, J. W. 'Psychological Theories and Teacher Training' in *The Education and Training of Teachers* (Year Book of Education, 1963). *op. cit.*

[3] Byrns, R. H. 'The Pragmatic Barrier', *Improving College and University Teaching*, VIII:4, Autumn 1960.

qualifications that would enable them to teach the component strands of the Education course to a high level.[1] What specialist knowledge of psychology, sociology or philosophy they possessed was secondary to their experience in schools and their capabilities as infant, junior or secondary teachers. We can add to this the effect of the progressive, child-centred approach to education in schools, itself partly based on psychological insights, which emphasized the needs of the child as the validating principle or curriculum design. Although this approach had a tremendously liberating effect on the work of the infant and junior schools, it did not follow at the college level that educational studies were best pursued in accordance with the same student-centred principles of learning and development.

Because of the way in which the college curriculum grew up, a variety of disciplines that contribute to the understanding of the educational process came to be employed together in a single college course and under the control of a single group of tutors. But this is not the same as saying, as have some defenders of the unitary approach to educational studies, that this course constituted a discipline in its own right; such a claim seems little more than what Jacques Barzun calls a 'dogma of rationalized habit'.[2]

One of the more sophisticated arguments for the recognition of Education as a distinct discipline is that its constituent elements are synthesized by being related to certain uniquely educational points of reference, such as 'the child', 'the learning process', 'the school' and so on. This indicates a teaching approach that is both child-centred and topic-centred, and which works outwards from the students' own experience of life and educational situations.

'Many of the student's early discussions will lead into topics of educational history and the relationship between the school and society. Towards the end of the course the student should have gained a conceptual framework in which to set these topics. It is doubtful whether excessive reliance upon textbooks or

[1] See Chapter 8 *passim* and also *Teaching Educational Psychology in Training Colleges*. Report of a Committee of the British Psychological Society and the A.T.C.D.E., London, 1962.

[2] Barzun, J. *The House of Intellect*. London: Secker and Warburg, 1959, p. 189.

attendance at lectures on educational history or sociology will base that framework on an intelligible foundation; but the discussion of students' experiences in a variety of schools and other institutions, such as factories, youth clubs, or in welfare work, will give purpose and meaning to their studies.'[1]

This approach can be linked with the notion that the distinctive character of a discipline is determined by the uniqueness of its point of view.

'These then are two of the senses in which discipline refers to mental processes. The one sets limits to the view but gives it a unity by putting it within a frame. The other sets limits to wandering thought and confines it in a net of logic. In these senses at least education as a separate study should be considered a discipline at training college or at university levels.

'What, first, is the unique point of view of the educationalist? In University Departments of Education and in training colleges he is primarily concerned with the introduction of children to their world, whether physical or social. He wants to know how children learn about the world, how they adapt themselves to living in it, and how they accommodate themselves to it. . . .'[2]

But such a point of view is by no means restricted to educationists. Sociologists, psychologists and anthropologists are equally interested in such matters. What *is* unique about the educationist's point of view is his essentially *practical* concern; he wants to know more about child development, socialization and so on in order to improve the practice of teaching. But this practical orientation does not invest the approaches and methods of study that he employs with an existence independent of the disciplines from which they are drawn. The fundamental question, as Paul Hirst has pointed out, relates to the criteria by which we are to assess the contributions that other branches of knowledge make to educational study. Those who support the view that Education is an autonomous discipline imply that these criteria arise from within the educational study itself. Countering this view, Hirst states:

'Because of the nature of the questions with which it deals

---

[1] *The Study of Education in Colleges of Education for Teaching*, A.T.C.D.E. Education Section. London: The Association, 1962.

[2] Bramwell, R. D. 'Education as a Discipline', *Education for Teaching*, November 1962, p. 24.

educational theory is dependent upon a particularly wide range of knowledge and experience. It does not however seem to me correct to speak of the theory as developing criteria of its own for assessing the knowledge and beliefs on which it draws. These forms of understanding are valid in their own rights and must therefore be accepted into the theory as they are. As their function is to provide a wider knowledge of what is involved in educational practice and so promote more responsible judgements, it is difficult to see how the knowledge itself can be assessed by criteria within the theory. The theorist has to recognize or discover the relevance of other specialist studies for education, taking these into account when he forms his principles.'[1]

The relationship of 'Education' to its underlying disciplines is in the same order as the relationship of the practice of medicine to the study of anatomy, physiology, biology and so on. Whether he is conscious of the fact or not, the medical practitioner is making use of such biological and physiological knowledge at every step of his diagnosis and recommendations for treatment; the teacher who denies the influence of social, psychological and philosophical assumptions in his own decision-making is merely the slave of unformulated and unsystematic patterns of habit.

A further consequence of a unitary approach to educational studies was that too much reliance on teaching in terms of topics, problems and lines of enquiry tended to minimize the differences between philosophical, psychological, historical and sociological kinds of judgement. Such topic-based teaching was probably more interesting for students than a more systematic analytical procedure, and avoided the charge of irrelevance and premature conceptualization. But in doing this it also ran the risk of encouraging a certain shallowness and confusion of ideas; the combination of disciplines that experienced tutors conceived as a 'mesh' was often received by students as an undifferentiated 'mush'.[2] In trying to avoid giving too much attention to 'tips for teachers' at the one extreme, whilst rejecting the 'arid intellectualism' of the disciplines at the other, Education lecturers ran

[1] Hirst, P. H. 'Philosophy and Educational Theory', *British Journal of Educational Studies*, November 1963, p. 58.
[2] For which distinction I am indebted to R. S. Peters.

IN THE COLLEGES OF EDUCATION

the risk of their courses being perceived as a rather aimless wandering among intellectual topics, in which hortatory injunction and a concern with group process took the place of systematic analysis. As Conant has stated with respect to teacher education in the United States:

'School people are under incessant pressure from ideological, economic, political, and other social groups to mold the schools in their interests. An understanding of the values of such groups as they bear on educational practice seems an important part of the equipment with which teachers should be provided. Skill in the analysis of propositions used in these debates is also of value. To develop this understanding and skill—rather than, as is often attempted, to produce by indoctrination partisans of a particular point of view—should be the aim of the college or university. If I can rely on the complaints I have often heard expressed, professors of education spend too much time mouthing platitudes about what a "democratic education" ought to be and too little time teaching their students to understand, analyse, and criticize the functions that various competing social groups (including educators) would impose on the schools as conditions of "democratic" education.'[1]

A second consequence of regarding Education as a unitary discipline related to the methodology and status of educational research. A background of study in Education so conceived did little to provide an adequate basis for the work of a student who wished to investigate some educational problem. He soon found it necessary to retrace his steps into more elementary areas of the underlying disciplines relevant for his purposes. This helps to account for the poor reputation of a good deal of research in Education, and provides many difficulties for the members of Department and Institute of Education staff responsible for guiding and supervising work for higher degrees. What begin as educational questions turn out on closer examination to be essentially psychological, sociological, historical, political or philosophical problems. Conant has recommended that 'the professors of educational philosophy, educational history, educational sociology and educational psychology should be professors of philosophy, history, sociology and

[1] Conant, J. B. *The Education of American Teachers.* New York: McGraw Hill, 1963, p. 121.

121

psychology who have a commitment to the public schools and their improvement.'[1] Whilst to implement fully such a recommendation would create impossible staffing problems for the colleges and departments in this country at the present time, some steps have been taken in this direction in recent years.[2]

The growing social and economic importance of education in a complex industrial society, and the need to secure useful answers to important practical questions have been among the factors that have helped to change the face of Education as a field of study in recent years. Another has been the expansion of the colleges and departments, which has enabled larger numbers of staff with specialist qualifications in particular disciplines to be recruited. The increase in the volume of educational research undertaken, the larger number of advanced qualifications available which involve study in depth, and the introduction of the B.Ed., have also played some part. Such systematic experimental work as existed in Education during the inter-war and early post-war periods was primarily psychological, and was heavily concentrated upon the measurement and prediction of cognitive performance; such work owed much to the problems of the period, in which a restrictive rather than an expansionist educational strategy was the rule.[3] Whilst the educational psychologists have retained a position of importance within the framework of educational studies, their pre-eminence has been challenged by the rise in the importance of sociological, and more recently still, philosophical studies. Post-war analyses of educational opportunity by sociologists such as Floud and Halsey showed that the use of objective measures of attainment and potentiality had failed to provide the equalization of opportunity towards which educational reforms had been directed, and subsequent work by Douglas, Fraser, Bernstein and others has helped to clarify why this has been so.[4] A beginning has

[1] *Ibid.*, p. 122.

[2] See the discussion of Conant's ideas in Holmes, B. 'The Education of Teachers: The Conant Report', *Education for Teaching*, February 1964, p. 55.

[3] For a discussion of such strategies and effects see Vickers, G. *The Art of Judgement*. London: Chapman and Hall, 1965.

[4] Taylor, W. 'The Sociology of Education' in Tibble, J. W. (ed.) *The Study of Education*. London: Routledge, 1966.

also been made in the study of social process within schools and other educational institutions.[1]

The impact of a new kind of philosophical thinking about educational issues has been even more recent. Scheffler and others in the United States, and Peters, Hirst and their pupils in this country have done a good deal to introduce a more stringently analytical character to contemporary studies, and through the medium of courses and conferences, the Philosophy of Education Society, and former higher-degree students who have obtained college and department posts, a good deal of this new approach has rubbed off on to courses in Education for students in training.[2]

The tendency today is to see Education as an area of study in which the distinctive contributions of Psychology, History, Sociology, and Philosophy are used to obtain understanding of the activities and problems of pupils, teachers and schools. The clearest statement of this point of view appears in Tibble's *The Study of Education*,[3] in which representatives of each discipline spell out the way in which each of the forms of thought with which they are concerned plays its part in the overall pattern of Educational studies.

The effect of all this on the college courses is by no means yet fully worked out; there are still some places in which 'mother-hen', tutorially based courses are general, and where there is no one on the Education staff who has had recent experience of advanced study in one of the disciplines that underlie Education. There are in particular shortages of well-qualified sociologists in the colleges and departments. But it is clear that the climate of thought about the position and scope of Education has changed a good deal. The report of the Education Section of the A.T.C.D.E. entitled *Bachelors of Education : The Undergraduate Study of Education in a College of Education*, issued at the end of 1966, reads very differently from the 1962 statement *The Study of Education in Colleges of Education for Teaching*, and the difference is by no means entirely due to the fact that one of the documents

---

[1] *Ibid.*

[2] See Hirst, P. H. *op. cit.*; Archambault, R. D. (ed.) *Philosophical Analysis and Education*. London: Routledge, 1965; Peters, R. S. 'What is an Educational process?' in Peters, R. S. (ed.) *The Concept of Education*. London: Routledge, 1967.   [3] *Op. cit.*

deals only with students working for the B.Ed. An example of a College Education course based upon the new approach to Educational study is included as an appendix to this chapter.

The Organization of the Three-year Course

It may be useful at this point to look briefly at the overall college course to which the elements that have been discussed make their contribution. It has already been emphasized that there are very considerable differences in detail between the arrangements of the various area training organizations, and between the colleges within a particular area—and even within the college itself according to the age group for which the student is preparing to teach. It is thus very difficult to provide an overall picture that can be classed as 'typical'. The total timetable load for students varies between about 15 and 27 hours per week, the number of timetable periods tending to be rather less in the third year. In some colleges educational studies (which in the United States would be known as the 'professional sequence') take up as much as one-third of the timetable periods in each year, but in these cases such studies often include some work that would elsewhere come into curriculum courses. Practical teaching—in the form of study practice, observation and child study as well as block teaching practices—occurs in each of the three years of the course, with the longest practice period often coming in the seventh or eighth term. There is some evidence that block time-tabling is becoming more common—a whole day is set aside for Education or main-subject work rather than single periods scattered throughout the week. This procedure simplifies time-tabling and facilitates the introduction of the kind of team teaching implied in the preceding section. Curriculum courses present the greatest variety of arrangements; sometimes there are Institute requirements relating to English and Physical Education, sometimes there are obligatory college courses; other teaching subjects may be brought together within a single organizational framework as 'curriculum studies' or as a 'combined course'.

For a student preparing to reach in secondary schools it is possible for the three-year course to contain little beyond a single main subject, a qualifying course in English, practical teaching and Education courses, and perhaps one or two curriculum courses. It is perfectly possible for the intending primary teacher to follow an almost similar programme, the main differences being in the number of curriculum courses—perhaps three or four instead of one or two—and the orientation of the educational studies undertaken. In contrast to the United States, the chief distinction in this country is not between the courses followed by students preparing for work in particular types of schools, but between the courses provided by the different types of institution in which teachers are trained—concurrent programmes in three-year colleges of education, and one-year professional courses for the university graduate in departments of education or in special groups in the colleges. These differences are not therefore functional, but historical and traditional, owing more to the institutional separation of élite and mass education than to age-group differences.

A feature of many college courses of particular interest is the 'foundations' or 'introductory' course that students pursue during their first weeks or first half-term. Such courses frequently include work of a kind with which students are unlikely to be familiar from their sixth-form experience, and are clearly intended to facilitate a reorientation towards the goals and values of teacher education and away from the academic and subject-centred attitudes with which they are assumed to have been imbued at school. In one such introductory course in a voluntary college, the Religious Education element is represented by the showing of feature films and a discussion of the moral issues to which these give rise, the Education section by the making of individual and group models suitable for use as teaching aids in schools, and the main-subject sections by projects and group enquiry work culminating in displays.[1] Such introductory

---

[1] Commenting on the introductory course in a Catholic college in the North of England one mature student wrote, 'Convents have changed. Whether it is the ecumenical spirit or the progress of education is not yet discernible to me. In my era it was a red-letter day to see lantern slides of the Holy Land. In my first week here I have viewed "The L-shaped room" and "Saturday Night and Sunday Morning", the latter being our first English lecture. . . . The next conference informed the girls that expulsion was automatic should anyone remain out all night. Could it be that psychology is lurking about somewhere?' Lambkin, R. 'My Return to Good Lunches and Luxury', *The Student Teacher* 2, Spring 1966, p. 14.

courses may be likened to the procedures whereby newcomers to hospitals, prisons, the army and other 'total institutions' are resocialized to the norms of their new environment.[1]

In contrast to the English situation, and despite the fact that programmes of preparation for elementary and secondary school teachers in the United States have come in for a good deal of criticism in recent years, few of the remedies there suggested indicate any tendency towards a stringent limitation of course requirements.[2] On the assumption that despite team teaching and the introduction of other organizational innovations, 'self-contained classrooms will continue to be the dominant pattern for kindergarten and the first three grades during the next ten years' whilst 'there will be an increasing tendency to use specialists in grades four through six', Conant[3] recommends that teachers of the lower grades should receive preparation in *all* subjects taught in these grades, whilst teachers of grades four to six should have only an introduction to elementary subjects outside the particular subject or cluster of subjects in which they have chosen to specialize.

But this difference in approach is to apply only to the number and range of intensive teaching-subject workshops that students undertake. The curriculum set out below is proposed by Conant as a basis for the preparation of all elementary school teachers. Approximately half of the time available in the four-year course is devoted to General Requirements, a quarter to an area of concentration in one or more of the areas listed, and a further quarter to the professional sequence.

This contrasts sharply with some of the programmes of study of teachers preparing for primary teaching in this country, where from the beginning the degree of specialization goes far beyond that typical of the United States. Conant's recommendations for the education of the intending secondary school teacher involve a parallel degree of breadth, although more of this is in academic fields than in the case of the elementary major; about half of the secondary students' four years should be spent on general education, three-eighths on an area of academic con-

[1] Goffman, E. *Asylums*. New York: Doubleday Anchor, 1962.

[2] For a survey of the current position see Beggs, W. *The Education of Teachers*. Englewood Cliffs, N.J.: Prentice Hall, 1965.

[3] Conant, *op. cit.*, p. 159.

centration and only one-eighth on Education courses and practice teaching[1]—although it is likely that there could be room in the general education programme for some of the work that forms part of education courses in this country. Two typical programmes as recommended by Conant, one for a future high school teacher of history, the other for a biologist, may serve as illustrations.[2]

A Proposed Curriculum for the Education of
U.S. Elementary School Teachers[3]

	Semester Hours
Summary	
General Requirements	60
Concentration	30
Professional	30
Total	120

General Requirements:

The English Language	6
Western World's Literary Tradition	6
History (at least one half other than American)	9
Mathematics	6
Philosophy	3
Science (physical and biological studies consecutively)	12
Economics, Political Science, Sociology and Anthropology	9
Introduction to General Psychology	3
Fine Arts (art or music)	6
Physical Education (non-credit)	–
Total	60

[1] *Ibid.*

[2] For a survey of the courses required in common by both primary and secondary majors in institutions accredited by the National Council for the Accreditation of American Teacher Education see Humphry, B. J. 'A survey of Professional Education Offerings in N.C.A.T.E.-Accredited Institutions', *Journal of Teacher Education* XIV:4, December 1963.

[3] Conant *op. cit.* p. 159, p. 176 and p. 172.

THE THREE-YEAR COURSE

Secondary School Biology Teacher

	Semester Hours
General education, including 6 hours of biology, 6 hours of physical science, 6 hours of mathematics and 3 hours of general psychology	60
Educational psychology	3
Philosophy or history or sociology of education	4
Additional physical science	9
Biology	36
Practice teaching and special methods	9
	120

Secondary School History Teacher

	Semester Hours
General education, including 9 hours in history, 3 hours of sociology and anthropology, 3 hours of political science, 3 hours of economics, and 3 hours of general psychology	60
Educational psychology	3
Philosophy or history or sociology of education	3
Further history	33
Further political science	3
Further economics	3
Geography	6
Practice teaching and special methods	9
Total	120

In this country there is a need for a systematic enquiry into the actual programmes of the colleges of education, with a view to providing firm data on which recommendations for reform might be based; nearly all the attention the college courses have received has been in relation to their length and place in the overall educational structure, to the recruitment of appropriate numbers of students, to goals, aims and values, rather than content and standards. Within the next few years a variety of changes are likely to occur in the work of the schools that will require a reappraisal of the work of the colleges. Closed-circuit television, a greater stress upon individual rather than group learning, teaching machines, team teaching and secondary reorganization all have implications for the work of the teacher and the type of training that he requires and have as yet hardly begun to be taken into account.

The Assessment of Performance

The traditional mode of assessment in higher education has been performance in written papers, sometimes accompanied by an oral examination. These have been institutionalized to a greater extent than in the United States, where the teacher of a particular course usually has sole responsibility for the examination of the students taking it. In most area training organizations the complex procedures of internal and external assessment, the determination of the content of common papers, the arrangement of examiners' meetings and the consideration of border-line cases require a formidable bureaucracy, and Institutes of Education usually have a full-time secretary for examinations or an examinations officer with an appropriate number of clerical staff. The area training organization is responsible for recommending to the Secretary of State the award of qualified-teacher status to a student who has successfully completed a course of study in one of its recognized institutions; in practice, the assessment of substantial parts of the course is delegated to the college authorities who, for example, are required 'to certify in respect of every candidate presented for examination that the candidate has pursued an approved course of study for the Teachers' Certificate to the satisfaction of his teachers. Without this certification a student will not be eligible to take the examination. College authorities are [also] required to certify to the Institute that a candidate has attained a satisfactory standard in written and spoken English and in curriculum subjects. . . .'[1]

Even in connection with those aspects of the course that are formally examined by the Institute, the staff of the colleges play a considerable part in setting the papers, marking the completed scripts and selecting those candidates whose papers are to

[1] University of London Institute of Education *Regulations*, p. 11.

receive more detailed consideration or who are to be interviewed by the external examiner. External examiners are
appointed by the Institute of Education, but again, nominations
and recommendations are often provided by the individual
colleges; sometimes the subject department of the college
names its own external examiners and these are formally approved by the Institute. Sometimes the external examiner
makes the final selection of questions to be included in the
papers from lists that may or may not have been approved by
the relevant Institute Board of Studies, but are likely to have
originated from the colleges themselves. Common papers for all
the colleges in an Institute area are still retained in some subjects, but in a growing number of cases the individual college
departments have their own papers based upon the particular
content and needs of their course. Whilst there is considerable
diversity of practice in all these matters, the general pattern is
one in which the college lecturers exercise considerable control
over the final assessment of their students, subject to the
moderation of the Institute Boards and external examiners.

The proportion of students entering the colleges of education
who fail to complete courses successfully is small. Between 1954
and 1964 the overall figures remained practically stationary at
around 3 per cent, although the proportion of men failing both
three-year general and two-year shortened courses in 1963-4
was higher than in earlier years. A large proportion of those
failing at the first attempt resit and are successful in subsequent
years–most A.T.O.s allow two attempts to redeem initial
failures in the written papers.[1] Wastage during the course is
small by university standards, but, as the Robbins Committee
predicted, has risen somewhat with the lengthening of the
college course to three years; losses were particularly high
during the first full three-year course which began in September
1960, some 9 per cent of men and 11 per cent of women
entrants withdrawing before the end of the course.[2]

[1] *Statistics of Education* and *Reports and Statistics* of the Department of
Education and Science and the Ministry of Education for the years concerned.

[2] *Higher Education: Students and their Education*, Appendix 2(A) of the
Report of the Committee on Higher Education (Robbins Committee).
London: H.M.S.O., 1964, p. 157.

The assessment of a student's performance during the course
by means of written papers has come in for a good deal of
criticism on the part of college lecturers, who are particularly
conscious of the backwash effect of examinations of all kinds on
the courses that precede them. In many respects the colleges
are remarkably free of the usual drawbacks of the external
examination, imposed by some outside body that has no first-
hand knowledge of the types of work the students have undertaken during the course. The manifest functions of the written
examination are to provide a basis for the comparison and
ranking of student performances, some structure for the course
and motivation for the individual student, and to help to ensure
some pattern of common expectation within and between
colleges and Institutes. Among their latent functions is the legi-
timation of the academic work of the college and the provision
of evidence that certain standards have been adhered to. This
last point raises certain difficulties. It is clear that in all types
of examination there is a considerable element of unreliability,
and differences in standards are bound to exist in any system
that employs more than one examining body, one examiner
and one examination paper. Sometimes this is a matter for serious
anxiety—in relation to the eleven-plus examination within a
county area for example, where a substantial degree of both
reliability and validity are necessary if the procedures are to be
regarded as tolerable by those who are subjected to them. By
dint of very considerable efforts of time and money, the use of
objectively scored tests wherever possible, and very carefully
evaluated methods of assessing the non-objective items in the
test battery, a fair degree of reliability and validity have been
obtained in respect of this particular examination. But no
such claims can be made for the other, non-objective examinations that come later in the individual's educational career.
There is a substantial literature on this topic which it is not
within the scope of this book to review; two recent examples
must suffice. Clegg quoted during 1965 the case of a headmaster who, anxious about the equivalence of standards in
'O' level English papers between examination boards, allowed
his pupils to enter for the examinations of two separate
boards. Out of twenty-eight candidates, twenty-seven passed
the examination of one of the boards, three that of the

other.[1] Drever has drawn attention both to the lack of reliability of university examinations—marking the same answers in
three different contexts in the course of six months he correlated
only 0·57 with himself—and to the phenomena he calls 'drift'.

'In marking, if the quality of candidates changes, examiners
tend to adapt, and the range of marks and the proportion of
passes hold remarkably constant. They seem characteristic of a
person or a department rather than closely related to the
quality of scripts. Sometimes adaptation proceeds by changes
in the difficulty of the questions . . . more commonly the changes
are in the examiners and their standards. . . . Performance in a
certain subject was shown over a period of years to correlate
quite well with performance in the matriculation examination.
The coefficient ranged from 0·62 to 0·65 for the preliminary or
first degree examination. The nature of the relationship was
such that a rise of 10 per cent in the pass level at the matriculation stage should have cut the university failure rate from just
over 50 per cent to under 30 per cent. Administrative changes,
brought about partly by the first stage of this investigation, in
effect eliminated from the class nearly all those whose matriculation mark was less than 60 per cent. The first year after this
happened, when the class—numbering some 300 incidentally—
still contained some 50–60 per centers, there was a drop in the
failure rate from 53 to 48 per cent. Then it went down to 43
instead of 28 per cent as it should have done, and since that time
it has been climbing back towards 50 per cent. Now this sort of
thing must be very common and can make nonsense of improved
selection, or better teaching. It is probably true that as the load of

[1] '. . . the Headmaster of Otley Grammar School put 28 pupils in for
the English Language "O" level examination under two different boards.
These were not borderline candidates, may I say. In one case 27 passed and
one failed; in the other, three passed and 25 failed. In the one case, the
average grade was four; in the other it was eight. Two candidates only out
of 28 were placed in the same grade by both boards, and one candidate was
placed in the top grade by one board and the bottom grade by the other.
Let me say at once that this is not an isolated case nor confined to one
subject—though it is interesting that the case I quote is English language,
the one subject which is regarded as essential for so many purposes. May I
add that the correlation between the two lists that I have quoted was
about 0·2. What I am interested to know is with which of these "O" level
passes is the grade 1 of the C.S.E. to be equated' Clegg, A. B. 'Dangers
Ahead', *Education*, 5 February 1965, p. 238.

examining becomes heavier, and the opportunity for reflective scrutiny of individual papers diminishes, habit and adaptation will play an even greater part. The trouble is that we in the universities have so long been used as a criterion to determine the validity of other people's examining that we are reluctant to admit all this. To call into question an examiner's standards in his own subject is about as acceptable as criticizing his sense of humour.'[1]

Drever's points find ample confirmation in those sections of the Robbins Committee's Report that deal with student wastage—withdrawal and failure—from undergraduate courses; there is much greater consistency between a particular faculty within a particular university over time than between universities as a whole, as can be seen from the table on page 134.

All this evidence supports the view that there is great difficulty in assuming the existence of common standards. In this country there exists no overall means of assessing the differences that exist between areas and institutions. In the United States certain national examinations permit more direct institutional comparisons to be made. Conant quotes from the reports from the Graduate Record examinations in Natural Science taken in a variety of colleges and universities by seniors who are candidates for graduate schools. He notices that in the institution that had the highest mean score, 98 per cent of the students had made a score better than that made by some 25 per cent in the lowest-ranking institution. He has calculated that if this score had been taken as a pass mark, only two per cent of the seniors in the first institution would have failed, against some three-quarters of those in the second. Records show that 'no such mortality rate was recorded'.[2]

In a single state in which students from several colleges took the National Teacher Examinations a similar pattern appeared; with a score of 500 taken as the pass mark, only 1 per cent of the students in the state university would have failed, against 40 per cent of those from a private college and 75 per cent from two other institutions of higher education.[3]

[1] Drever, J. 'Universities and the Social Fabric', *The Advancement of Science*, 22 : 95, 1966, p. 32.   [2] Conant, *op. cit.*, p. 77.
[3] *Ibid.* For an extensive review of the literature on examining in British universities see Cox, R. 'Examinations and Higher Education', *Universities Quarterly* 21 :3, June 1967.

TABLE VI
Wastage Rates of Undergraduates

Percentages

University	ARTS			SCIENCE			TECHNOLOGY		
	1952 entrants	1955 entrants	1957 entrants	1952 entrants	1955 entrants	1957 entrants	1952 entrants	1955 entrants	1957 entrants
C	6	5	3	4	3	3	6	5	5
G	28	14	18	23	19	19	35	31	28
T	7	10	11	11	12	9	40	22	14
X	7	8	8	6	5	4	7	14	11
U	34	12	8	56	25	28	—	—	—

Source: Higher Education, Appendix Two (A). Part IV, Table 6, p. 130.

IN THE COLLEGES OF EDUCATION

There is no evidence that the rate of failure of colleges of education in this country differs substantially between individual colleges and area training organizations. It seems likely that if particular institutions or groups of institutions decided to fail a substantially greater proportion of students than the national average this would be regarded as requiring investigation by the Department of Education and Science and other interested bodies. As Simons has shown, there are in, fact substantial differences in the initial qualifications of students accepted by different colleges; some colleges are heavily oversubscribed by candidates naming them as first-choices, and are able to choose only those with superior academic and personal qualifications. The weaker candidates tend to find themselves accepted by those colleges that attract a smaller proportion of first choices. Although there is little evidence to support the existence of a close relationship between 'A' level results and final grades, it seems doubtful if the intellectual fare and type of teaching provided by the colleges at the lower levels of the entrance pecking order is sufficient to ensure that the mean end-of-course performance of their students is commensurate with that of colleges higher in the scale. The system of external moderation, even when – and these conditions are by no means always fulfilled – one or more examiners takes responsibility for seeing the work of several colleges, and meetings are held at which impressions are discussed and scripts compared, does little to ensure any development of common standards. It seems clear that no such standards exist in this country. An eventual failure rate of under two students in every 100, and in-course wastage for all reasons, personal, domestic and academic, running at just over six per cent, means that the vast majority of those who are offered a college place, and virtually all those who manage to occupy it for the full three years, are assured of qualified teacher status. The fact that the final grades obtained, in both theory and practice, play virtually no part in helping or hindering the student to obtain his first appointments, are never taken into account subsequently, and have been shown to have no significant correlation with later promotion and teaching success, reinforce the impression that the final examinations have a purely nominal function as far as the maintenance of standards and the predictive ranking of teacher competence is concerned.

THE THREE-YEAR COURSE

Yet a very considerable amount of time and resources are devoted to the business of examining and assessing; most people who have worked in teacher education will have had experience of the long-drawn-out discussions as to whether Miss X's work deserves a B+ rather than a B, or whether Mr. Y's C− should be downgraded to D. In many Institutes there have been attempts to simplify procedures and to concentrate attention upon the borderline failure and borderline distinction cases, and also to allow an overall assessment of work during the course to play a part in the final grade.

In a few places this has led to the adoption of a system of *continuous assessment*, the final examination being dropped altogether. Either the whole of a student's work during the course—essays, participation in discussion, quantity and quality of private study and so on – is taken into account, or specified parts of this work–particular essays, a special study or dissertation. Continuous assessment has been the norm in the University of Bristol Department of Education for the last 45 years; writing about how the system operated in 1958, Humphreys makes clear that the system demands a substantial measure of personal contact between student and tutor if it is to be effective.

'In the first term, there are two "foundations" essays plus the student's work in and for the weekly tutorial, for which the tutor gives a personal assessment. When the staff meet early in February to consider the work of the first term they have before them these three assessments made by at least two, or more often, three people. Thanks to the fact that all of the work other than foundations lectures is done in small groups each student will be personally known to quite a number of the staff . . . the assessments can thus be considered in the light of several people's personal knowledge of the student. . . .'[1]

Not all students respond favourably to this type of assessment—expecially at the beginning of the course, when the experience of school and, in the case of the university department of education, of university undergraduate work, have established a different framework of expectation. The feeling may exist among them that they are under observation all the

[1] Humphreys, D. W. 'The Continuous Assessment of Theoretical Studies in the University of Bristol Department of Education', *Education for Teaching*, November 1958, p. 26.

time, that everything they say and do may well be taken down to be used as evidence for or against them. Richardson suggests that 'some of those in a position to judge have come to the conclusion that this apprehension produces a sense of pressure, varying with the temperament of the student, which is at least as severe as that produced by the traditional method of assessment by a single final examination.'[1] In attempting to refute this view Richardson states that the purpose of course assessment ' . . . is not to add up marks for individual pieces of work but to look at the student's work as a whole, particularly as an indication of the rate and rhythm of his development and of his ability to make progress by fostering his capacities and eliminating or minimizing his weaknesses. *The significant thing is, not the sum of the student's work, but the progress he has made from first to last which, when considered in all its aspects, is an index of his personality.*' (My italics.)

This last sentence quoted is important from several points of view. In the first place, it exemplifies that aspect of the ideology of teacher education that stresses the total process of exposure to an appropriate educational environment, rather than the acquisition of a certain pattern of skills and knowledge legitimized by examination success. Secondly, it bears upon some of the tensions that exist between, on the one hand, what can be called the *open system* of the technical college or the American university, with its minimal stress upon entrance qualifications and emphasis upon a competitive examination structure and, on the other, the *closed system* of the Oxbridge college, the theological seminary and, to a lesser extent, the college of education, with high entry thresholds that pay explicit regard to personal and social as well as intellectual factors, a concern with the total pattern of the individual's development during the course and a comparative disregard for the processes of formal certification. It is these tensions, linked with the more mundane considerations of status, that are important for an understanding of the relation of teacher preparation to other forms of higher education; this topic receives more extended treatment in Chapter 10. The effect of continuous assessment on staff/student relationships is also examined more fully in Chapter 9.

[1] Richardson, E. 'Personal Relations and Formal Assessment in Graduate Courses in Education', *Education for Teaching*, May 1965.

The Course for the B.Ed.

Discussions about the establishment of the B.Ed. degree began
immediately after the Robbins Committee's Report containing
a recommendation to this effect was published. The Committee
had considered various types of degree structure, including a
three-year and a four-year degree for all trainees, but finally
came down in favour of a four-year concurrent course, in which
Education would be studied alongside academic subjects, for
up to a quarter of college entrants. Such a degree would be
comparable in standard to other first degrees, and capable of
being accepted as a suitable qualification for higher degree
work. The universities reacted favourably to these proposals,
although for a time there was a fear that the colleges would be
forced by government pressure to seek their B.Ed.s from the
Council for National Academic Awards. The 'Woolwich'
speech of April 1965 did nothing to allay this fear. In the event,
however, the universities, Institutes of Education and colleges
went ahead with their discussions and by June 1966 arrangements had been approved everywhere except in Cambridge.
There, the fact that the Institute of Education had never been
a constituent body of the university complicated the issue, and
Cambridge only accepted B.Ed. in March 1968.

Perhaps the most vital difference between the schemes put
forward by the universities is the fact that in some places it will
be possible for an Honours degree to be awarded, which will
entitle graduates with a second-class or better degree to a
substantial annual addition to their teaching salaries, whilst
elsewhere only a pass or general degree will be available. It
remains to be seen if this will have any effect upon the pattern
of recruitment of well-qualified students to the colleges in the
Institute areas concerned.

Other important differences relate to the requirements for
entry to B.Ed. courses, the point at which registration becomes
effective, the range of subjects available and the number
requiring to be studied, the method of assessment and the extent
to which the colleges will remain responsible for teaching B.Ed.
candidates.

With respect to the first of these, in some places it will be
necessary for potential candidates to satisfy normal matricula-

tion requirements *and* faculty requirements in the subjects chosen, usually involving a number of passes at 'A' level in particular subjects and at a specified grade. Elsewhere, no pre-college requirements are made, and entry to the fourth year of study will be dependent upon performance in the Teacher's Certificate examination at the end of the third year. The Certificate course will remain very much as it is for both degree and non-degree students in some areas, with a certain amount of B.Ed. supplementation in the third year in certain cases, but elsewhere the Certificate and degree courses diverge from the beginning of the second or third years.[1]

There has been a good deal of anxiety regarding the position of those subjects which are not at present taught in most universities, but which have formed an important part of the offerings of the colleges, such as Physical Education, Home Economics and Art and Craft. Again, there are differences in the extent to which universities have been willing to recognize these as part of the degree course, and it will be interesting to see what happens as a result to the applications received by a specialist Home Economics college that is able to offer an Honours degree in the subject and a similar college elsewhere that can offer no such degree.

Education forms part of the fourth-year work in all universities, although practical teaching has generally to be completed by the end of the third year, as the award of the Teacher's Certificate will be dependent upon a satisfactory performance in the classroom. Most universities seem likely to require that B.Ed. students will have obtained a good mark in the practical part of the Education course before commencing degree work proper. Two main subjects, or one main and a subsidiary, or one main only, constitute the range of academic requirements in the fourth year.

The extent of participation by the academic staff of the colleges in the control of syllabuses, and the teaching and the examination of degree students show very considerable discrepancies between one university and another, and the restrictiveness of some in this respect has caused a great deal of anxiety and concern in the associated colleges. In one area all the

[1] See *Bachelor of Education Degree Courses in Colleges of Education in England and Wales.* London: Central Register and Clearing House Ltd., June 1967.

fourth-year work will be undertaken within the university by university staff, whilst there are other places where a precisely opposite arrangement has been agreed upon. Syllabus committees usually include both university and college representatives, although the balance of numbers again varies. Some universities have felt the need to give official recognition to those college lecturers who will prepare students for the B.Ed., and this may introduce a potentially divisive factor into staff relationships within individual colleges.

There seems little doubt that the B.Ed. has had, and will continue to have, a considerable influence on all the work of the colleges, and not just on that part concerned with the direct preparation of a selected minority of students for the degree. Where the Certificate examination is to constitute Part I of the degree it will be necessary for greater attention to be paid to syllabuses and standards than in the past, and this will affect the work done by all students. The new links with the universities, over and above the usual Boards of Studies and other joint committees, may also help to create a broader basis for future co-operation, although in a few places the clash of interests that closer contact has revealed may make this more difficult.

APPENDIX

A Three-year Course in Education

The three main aspects of the Education course—Educational studies, Curriculum studies and Practical teaching—are regarded as constituting an interrelated whole. All students take the same course, but there are opportunities to specialize in particular aspects of junior and secondary teaching during the curriculum studies work.

Most of the teaching is organized in terms of 'course units' of approximately half a term's duration. Each unit comprises six lectures to the entire year, together with six associated small group meetings, six linking written assignments, an essay and/or a group or individual display or some other form of practical work, and an objective test or quiz.

Students are given an outline syllabus for each unit and, at each lecture, a background sheet comprising quotations, statistics, discussion points, suggested reading and a short written assignment. The lectures are linked with the small group meeting of the following week by means of these assignments, which provide a basis for informed discussion of the topic under consideration. At the end of each course unit there is usually a forty- or fifty-question 'quiz', designed to be used diagnostically by both staff and students.

Linking of the various course units is achieved through the small group work, by various forms of practical assignment, including 'cross-unit' group and individual displays in the Education room, by group study practice in the second year and dissertation work in the third, and by drawing upon students' experiences in schools, which are proceeding throughout the course except for terms seven and eight.

Some measure of integration is also sought through close and continuous departmental collaboration. Department meetings occupy a minimum of two hours each week. Each course unit is the responsibility of the lecturer particularly qualified and experienced in the field concerned, and he briefs his colleagues regarding the group discussions and written work associated with his unit. All members of the Education staff attend the year lectures. No one individual is expected to organize more than two course units in a single year, i.e no one gives more than twelve to fifteen lectures per year. Tutors from other departments also participate in the curriculum studies and third-year dissertation work, and the whole staff is involved in group study practice and the supervision of block practices. The following is a summary of the content of the course.

First Year

Term One — Observation in Infants' and Junior Schools.
Psychology 1: Child Development.
Curriculum Studies 1: Basic work in the Primary school.
Curriculum Studies 2: Basic mathematics.
Curriculum Studies 3: Options (History, Geography, Drama, Art, Craft, Junior Science, Film, French).
Health Education 1: First-aid–programmed course plus practical sessions.

THE THREE-YEAR COURSE

Term Two   One-day-a-week observation and group teaching in schools.

School and Society 1: Elements of social structure.

Psychology 2: Principles of learning.

Curriculum Studies 1, 2 and 3 continue.

Health Education 2: First-aid course continues.

Term Three   Examinations.

Preparation for School Practice.

Three weeks' block practice (in same school as for one-day-a-week observation in term two).

Preparation for vacation assignments.

Second Year

Term Four   Group study practice in schools (one half day per week).

School and Society 2: Development of English Education.

School and Society 3: The Sociology of the School.

Curriculum Studies 4: Classroom organization.

Health Education 3: Social Aspects.

Term Five   Group study practice continues.

Psychology 3: Mental measurement.

Philosophy 1: Values and assumptions in educational practice.

Curriculum Studies 5: Film and television in the school.

Health Education 3:

Term Six   Examinations.

Preparation for school practice.

Four weeks' block practice.

Preparation for vacation assignments.

Third year

Term Seven   Psychology 4: Dynamics of Behaviour.

Philosophy 2: Contemporary Educational Issues.

Visual Aids Operators course.

Dissertation and topic groups. Individual topics selected from a wide range, according to student interests and the specialist background of the staff concerned.

Term Eight   Philosophy 3:   Authority and Integrity.
Revision courses: Sociology and Psychology in relation to contemporary issues.
Dissertation work continues.

Term Nine   Final examinations.
Preparation for school practice.
Six weeks' block practice (in type of school of choice).

6

PRACTICAL WORK IN THE EDUCATION OF TEACHERS

There are a number of reasons why the problems of practical work in the training of teachers are of particular importance and deserve separate consideration. Firstly, it seems likely that the time that the student spends in schools during the college course may have a greater influence on attitudes and personal development than any other single aspect of post-school education. It is during this time that what has been called the 'pragmatic barrier' between theory and practice can be broken down or reinforced;[1] the inconsistencies, misunderstandings and conflicts between school and college in respect of ideas and methods exposed; the student's professional models and identifications established. Secondly, each year brings fresh difficulties in finding suitable schools in which students can practise. When the McNair Committee reported in 1944, they estimated that on the basis of 30,000 schools being available and 14,000 students in training, there would be enough choice of schools to ensure that every student could be suitably placed for 'practical training' and 'school practice'. Today there are about 34,000 schools, although many of them are much larger than was the case twenty years ago, and some 90,000 students in training. Within a few years this number will be in excess of 110,000. It is clear that the demands of school practice are going to bear more hardly upon the schools during the next few years than ever before. It is already necessary in some areas for colleges to use every school that is willing to take students for practice purposes, irrespective of whether the school provides a good, bad or merely indifferent learning environment.

[1] Byrns, R. H. 'The Pragmatic Barrier', *Improving College and University Teaching VIII:* 4, 1960.

A third reason for separate consideration of this topic is that school practice provides the principal setting in which the schools and the colleges meet face to face. In so far as the colleges are innovatory and the schools conservative institutions – and the balance is not always this way round – the acquisition and trial of new ideas and techniques by students during the college course may be hampered by the slower pace of change in the schools where teaching practice is undertaken. Any gap between what the college tutors seem to recommend and the teachers and the schools to value may produce a conflict in identification for the student. This is likely to be resolved in favour of the schools, which constitute a reference group of greater long-term importance than the college, where the student spends only a limited period.

Practical Teaching in the Early Colleges

The earliest forms of teacher training provided in this country were within existing schools, and for many years all training colleges had attached to them 'model', 'demonstration' or 'practising' schools. Kay-Shuttleworth's Battersea Training College had available the village school for its practical teaching work, and by all accounts this was an admirable institution, well in advance of its contemporaries.

'On entering the school-room, the attention of the visitor is at once attracted by its cheerful aspect. Accustomed to see poor children taught, standing, with a scrupulous regard to their symmetrical distribution upon the school-room floor, and to associate these circumstances with a high state of discipline and mute attention, he is surprised to find the children of this school *seated* (as he probably sat himself when a boy at school) in easy attitudes, at desks – arranged with little regard for regularity – in groups three or four deep; each little group of desks giving space to a class of about twenty, entrusted to the charge of a single teacher.'[1]

The excellence of the method work at the Borough Road College also attracted attention in the early inspectorial reports. Here the art of teaching was facilitated in three main ways. All the students attended the model school attached to the college

[1] *Minutes of the Committee of Council 1845*, Vol. II, p. 26.

for four and a half hours each day. At a time when the length of the working day was so onerous, this left plenty of time for students to attend lectures and perform their studies. Secondly, each student gave criticism lessons in front of his fellows and the master. Thirdly, students gave lessons to each other, and heard each other's comments, which were 'all but universally' received with good temper. 'On the entrance of some students', the Principal noted, 'the observations have been rather intended to show the acuteness of the speaker than to benefit the teacher who has given the lesson. But this has soon righted itself. . . .'[1]

As we have seen in an earlier chapter, the weaknesses of the students' pre-college education required a system that would not only provide practical instruction in teaching, but would also furnish something by way of a secondary education. This need was fulfilled by the establishment in 1846 of the pupil-teacher system, by which boys and girls of not less than 13 years of age were apprenticed in charge of elementary school head-teachers for a period of five years prior to entering training college. Such entry was by no means guaranteed, and large numbers of pupil-teachers failed to obtain the scholarships that would secure a college course. On entry to college, many of the students were already, in Rich's words, 'well pleased with their teaching powers, and the college authorities did little to disillusion them and point the way to better things.'[2] There was very considerable variation in the amount of time devoted to practical teaching during the college course. In a sample of women's colleges surveyed in 1855 the time so spent by students of at least fifteen months' standing varied from 70 hours at Salisbury to no less than 340 hours at Whitelands and the Home and Colonial Training College.[3] The pupil-teacher system, although modified from time to time, continued for many years to be the principal avenue to a career as a qualified teacher.

'For more than half a century many of the brighter children passed into the profession by way of pupil-teachership, and supplied the training colleges with a succession of hard-working

---

[1] *Ibid.*, 1846, Vol. II, p. 385.

[2] Rich, R. W. *op. cit.*, p. 165.

[3] *Minutes of Committee of Council, 1855–6*, p. 741, quoted Rich, R. W. *op. cit.*, p. 165.

students of whom, whatever their academic attainments, it might be certainly said that they knew how to teach.'[1]

By 1902 the minimum age for apprenticeship in urban areas was raised to 16, and by 1925, the five years had, at least in the towns, shrunk to only two, the first of which was often an indistinguishable part of a secondary school course. But even by this date over half the students entering colleges had at least one year's teaching experience in schools, and this inevitably affected their attitude towards the practical teaching work during the course itself.

The Twentieth Century

The training college course remained fixed at two years for just over a century, from 1856 to 1960. During the first three decades of this century, students spent an average of twelve weeks, or one term out of six, on practical teaching in schools. The Voluntary Colleges frequently had demonstration schools attached to them, as did some of the l.e.a. colleges that were established after 1904. The Departmental Committee of 1925 felt that every college should have a special relationship with a local school.

'The ideal would seem to be a school, forming part of the Elementary school provision of the area, where the Training College authorities co-operated with the Local Education Authority in appointing the staff and in arranging the curriculum and timetable, and where methods could be tried and demonstrated as if in a teaching laboratory.'[2]

But educational opinion failed to endorse this recommendation. Model and demonstration schools had been universal among the early training institutions, but some of the smaller provincial colleges set up during the second half of the nineteenth century had no such accommodation, and were forced to use local schools for teaching practice.[3]

[1] *Report of the Departmental Committee on the Training of Teachers in Public Elementary Schools*, 1925, Cmd. 2409, p. 12.

[2] *Op. cit.*, p. 97.

[3] The 1926 *Yearbook* of the American Association of Teachers' Colleges included the following standard, 'Each teachers' college shall maintain a training school under its own control as part of its organization, as a laboratory school, for purposes of observation, demonstration and supervised study on the part of students. The use of an urban or rural school

The day training colleges that were established after 1890 also had no model school facilities, and the profit that their students appeared to derive from working in ordinary schools was another factor that led to a decline in favour of the model school idea. Demonstration and model schools were the product of a period when children of all ages had been educated under one roof. As reorganization into separate primary and secondary stages took place, colleges were sometimes left with only the junior complement of their model school, a state of affairs inappropriate to the preparation of teachers for both primary and post-primary work. Rich sums up the position by suggesting that the system 'suffered from the inherent failing that a practising school could never be a model, and a real "model school" was a static thing, often little related to the reality that the teacher would have to face when he left college.'[1]

It is of interest to compare the disappearance of the model school from the training college scene in this country with the situation in the United States, where the 'campus school' has enjoyed a much longer run, albeit sometimes in a form very different from that intended by its founders. Whilst it has been common for 'model school', 'demonstration school', 'laboratory school' and 'campus school' to be used synonymously, the term 'laboratory school' can be held to apply to a distinctive type of provision that need have little in common with the other three. In an early statement, Dewey summed up the advantages of a laboratory approach to practical teaching in terms that still have a great deal of relevance for today.

'On the one hand, we may carry out the practical work with the object of giving teachers in training command of the necessary tools of their profession; control of the technique of class instruction and management; skill and proficiency in the work of teaching. With this aim in view, practical work is, as far as it goes, of the nature of apprenticeship. On the other hand we may propose to use practice work as an instrument in system, under sufficient control and supervision of the college to permit carrying out the educational policy of the college to a sufficient degree for the conduct of effective student teaching, will satisfy this requirement.' Quoted Williams, E. I. F. *The Actual and Potential Use of Laboratory Schools*. New York: Bureau of Publications, Teachers' College, Columbia University, 1942.

[1] Rich, R. W. *op. cit.*, p. 198.

making real and vital theoretical instruction, the knowledge of subject matter and the principles of education. This is the laboratory point of view . . . there is a fundamental difference in the conception and conduct of the practice work according as one idea or the other is dominant and the other subordinate. If the primary object of the practice is acquiring skill in performing the duties of a teacher, then the amount of time given to practice work, the place at which it is introduced, the method of conducting it, of supervising, criticizing and correlating it, will differ widely from the method where the laboratory ideal persists; and vice versa.'[1]

The clear and important distinction made by Dewey between 'apprenticeship' and the laboratory approach was not maintained in the practice of teacher-preparing institutions in the United States during the following half century. As already noted, there has been a tendency to use the term 'laboratory school' indiscriminately to describe all the campus and some of the off-campus schools in which the student practicums take place. The term has also come to be associated with a stress upon human relations in the teaching situation rather than upon the wider understanding and experience to which Dewey refers. A recent definition of 'professional laboratory experiences' suggests:

'1. It is a guided experience which makes a direct contribution to the student's understanding of individuals and competence in their guidance in teaching-learning situations.

'2. It requires the student's involvement in interaction with children, youths and adults.

'3. It provides opportunity for the student, in terms of his level of readiness, to participate in representative activities of the teacher.'[2]

The words used in this passage—guidance, involvement, interaction, readiness, participation—are typical of a great mass of the literature of teacher education in the United

[1] Dewey, J. 'The Relation of Theory to Practice in Education' in *Third Yearbook* of the National Society for the Scientific Study of Education, edited by C. A. MacMurray. Bloomington, Indiana: Public School Publishing Co., 1904.

[2] Sharpe, D. M. 'Professional Laboratory Experiences' in Cottrell, D. P. (ed.), *Teacher Education for a Free People*. Oeneonta, N.Y.: American Association of Colleges for Teacher Education, 1956, p. 183.

States during recent decades, and reflect a conservatism of role-conception on the part of teacher educators that is very far from the clarity and radicalism of the earlier statement by Dewey.

A survey of 294 teacher-preparing institutions in the United States carried out by the National Council for the Accreditation of Teacher Education during the academic year 1957–8 showed that whilst the predominant practice was for student-teaching programmes to be conducted in schools away from the campus, the next largest group of colleges used a combination of campus and off-campus schools, and some used their own schools exclusively.[1] Quoting individual and association support for the campus school, one author suggested that

'These and other persons familiar with the requirements of high-quality programmes are justified in their conclusions for good reasons. They know that without a college-controlled school located on the campus, the following essentials of a good teacher education programme are obstructed: (1) Co-ordination, (2) Appropriate staff, (3) Standard setting, (4) Experimentation and Research, (5) Observation and participation.'[2]

Whilst special model or demonstration schools have many disadvantages–not least for the pupils who are educated in such educational hothouses–there are a number of ways in which the ready availability of classroom laboratory situations could be of value to the college of education, especially in a period of rapid educational change. There is no mention of the laboratory school as such in the report of the McNair Committee on the Supply and Training of Teachers, but the Committee's recommendations regarding practical work in schools have a good deal of bearing on the way in which laboratory situations might be employed.

The McNair Committee recommended that there should be 'two distinguishable types of school practice . . . (a) Practical training in schools, (b) Continuous teaching practice.' The first of these should include 'comparatively discontinuous periods of teaching and observation in the schools, visits, minor investi-

[1] Hodenfield, G. K. and Stinnett, T. M. *The Education of Teachers.* Englewood Cliffs: Prentice-Hall, 1961, p. 276.

[2] Bryan, R. C. 'The Vital Role of the Campus School', *Journal of Teacher Education*, XII:3, September 1961, p. 276.

gations and so on', whilst the purpose of continuous teaching practice would be to provide 'a situation in which the student can experience what it is to be a teacher, that is, to become as far as possible a member of a school staff.'[1]

The practical training thus recommended is in direct line of succession from the criticism lessons and demonstration school work of an earlier age, whilst the continuous teaching practice simulates the experience that entrants to the profession had formerly received as student and pupil teachers. The Committee recommended that a total of about twelve weeks in the three-year course should be devoted to 'practical training', with a further full term given up to teaching practice, preferably in a school some distance from the college and under the control of the schools and the teachers rather than the training college staff. Throughout their remarks, the Committee used the term 'selected' when referring to the schools in which students will practise, and it is proposed that in such schools, in the choice of which 'quality of staff and adequacy of premises and amenities would be the main considerations', a member of staff should be appointed to a post of special responsibility for the supervision and guidance of students' work.

'It will, of course, be a distinction for a school to be selected for training purposes, and the new responsibility might prove to be a valuable stimulus, especially to those schools which have had little contact with training. There should be one member of staff, not necessarily the headmaster, entrusted with special responsibility for supervising the student's work during his term of apprenticeship.'[2]

The McNair Committee's recommendation that the training college course should be extended from two years to three was not implemented until 1960. During the intervening fourteen years students continued to spend about twelve weeks of their six-term course in the schools, but there was increasing experiment with various forms of observation work and small group practice.[3]

[1] *Teachers and Youth Leaders.* H.M.S.O.: 1944, p. 78.
[2] *Ibid*, p. 80.
[3] See Collier, K. G. 'The Rhythm of Theory and Practice: An Experiment', *Education for Teaching*, May 1955.

Practical Work in the Three-year Course

As the date for the implementation of the three-year course grew near, the Ministry of Education, the A.T.C.D.E. and other interested bodies made known their views regarding the content and scope of the lengthened programme of education and training that the colleges would provide. The Sixth Report of the National Advisory Council made two points of some importance regarding the place of school practice in the course. It was suggested that since much 'practical skill must perforce be acquired after the student leaves college', it would be wrong to accept uncritically the need for devoting more time to practical teaching; the student who did not come to grips with fundamental educational problems while at college might never do so. Secondly, the Council emphasized the need for a gradual introduction to the full responsibilities of the classroom, perhaps beginning with periods of guided observation and visits rather than the 'in at the deep end' first school practice which was still customary in some colleges. Doubts about the wisdom of this early induction to the responsibilities of the classroom teacher had been mounting during the post-war years.

An Australian observer of the English teacher-training scene has suggested that premature introduction to the classroom has three main effects. First, the student will tend to reproduce the teaching formulæ which his past experience as a pupil suggest; this may be good, bad or indifferent, depending upon the quality of his own previous education, but, since it has been obtained in a grammar school setting, is unlikely to be much use in primary schools. Second, the student tends to be forced immediately into formal class teaching, where the class is treated as a unit and little attention is given to individual differences. Third, early experiences can become 'fixated'. Methods that appear to work, often because of particular situational factors, are accepted as panaceas.[1]

Another factor that has been held to limit the benefit that the student obtains from school practice early in the course is his inability 'at first to be able to concentrate ... attention on the right things—the social situation of the classroom, the observa-

[1] Katz, F. M. 'Some Problems in Teacher Training', *Education for Teaching*, February 1959, p. 32.

tion and interpretation of children's reactions to the teacher and to each other. The young teacher tends to be preoccupied with the content of the lesson and with methods of preparation and these other things feature at best only in the background of his consciousness.'[1]

In the United States most of the school practice is concentrated into the fourth year of the course, and one observer has stated:

'It is obviously impossible to drop student teaching down to the freshman or sophomore year, when the student would know neither what to teach or how to teach it. Neither is he likely to be well enough prepared during his junior [third] year. The solution would seem to be to "expose" prospective teachers to the classroom early in their college courses to see if, like the measles, it will "take".'[2]

In this country the stress has been upon the interpenetration of theory and practice that concurrent academic and practical work permits, and the importance of this was stressed by the A.T.C.D.E. and other bodies that presented evidence to the Robbins Committee on the structure of the B.Ed. degree.

The Ministry of Education's Pamphlet No. 34 *The Training of Teachers: Suggestions for a three-year training course* proposed that the first block practice should follow periods of observation and not take place until the end of the first year. Group and individual work with children might continue during the second year, followed by a second period of continuous practice. The final period of school practice might be longer and extend 'in a few cases, to a whole term, but in certain areas a period longer than six to eight weeks would probably place too great a strain on the schools and on the student.'[3] The pattern suggested by the Ministry has become standard practice in a large number of colleges, although there is still a very great variety of organization, as can be seen from the examples overleaf.

The detailed organization of observation, group practice and school practice is usually undertaken by individual colleges. In some areas the university Institute of Education exercises a

[1] Tibble, J. W. Review of T. H. Newcomb's *Social Psychology; Education for Teaching*, November 1954, p. 55.
[2] Hodenfield and Stinnett, *op. cit.*, p. 83.
[3] *The Training of Teachers*, Pamphlet 34. London: H.M.S.O., 1957.

Term	College A	College B
1	Nine days' guided observation in infants, junior and secondary school.	—
2	Half a day each week in the same school as that in which the first block practice will be carried out.	Four weeks' block practice.
3	Three weeks' block practice.	—
4	Group work with children in a local school for half a day each week.	—
5	Group work in schools (cont.).	—
6	—	Six weeks' block practice.
7	—	Group work with children in a local school for half a day each week.
8	—	Group work (cont.).
9	Six weeks' block practice.	Group work (cont.).

co-ordinating function, and the available schools are shared out among the colleges in accordance with their particular needs, travel facilities and so on. The local education authorities co-operate with the Institutes of Education and the colleges, and in some cases chief officers authenticate and support the approaches that are made to the schools for practice places. Elsewhere, however, effective co-ordination is still lacking, and colleges compete against each other to secure favourable placings for their students. There have been pressures during recent years for students to undertake longer periods of practice during which they might take over the full responsibilities of a teacher, but these have on the whole been successfully resisted by the colleges.

The administrative work associated with the organization of practical work is very considerable. Few colleges have adequate clerical help available, and in most cases it is the members of the Education department who arrange practices in addition to their normal teaching commitments. There is no equivalent in this country of the 'Director of Student Teaching' of the American College of Faculty of Education.[1] School practice

[1] See Stiles, L. J. *et al*, *Teacher Education in the United States*. New York: Ronald Press, 1960, p. 267, for a description of the role of the Director of Student Teaching.

organization tends to be carried out by the quickest and most convenient means, with mimeographed circulars and pro-formæ taking the place of personal visits and individual letters. Efficiency of communication is in some cases low, and this exacerbates the tensions that are inherent in the school/college, teacher/tutor relationship.

Some of the tensions derive from the kind of separation of trainers and practitioners that a working party of the Head-masters' Association saw as greater in relation to teaching than in any other profession.[1] A frequent and familiar criticism is that the staff of the colleges have an excessive concern with theory, and there is a measure of resentment among teachers at the good fortune of those colleagues who have escaped into apparently less arduous and demanding work. Another source of difficulty derives from the inability of anyone outside the class-room situation to appreciate the importance of day-to-day 'system maintenance' for the practising teacher. Once out of the classroom the lecturer or administrator becomes subject to new and different sets of institutional pressures and demands, and it is not easy to enter fully into the kind of situational press to which the teacher is subject.

Efforts on the part of a college to maximize understanding between tutors and teachers do not always guarantee that the student receives maximum benefit from his period of prac-tice. Good relationships can sometimes be bought at the cost of expensive compromises, which diminish the influence that the college brings to bear upon the student while he is in training, and enhance the deleterious impact of the norms and values of the poor school on the student's work and attitudes.

Supervision and Assessment of Practical Work

The meagre literature available on this topic in this country can be contrasted with the situation in the United States, where Purpel has suggested:

'Perhaps we ought to declare a moratorium on published material that does not advance our thinking (in the area of student teaching and supervision). Instead of publishing articles

[1] Headmasters' Association *Report of the Working Party on the Training of Teachers.* London: The Association, May 1965 (mimeographed).

that are intended to inspire, to give hope, to exhort, and to warm and gladden the heart, perhaps professional journals ought to publish only two kinds of material about student teaching: (1) those which report on rigorous analytical and/or empirical investigations and (2) those that proclaim the current scandalous nature of student teaching conditions and the state of research on supervision.'[1]

Until recently, nearly all the practical work undertaken by students in training could be classified under three heads – observation, group practice and block practice. New patterns of organization are now emerging, which raise fresh problems of supervision and assessment. The traditional observation was largely unsupervised, in the sense that the college tutors did not visit the school to see how the student was getting on. Group practice, on the other hand, involves the tutor in working closely with students in the classroom, and supervision is thus a continuous process. Supervision raises most problems in connection with periods of block practice, which still constitute the most important type of practical work undertaken by students.

The recommendations of the McNair Committee that some practical work should be done away from the college, under the control of head-teachers and school supervisors, has received little favour since 1944. Most students still practise in schools that are within daily travelling distance of their colleges or from special school practice residential centres that some colleges have established. College tutors visit their students at regular intervals during the practice, but there is considerable variation in the pattern of this supervision. In some cases the student is seen several times by a single tutor, while in others, especially when the practice is being carried on in a secondary school, a number of specialist tutors may pay visits to the same student. The cost of supervision of this kind is very high, especially when long distances are involved. The average cost per student in voluntary colleges for all school practice expenses in a recent year was £9·8, but the range was between £16·8 and £4·0. Clegg has stated:

[1] Purpel, D. E. Review of *Concern for the Individual in Student Teaching* (42nd Yearbook of the Association for Student Teaching, 1963) in *The Journal of Teacher Education*, XV:1, March 1964, p. 107. See also Purpel, D. E. 'Student Teaching', *Journal of Teacher Education*, XVIII:1, Spring 1967.

'I cannot believe that a visit to a school or a small group of schools, which can cost as much as £20 in the tutor's salary and a further £20 in travelling expenses, is not something which we could not do as efficiently in other ways.'[1]

The following description of the arrangements for supervision in one college illustrates the non-specialist tutorial approach:

'On entry, students are allocated to one of seven Education groups according to the age range that they are going to teach. Each group contains from twenty-two to twenty-five students, and is sub-divided into three tutorial groups. One Education lecturer is responsible for each Education group and acts as Chairman of the group of specialist tutors associated with her group. In the first practice and sometimes in the second, the tutors supervise their own tutorial groups. This means that the tutors have had nearly two months' opportunity to get to know the students in informal discussion, that they have frequently worked with their group in week-to-week observation and practical work in schools, that they have had discussions with the Education lecturer and know, therefore, the kind of guidance she is giving the students in their Education classes. . . . Basic to this procedure is the interpretation of the supervisor as a "general" supervisor and not a specialist.'[2]

The frequency of the visits that supervising tutors make to their students varies considerably from college to college, and even from individual to individual, but on average not less than one full lesson each week is seen. The customary pattern is for the tutor to remain in the classroom for the whole of a student's lesson, and to discuss with him at the end of the period the strong and weak points of his teaching, providing guidance as to the future planning and conduct of work. Frequently the supervising tutor discusses the student's performance with the class teacher, who sometimes remains in the room while the student is teaching, especially in the case of those on their first practice. Some teachers do not find it easy to adopt an assessment role in relation to someone whom they regard as a potential colleague, and will sometimes try to help the student by 'putting the class straight' before the tutor's visit.

[1] Clegg, A. 'Dangers Ahead', *Education*, 5 February 1965, p. 240.
[2] Fletcher, C. M. 'Supervision and Assessment of Practical Teaching', *Education for Teaching*, November 1958, p. 19.

Eggleston and Caspari have suggested that there are severe drawbacks to the customary procedures of direct tutorial supervision. The presence of the tutor in the classroom distorts the teaching situation, by generating anxiety in the student and encouraging him to adopt approaches that are likely to 'please' in terms of his perceptions of the tutor's norms and values. They discuss an experiment in which students were asked to provide detailed written records of specified lessons, which were then discussed with a tutor outside the school setting; it is claimed that this method enabled students to recognize and cope with their feelings in the classroom more effectively than direct supervision would have permitted.[1] Elsewhere, Richardson has described the inter-personal tensions that arise in the tutor/ student relationship both with respect to school practice supervision and the continuous assessment of theory work.[2]

The formal intention of the colleges is to emphasize the tutorial role of supervision at the expense of assessment. Assessment is in fact going on all the time, and both tutor and student know this. Assessments are demanded for a variety of motives—to sort out the failures early in their course, to have something to put on paper that other members of staff can refer to, to satisfy lecturers' consciences regarding the proper performance of their duties, to motivate students to improve their performance, and, in the final practice, to provide a mark for the testimonial that will be demanded by headmaster and local authority. In giving these assessments a whole series of assumptions are made about the supervisor's objectivity, the homogeneity of different tutors' grades, the way in which performances can be isolated from the settings in which they occur—or the extent to which staff are capable of making allowances for certain characteristics of these settings—and the consistency of an individual's performance from one hour to the next. Surveying one thousand grades awarded to students practising in ten primary and ten secondary schools over a period of years, Shipman has shown that placement is a major factor in determining the degree of success achieved by the individual student—the chance of securing a

[1] Eggleston, J. and Caspari, I. E., 'Supervision of Teaching Practice', *Education for Teaching*, November 1965, p. 42.

[2] Richardson, E. 'Personal Relations and Formal Assessment in Graduate Courses in Education', *Education for Teaching*, May 1965, p. 43.

credit or a distinction is much greater in some schools than in others. He concludes that 'practice enables the best and worst to be sorted out. But it is probably useless to try to discriminate among the majority of students'.[1]

With a growing recognition of the hazards involved in practical work assessment has come a scepticism regarding the value of spending long periods discussing the grades that shall be given to a student, haggling over whether a particular individual's mark should be B or B+; such fine distinctions are of little use at any stage of the course, and the only differential that matters to many local authorities today is that between pass and fail–and in some areas even this influences only the salary the individual will receive, not the fact of obtaining an appointment. Thirteen-point scales have been simplified into five-point scales, five into three—Distinction, Pass and Fail, with perhaps an additional grade to indicate those students who have *just* passed, but require additional help and guidance if they are to overcome the handicaps with which they set out on their teaching careers.[2] The visit of an external examiner to see the work of certain students is now taken rather more in the stride of the practice than before, although it still gives rise to a complex student form book, since it is assumed that the external examiner sees only the potential distinction and fail candidates. It is clear that assessment and grading of performance and potential–by no means the same thing, as follow-up studies have shown–will continue, but a very much more simplified form of grading than has sometimes been used in the past will serve to: (a) sort out those students who are so weak that they should fail or discontinue the course, (b) register the fact that some students will require special help and guidance from the head-teacher and inspectorate during their early years of teaching, (c) show that the student has been visited by a tutor or tutors on previous

[1] Shipman, M. D. 'The Assessment of Teaching Practice', *Education for Teaching*, May 1966, p. 38. See also Collier, K. G. 'The Criteria of Assessment of Practical Teaching', *Education for Teaching*, February 1959.
[2] Wiseman, S. 'Measuring success in the teaching profession', *Proceedings of the International Congress of Psychology*, Washington, 1963: Wiseman, S. and Start, K. B. 'A follow-up of teachers five years after completing their training', *British Journal of Educational Psychology*, XXXV:4, November 1965: Start, K. B. 'The Relation of Teaching Ability to Measures of Personality', *British Journal of Educational Psychology*, XXXVI:2, June 1966.

practices and (d) indicate the student whose work in schools during the course has been of outstanding quality.

The Co-operating Teacher

The McNair Committee's proposals regarding the status that should be given to selected teachers supervising students' work in schools have never been implemented in any general way. Some of the latest schemes for practical work in schools, referred to in the following section, do involve teachers much more in the guidance and assessment of students, but these are still exceptional arrangements. In large schools, head-teachers generally attach students to particularly well-qualified and experienced members of staff, although a highly specialized timetable means that the student may sometimes encounter a large number of different classes, form and subject teachers in the course of a week, and this may reduce the influence that a particular teacher can have on his work. In small schools, especially those with only three or four teachers, the student can find himself working with a member of staff who has only recently qualified, although in such cases the head is usually able to have a good deal of contact and to give advice and help.

There have been no formal attempts in this country to assess the impact of the co-operating teacher on the work and attitudes of the student, although American studies indicate that this may be considerable. Reporting a study in this field, Price[1] states that 'the correlation between supervising teachers' and student teachers' classroom teaching performance indicated that student teachers seem to acquire many of the teaching practices of their supervising teacher. . . . The most logical conclusions for this finding reinforces the belief that only the best available teachers should be used in student teaching programmes.' Another small-scale study suggested that 'the more formal the co-operating teacher . . . the more influence she seems to exert on the student teacher assigned to her classroom'.[2]

Where teachers have undergone the more formal type of

[1] Price, R. D. 'The Influence of Supervising Teachers', *Journal of Teacher Education*, XII:4, 1961, p. 471.

[2] McAulay, J. B. 'How much Influence has a Co-operating Teacher?', *Journal of Teacher Education*, XI:1, 1960, p. 79.

training that was general a decade or two ago, or have absorbed certain beliefs about the nature of ability and the limits of performance, and have since had little in-service education, it is almost inevitable that their own ideas and practices will fail to reflect the contemporary attitudes and influences that are communicated to the student through his training course. Many of these teachers will sympathize with the student's efforts to establish his own techniques and experiment with the classes that he takes. When he fails, teacher and student will be able to agree that it was the technique that was defective, rather than the student's immature use of it.

Because the status of co-operating teacher does not exist in other than local arrangements and on-going experiments, colleges in England and Wales have in general been able to do little to make contact with the teachers who help and guide their students, other than in the encounters that take place during the actual process of student supervision and assessment. Where meetings between school and college are held these generally involve the heads rather than the staff. In the United States the formal role of co-operating teacher is recognized in a number of ways—listing in the college catalogue, honoraria, invitations to tea parties, lunches and a variety of campus meetings and conferences, the granting of library facilities, free or reduced tuition for in-service courses, even reduced prices for university football games.

New Approaches to Practical Work

This chapter has concentrated upon the practical work that students undertake in schools, but a large number of colleges now encourage active participation in the work of youth centres, clubs and a variety of community agencies for people of all ages. It is claimed that this is of particular value in giving students some experience of the leisure interests and activities of the 'non-academic' children, with whom they may have had little previous direct contact.

A common feature of many of the new approaches that have been made to the organization and supervision of practical teaching is an increase in the importance of the role of the teacher and the school. The Headmasters' Association have gone so far as to suggest that the training of graduate teachers might be school-based, with students spending a month during the long vacation after graduation in the university department, the whole of the autumn term in the school, the spring term back in the Department and the summer term again in the school. They also propose that the probationary year should become part of the training period, during which studies would be continued alongside actual employment in the school, with full qualification being dependent upon the satisfactory completion of these studies as well as on a satisfactory standard in the classroom.[1] There is a good deal of sympathy with the idea of making better use of the probationary period among educators of teachers, but few would go all the way with the Headmasters on the issue of school-based training. Most of the other suggestions for greater school participation that have come forward in recent years have been a good deal less radical than this.

Some suggested schemes have been motivated as much by a desire to make effective use of the teacher-training plant as to improve the organization of practical teaching. Pedley has outlined a pattern whereby one-third of the students in any particular college would be on school practice throughout the year, each teacher spending two half-terms in school annually. During the practice halves students would live in lodgings or at home, thus freeing the college to take some 50 per cent more students each year. Supervision in the schools would be provided by 'master teachers', approved by the local Institute of Education, local education authorities, Heads and H.M.I.s, who would have student apprentices attached to them throughout the school year. Groups of master teachers would hold regular meetings with college tutors to discuss students' progress and to work out a common approach.[2] Clegg thinks that '. . . it would be sensible to make all teacher-training courses sandwich courses by letting the teaching practice extend over a whole term and even a whole year, and giving the responsibility for it to the schools. The teachers charged with the task of supervision would, of course, be given time and a responsibility allowance for doing it. We could at once by this means increase the capacity of the training colleges and stop a lot of grossly expen-

[1] *Report of the Working Party on the Training of Teachers, op. cit.*
[2] Pedley, R. 'Teacher Training: A new approach', *Education*, 4 June 1965.

sive waste of tutors' time in travelling.'[1] Schemes of this kind were urged upon the colleges during 1965 as part of the government's effort to increase the output of teacher training, but it appears that only a minority of colleges have made such organizational changes.[2]

There are some other experiments that, although they may make better use of college plant and of the available practice places in schools, are principally of interest because they involve a real difference of approach and are directed towards improving teaching practice itself. In a Department of Education and Science Circular issued in December 1966 reference is made to the possibility of using students two to a class during periods of block practice, and some work along these lines has already been done in colleges within the university of London Institute of Education.[3]

The philosophy behind the experiment has been outlined by Martin and others.[4]

'If there is to be a shift of emphasis in secondary education from teaching to learning, new patterns of classroom relationships will need to be explored and teachers will need to work more with pupils rather than to instruct them. As an experiment in training ... co-operative teaching ... seemed to develop a more flexible and less authoritarian attitude in the students, and this suggests that in working together in the classroom they learn more from one another than they do from someone not actively engaged in the lesson. . . . In the second place, and perhaps more importantly, the experiments suggest that children learn better when the teacher is sometimes a participant in the class. . . .'

With the increase in the number of those in training, the presence of students in the school has come to be a normal part of the school's activities, and not an exceptional once-a-year event. An experiment of particular interest in this respect is the Culham College–Crown Woods (London) Comprehensive School

[1] Clegg, A. op. cit.
[2] The majority succeeded in increasing numbers by 'crowding up' rather than organizational change.
[3] Circular 24/66, 13 December 1966.
[4] Martin, N. B., Hagestadt, M., Thompson, V. and Newsome, B. 'Two in a Classroom—new forms of co-operation', Bulletin of the University of London Institute of Education, New Series, No. 7, Autumn 1965, p. 14.

arrangement, whereby a substantial group of Culham students spend a full term in the school under the supervision of selected teachers. It is envisaged that this large school, with some 2,000 boys and girls on roll, may be able to accept as many as thirty students at one time, assist in their professional and personal studies 'and so integrate them into the life of the school that, instead of being an additional burden to the staff and a reason why the pupils are less well taught than they should be, they become a useful addition to the teaching strength of the school.'[1]

The University of Sussex School of Educational Studies has been operating a system of school based post-graduate training, in which the theoretical and practical elements of the course go on alongside one another, with the student attached to a school for the whole duration of the course.

Several university departments of education have made use of teacher-tutors in recent years, whereby teachers in particular schools which the department uses for practice purposes are given some status in the department, assist with tutorial work, and sometimes receive an extra payment for the work involved. Such arrangements have been easiest when students spend a whole term in the school, as is the usual pattern in a number of departments.[2]

The Impact of Practical Teaching

One of the weaknesses of school practice as it is so often organized is that the feedback that the student receives is inadequate and sometimes contradictory. Feedback is received from three main sources—the children in the class, the head and class teacher and the supervising tutor from the college. The latter's help is probably the most systematic and can often utilize existing knowledge about earlier weaknesses and problems in giving advice for future work. But where several tutors are involved, there are opportunities for inconsistent advice to confuse the the student—at a National Union of Students' Conference reference was made to the need for 'greater uniformity in

[1] *Culham-Crown Woods.* London: Crown Woods Secondary School, December 1966 (mimeographed).
[2] For accounts of such schemes see Tibble, J. W. *Education for Teaching,* May 1966, and Bell, J. *Times Educational Supplement,* 14 October 1966.

tutorial supervision, if possible the tutors in a college should decide in agreement among themselves what they wanted to tell students, what methods and theories they wished the students to try. . . .'[1] Furthermore, the tutors' advice is largely divorced from the school culture in which the student is operating, and it may be difficult for the student to act on the advice given, not simply because of inexperience and lack of knowledge, but because the school is antipathetic to the success of the particular procedure or technique that has been suggested. The impact of school cultures upon the success and failure of different types of teaching is as yet unexplored, and a more subtle analysis than the conservative/innovatory dichotomy between school and college is required.

Feedback is also provided by the head and class teacher and other teachers in the school, not all of this being overt and direct. The lifted eyebrow at a chance remark, the word of praise— sometimes bantering or facetious, but important none the less— when a difficult class appears to have been well handled, the silent approval that goes along with an apparent willingness to conform to the norms and values that the school and individuals within the school represent—all these may be significant ways in which the student learns from his work in the school. This type of feedback is sometimes occasioned by behaviour that the college would regard as inappropriate. In schools situated in difficult urban areas, for example, the fulfilment of certain minimum task needs—'quiet classes, polite responses' and so on— that have become associated with an authoritarian regime, can sometimes earn the student a type of approval for which he is unlikely to receive much credit from the college authorities.

In addition to the feedback provided by tutors and teachers, there is also that provided by the children he teaches. Colleges tend to place a good deal of emphasis on increasing the student's sensitivity to class response, on the importance of treating children as individuals rather than as mere members of a class. The heavy perceptual load of the classroom situation sometimes makes this very difficult for the inexperienced student. Furthermore, the effects of increased sensitivity may not be in the intended direction.

[1] National Union of Students' *Report of Conference on Teaching Practice.* London: The Union, 1964 (mimeographed).

'(Crow) found that a group of senior medical students were somewhat less accurate in their perceptions of others after a period of training in physician/patient relationships than were an untrained control group. The danger is that a little learning encourages the perceiver to respond with increased sensitivity to individual differences without making it possible for him to gauge the real meaning of the differences he has seen.'[1]

It seems possible that feedback from the children can also have an important effect upon the way in which the student learns to perceive his own role. In the primary school the younger children are unlikely to distinguish the students from the full-time members of staff; given a minimum of effective teaching, they will provide the positive response that is characteristic of children of their age. The fact that the student will have close contact with only a single class during the period of practice in such a school, however short this may be, enables some degree of rapport and mutual understanding to be established. All this helps to strengthen the student's child-centred conception of her role, and responsiveness to the spontaneity and ideas of her class, neither of which constitute a threat to what is a relatively secure position.

At the opposite extreme, the older children in the secondary school are likely to be much more conscious of the temporary and unqualified status of their 'teacher', who may in any case not be much older than they are themselves. The student is unlikely to be given the unquestioned status of his primary school counterpart, and the classroom situation may be perceived as threatening to his attempts to establish his teacher-role on a sound footing. Within a specialized timetable he may see six or seven different classes in the course of each week, which during a three- or four-week practice makes it impossible for him to get to know any group of pupils particularly well. In the face of all this he may retreat behind his desk and lesson notes, ploughing remorselessly on through a carefully prepared lesson that has long since lost its power to hold the children's interest or attention, getting back as soon as he can to the company of his future peers in the safer haven of the staff room. The fact

[1] Zalkind, S. S. and Costello, T. W. 'Perception: some recent research and implications for administration', *Administrative Science Quarterly*, VII, 1962–3, p. 235.

that staff rooms are almost universal in secondary schools and not found in many of the smaller primary schools is itself a point of some importance in this context.

It follows that any increase in the primary school teacher's sensitivity to feedback is likely to have a positive effect upon his perception of his role, and to reinforce the child-centred interpretation that has been fostered during the college course. For the secondary school teacher, however, such sensitivity acts dysfunctionally, merely serving to increase the threat that the classroom situation presents, and encouraging a retreat into the subject and a tendency to identify with the school staff as a reference group rather than the educational philosophy represented by the college.

Finally, it is not unimportant that only during periods of teaching practice is the student provided with models and exemplars of the kind of role that he will be called upon to perform at the end of the college course. Oakeshott has drawn attention to the importance of such models in achieving an understanding of what such an activity as teaching is about:

'... in every ability there is an ingredient of knowledge which cannot be resolved into information, and in some skills this may be the greater part of the knowledge required for their practice. Moreover, abilities do not exist in the abstract but in individual examples; the norms by which they are recognized are afterthoughts, not categorical imperatives. And each individual example has what may be called a style or idiom of its own which cannot be specified in propositions. Not to detect a man's style is to have missed three-quarters of the meaning of his actions and utterances; and not to have acquired a style is to have shut oneself off from ability to convey any but the crudest meanings.'[1]

Despite the growth of study practice arrangements, and other means whereby students combine their work in the principles of education and teaching method with actual activity in the classroom and among children, there is still a substantial separation within the course of training between work in college and work in the school. As a result, there is no guarantee that the models with which students are provided in school bear much

[1] Oakeshott, M. 'Learning and Teaching' in Peters, R. S. (ed.) *The Concept of Education.* Routledge, 1967, p. 169.

relation to the principles and propositions that they have been taught in college. Hence, rather than contributing to the development of both a theoretical and practical grasp of the teaching role, the Education course and teaching practice may be seriously disjunctive in their effects on student development. Recognition of these dangers has led to the financing of substantial research projects on the place of teaching practice in the preparation of teachers, but it will be some time before the results of this research are known and begin to have an impact upon the organization of courses.[1]

[1] The Department of Education and Science have sponsored such projects in the University of Bristol Institute of Education.

PART THREE
STUDENTS AND STAFF

7

THE BACKGROUND OF STUDENTS
AND THEIR SELECTION

Any society that sets about providing some form of education for all its children needs a large and continuing supply of teachers sufficiently competent to fulfil the educational objectives of the time. It is therefore not surprising that, in the words of the McNair Report of 1944, the state 'has subsidized training for the profession of teaching for a hundred years. It has never subsidized training for any other profession in the same way or to the same extent'.[1] At a time when education played a comparatively small part in social mobility as compared with the accumulation of small capital and the hard work of individual industrial and commercial entrepreneurship, a willingness to train for teaching provided a way in which post-school education, of a sort, could be obtained with a minimum financial investment or sacrifice. The pupil-teacher scheme, bursarship, student-teachership and training college provided a way up for thousands of the sons and daughters of skilled workers, farmers and tradesmen. These occupational groups have traditionally made a contribution to the supply of teachers considerably in excess of their numerical representation in the population at large; the division of ownership and control that follows the death of the proprietor-farmer or proprietor-tradesman is a far more serious threat to the prosperity of a family than in the case of the joint stock industrialist or commercial operator, and the chance to attain a respectable and secure, if ill-rewarded, social position no doubt added to the attractiveness of a subsidized teacher-training course for these groups.

[1] McNair Report, *op. cit.*, p. 90.

Qualifications on entry

We have already seen that there was a good deal of variation in the age and background of students admitted to the earliest colleges, especially in the period prior to the introduction of a pupil-teacher system in 1846. At a time when the total of colleges was small, students were drawn from all over the country; on leaving St. John's, Battersea, they were appointed to schools as wide apart geographically and socially as Redruth and Reading, Manchester and Mauritius, Eton College and Parkhurst Prison. The educational background of the students at the pioneer St. Mark's College, Chelsea, at this time was superior to that of those of Kay-Shuttleworth's Battersea College. Of the seventy residents at St. Marks in 1844, sixteen had received previous education in national schools, two at British and foreign schools, three at grammar schools, and forty-six at various other day or boarding schools. Of the early days of the Colleges of St. Paul and St. Mary at Cheltenham it has been said 'the earliest students of the college were drawn into the teaching profession ... from all manner of trades and occupations. There were men of forty among them, and some of them were incredibly rough stuff intellectually.'[1] In respect of both the previous education and age of its student body, St. Mark's stood in contrast to the other colleges founded during the early forties, which were closer to the Battersea pattern and tended to place a greater emphasis upon attributes of character rather than intellect. Mosely felt it necessary to remark upon this contrast in his report on the Chester Diocesan College, where over half of the students had been previously employed as workmen, had left school at an early age and had acquired what they knew during the intervals of daily labour. Whilst this might be a testimony to a superior character and an inestimable degree of self-dedication and self-sacrifice, it was scarcely the sort of background that would 'exercise a prompt and facile intelligence, or cultivate a verbal memory and an opulent diction'. Mosely was obliged to conclude that 'from the laborious character of an elementary schoolmaster's life and its privations, it is improbable that many people would seek it, whose friends were in a position to pay for

[1] Beck, W. E. *A History of the Cheltenham Training Colleges*. Bath: Dawson and Goodall, 1947.

them an annual premium of £25, unless, for some reason or other, they be disqualified from pursuing with success other avocations in life.'[1] This told against the effort to make the college self-supporting, since it encouraged a lowering of the standard of ability and qualifications of candidates; the ability to find, or to have found for one, the necessary premium became the chief criterion of eligibility.

The introduction of the pupil-teacher system brought a new type of student into the colleges, some of whose characteristics were summed up by Her Majesty's Inspector in his report on the Church of England colleges for 1857.

'Before the year 1852 the students were obtained from a different source from that which at present supplies them. They were picked up, as it were, by accident; many with no previous training for their profession at all; none with more than they might have obtained by acting as voluntary teachers in Sunday schools. These men were in some respects a very inferior, in some respects an excellent, material for the purpose to which the colleges hoped to apply them. They had generally everything to learn; but having for the most part chosen their profession not simply as a means of livelihood, but from a real love of teaching, they showed often a zeal and aptitude not to be easily replaced by any other qualifications. Such a source of supply was easily exhausted, and certainly could not have filled the colleges now at work. . . . The new supply of teachers [those apprenticed under the pupil-teacher system of 1846] were in many respects different from the old. They were always much younger, much better taught, and much quicker to learn. The old students felt themselves unfairly matched against such competitors, who even when inferior in the more valuable qualifications for the office of teacher, steadiness and maturity of mind, were sure to excel in all that makes a show. The consequence might have been expected. Several principals have told me that they found it much harder than formerly to bring the old sort of man into their colleges, and they attribute this to the cause that I have mentioned.'[2]

Although the previous education of students entering the

---

[1] *Minutes of the Committee of Council on Education*, 1844, p. 635.
[2] *Minutes, op. cit.*, 1856–7. Report of the Revd. F. Temple on the Church of England Training Colleges, p. 685.

colleges continued to improve during the next half-century, and a much sounder basis for further advance was provided by the creation of maintained secondary schools after 1902, there was a continuing tendency to associate the qualifications expected of students with the level of work they would subsequently have to undertake in elementary schools. Since this would make few intellectual demands upon them, it was clearly uneconomic to require from them a high standard of previous education before they were admitted to professional training. By the time the Committee on the Training of Teachers for Elementary Schools came to report in 1925, there were three main ways of becoming a qualified teacher in such a school. The longest established was the pupil-teacher scheme, now with two variants, neither requiring education in a secondary school prior to the age of fourteen. In urban areas, pupil teachers transferred from the elementary school at fourteen to a secondary school or a preparatory class in a pupil-teacher centre, where a further two years were spent in full-time study. Between the ages of sixteen and eighteen the pupil-teacher spent most of his time working in the elementary school and the rest continuing his education in the secondary school or centre. Entry to the training course was at eighteen. In rural areas the whole period from fourteen to eighteen was spent working and studying in an elementary school under the super-vision of a competent head-teacher; sometimes this was com-bined with a certain amount of part-time attendance at the near-est pupil-teacher centre. The second main avenue to teaching was via a bursarship, awarded as early as eleven, twelve or thirteen to boys and girls intending to teach in order to enable them to attend a secondary school. There they stayed until reaching the age of seventeen, when their status changed to that of student-teacher and part of their time was spent in teaching elementary classes under supervision, entering the college at eighteen. Finally, an increasing number of entrants to teaching were receiving a normal and 'unpledged' secondary education until the age of eighteen, when they entered college alongside their pupil-teacher and student-teacher counterparts.

By the middle twenties a large proportion of the recruits to training colleges had received a full secondary education—in Humphreys' terms most of them 'had had a better general education by the time they entered college than their predeces-

sors had had by the time they left it.'[1] The departmental committee of 1925 considered the possibility of restricting the work
of the colleges to purely professional training, and a minority
report advocated that the college course should be limited to
one year, following the successful attainment of the secondary
school examination, the higher school certificate towards which
sixth-form work was directed. The majority, however, recommended that the college course should remain at two years and
should include the study of one or more academic subjects in
addition to professional courses, and that intending students
should prepare for college by means of full-time secondary
education rather than student and pupil teachership. In the
event, anxiety on the part of some local authorities regarding
the future supply of teachers obliged the Board of Education to
permit the continuance of these earlier schemes, although on a
much reduced scale.

When the McNair Committee came to survey the provision
of facilities for the training of teachers in 1943 the position had
been reached whereby nearly all students entering the colleges
had received their preliminary education in a secondary school,
had passed the first ('school certificate') examination and had
spent some time in the sixth form. A minority had also achieved
a higher school certificate.

During the two decades after 1944 there was a steady improvement in the academic qualifications of students preparing
for teaching, especially in the more popular colleges, and the *de
facto* requirements for entry rose a good deal beyond the statutory minimum of five passes at 'O' level. By 1967 some 63 per
cent of men and of women had at least one pass at advanced
level, and only 7 per cent of women and 9 per cent of men were
qualified at the minimum level of five ordinary-level passes.
Given that the formal minimum requirement for university
entrance is two passes at advanced level, 38 per cent of the men
and 37 per cent of the women entering colleges of education in
1967 were so qualified. Much has been made of this fact by those
concerned with upgrading the work of the colleges and giving
their students opportunities to work for degrees, but the overall

[1] Humphreys, D. W. *The Relationship between the Training Colleges and the
Universities before McNair*. Bristol: University of Bristol Institute of Education, 1965.

figures, encouraging as they are, conceal important detailed differences. One set of these relate to the *grade* of the advanced-level passes achieved by university and college entrants respectively. Recent data are difficult to obtain, but the Robbins Committee made available some figures relating to the 1961–2 entry (shown in Table VII) which enabled the advanced-level grades of teacher trainees to be compared with those of undergraduates, students in colleges of advanced technology and full-time students in further education.

TABLE VII

Grades of Passes achieved at 'A' level by Students
in England and Wales, 1961–2   (percentages)

1961–2	3 or more 'A' with passes at A or B				2 'A' with passes at A or B			1 'A' with A or B pass		All	N
	3	2	1	0	2	1	0	1	0		
Teacher Trainees	1	2	6	11	4	10	25	6	35	100	2,735
University (all)	25	25	23	13	5	5	5	1	–	100	7,074
C.A.T.S.	4	8	17	23	4	7	26	3	9	100	787
Other f.t. f-ed.	3	5	11	14	4	8	22	12	20	100	1,635

Source: Report of the Committee of Higher Education 1965, Appendix Two(B) Table 86, pp. 77 and 109, p. 98.

Although it can be argued that pressure of numbers and improved standards have enabled universities to raise their entry requirements during recent years, and that the qualifications possessed by many college entrants today would have secured them a university place a decade ago, it is clear from this table that comparatively few teacher trainees during 1961–2 had the *de facto* requirements for university entry. Seventy-three per cent of undergraduates had three or more passes at advanced level, with at least one of these at grade A or B, whilst only 9 per cent of teacher trainees were in this category. Seventy-one per cent of teacher trainees had no advanced-level passes at A or B grade, against only 18 per cent of undergraduates. There is little reason to believe that this situation has changed much

recently–the proportion of college students with various patterns of 'A' level and 'O' level qualifications altered only very
slightly between 1960 and 1967.[1]

A second set of problems surround the distribution among the
colleges of students with different levels of qualification. Although
academic qualifications are not the only criterion for entry to
college, they inevitably play a large part in determining the
applicant's chance of securing an interview and further consideration. Colleges that attract large number of first-choice
applicants can afford to be highly selective, and are likely to
give consideration only to those candidates who seem likely to
do well in their subsequent advanced-level examinations. Since
offers of places are not contingent upon achieving an appropriate number or level of passes, the ability of the college and the
applicant's school to predict successfully the likely outcome of a
sixth-form course is an important element in this process. All in
all, 'a college which admits large number of poorly qualified
candidates is much more likely to be doing so because it is
forced to, than because it has a definite policy of admitting only
good teaching personalities'.[2] If anything, the introduction of
the B.Ed. is likely to increase rather than diminish the stress
laid upon academic qualifications and potential.

Simons found that whereas in certain colleges over 70 per
cent of the students had two advanced-level passes or better,
and only 0·7 per cent were qualified at a minimum of five
ordinary-level passes, there were other colleges where nearly a
quarter of the student body were qualified only at the minimum
level. It appeared that Church of England colleges had men
students slightly less well qualified than in the local authority
colleges, whilst the men in the Roman Catholic colleges are
markedly less well qualified than those elsewhere, only 27·4 per
cent of the 1962–3 entry having two or more advanced-level
passes as compared with 42·2 per cent for the local authority
group. A similar pattern applies to women in Roman Catholic
colleges, with only 29·3 per cent having two or more advanced

[1] Calculated from Annual Reports of the Central Registry and Clearing
House for the years concerned.
[2] Simons, M. *Intercollegiate Differences between Students ·entering Three-year
Courses of Training for Teaching.* Unpublished M.Ed. thesis, University
of Durham, 1965.

levels in comparison with 39·3 per cent for the local authority institutions. Differences between individual colleges are much larger than those between groups–such as local authority, voluntary, men's, women and mixed, Northern, Midland and Southern and so on. Furthermore, some of the anticipated differences, forming part of the folklore of teacher education, which imply superior qualifications of students in the London area and the popularity of the London colleges, were not borne out for the entry under discussion; a group of colleges in the North Midlands showed a considerably higher level of student qualification than was true of other areas.[1]

Too much should not be made of the differences in the academic qualifications of students on entry to colleges as compared with other institutions of post-school education, or the difference between one college and another. Such evidence as we have does not suggest a very strong correlation between advanced-level results and subsequent academic performance, and it may well be that there is an even less relationship between these results and skill and competence as a teacher.[2] In terms of the rough-and-ready criteria that are used for the determination of public and professional images of quality, potential and status, it is clear that the colleges of education are drawing upon educationally inferior groups as compared with the university, and that some of them have student bodies who are markedly inferior in terms of academic qualifications.

A more detailed picture of the pattern of sixth-form work undertaken by college entrants can be obtained from the analysis of advanced-level passes made annually by the Central Registry and Clearing House and from the surveys undertaken by the Committee on Higher Education. Whilst only 15 per cent of men entering colleges in 1962–3 had not attempted some subjects at advanced level, the number of women in this category was much larger (25 per cent); over a third of the women from independent schools had not been 'A' level candidates.[3]

---

[1] *Ibid.*

[2] Himmelweit, H. T. 'What to do about Student Selection', *Sociological Review Monograph No. 7*. Keele, 1963.

[3] *Higher Education: Students and their Education*, Appendix 2 (B) to the Report of the Committee on Higher Education (Robbins Committee). London: H.M.S.O., 1964, Table 89, p. 79.

Some 42 per cent of men and 68 per cent of women with advanced-level passes had qualified in Arts subjects only, 41 per cent and 20 per cent respectively in Science and Mathematics alone, and a further 11 and 12 per cent in at least one Arts and one Science subject.[1] Only 9 per cent overall had passes in Mathematics. This concentration on the Arts side was also reflected in the ordinary-level qualifications of teacher trainees – 97 per cent of the 1966 entry had passes at this level in English Language, but only 59 per cent of women and 76 per cent of men in Mathematics.

Geographical Origins

From their earliest beginnings as denominational training colleges, colleges of education have been national institutions, drawing their students from all parts of the country. The promoters of the training school at Cheltenham (later the Colleges of St. Paul and St. Mary) made this clear in their proposal of 1845, which required that the school be 'neither local nor diocesan nor territorial in its operations'.[2] (To ensure truly national representation of interests the initial governing body was to comprise no fewer than two hundred persons, divided equally between clerics and the laity.)

Although local education authorities are now the providing bodies for the majority of the colleges, the system of financing through the 'pool', to which all authorities contribute in proportion to the size of their school population, irrespective of whether they maintain colleges of their own, emphasizes this national orientation. The setting up of day colleges in recent years, which are both cheaper to provide and which meet the needs of such groups as non-mobile married women and other mature students, has constituted a new development. As yet such colleges, and the local outposts that have been established by existing residential colleges, cater for only a small proportion of the total numbers of students in training.

Local authorities often appear to be of the opinion that a college in their own area is likely to improve the supply of teachers for their schools, and encourage students to train who might otherwise be unwilling to travel to a distant college. It is

[1] *Ibid.*, Table 93, p. 82.   [2] Beck, W. E. *op. cit.*

these reasons, rather than the undoubted prestige that maintaining a college of education brings, that have often been invoked by those authorities that have wished to initiate or expand their teacher-training provision.[1]

At present we know very little about the part that the college of education plays as a redistributive agency, its influence on the flow of students from their various home areas to teaching posts in the same or different regions. A small-scale study of the home regions and the regions in which teaching appointments were taken up, undertaken among two entry groups in a single college several years ago, showed that half the students returned to their home areas at the end of the college course. But there were sharp differences between regions. Some 20 per cent of the students came from Wales, but only 3 per cent went back to teach there, whilst some two-thirds of a rather similar proportion of students from the counties closest to the college obtained first appointments in these same counties.[2]

Regional differences in teaching mobility have also been borne out by a large-scale survey undertaken with the support of the Department of Education and Science at the University of Keele. Over four-fifths of primary school teachers working in a group of North Midlands towns were found to have been born and received their schooling in the same area, against about a quarter of such teachers in a Southern urban area. A recent study of deputy head-teachers in a number of North-Eastern authorities reveals a very low rate of mobility, the great majority having been born in the area.[3] In a study of nearly two thousand secondary school teachers in schools within a twenty-mile radius of Sheffield, Jay showed that two-thirds of the modern school teachers were born within the survey area, whilst two-thirds of the grammar school teachers came from elsewhere. A third of the modern school staff had also trained within the area, against a quarter of the grammar school staff.[4]

[1] Tunn, T. H. 'The Significance of 1970', *Education*, 4 February 1966.

[2] Taylor, W. *Regional Origins and First Appointments of Students at St. Luke's College, Exeter, 1956-8 and 1957-9.* Unpublished paper.

[3] Burnham, P. S. *The Role of the Deputy Head.* Unpublished M.Ed. thesis, University of Leicester, 1964.

[4] Jay, L. J. *The Mobility of Teachers.* Sheffield: University of Sheffield Department of Education, 1966 (mimeographed).

Until recently there has been very little information available about the areas from which college of education students come and the extent to which they choose, and gain admission to, colleges close to their homes. A survey of the regional origins of students in a single college in the North of England enabled comparisons to be made between the 135 students entering between 1860 and 1865 and those beginning courses in 1965. The proportion recruited from the area closest to the college had remained almost constant in the two periods at 64 per cent, but whereas in 1860 to 1865 only 7 per cent of students had come to the college from counties other than in the North, by 1965 this proportion had risen to 19 per cent.[1]

To test the view that colleges in the North of England are likely to have a larger proportion of local students than some of those in the South a detailed study was made of the 1964 entrants to two colleges, each admitting a similar total number of students, one on the outskirts of London, the other in a similarly urban area in the North-West. The expected contrast between North and South did not appear. Approximately half of each college intake was found to be from its own region, and a further substantial proportion from adjacent areas.

This small-scale survey was followed by an investigation of the relationship of entrants' home addresses to applications to, and acceptances by, a stratified sample of fifty-three colleges. The regions used by the Department of Education and Science were employed as a basis for the enquiry, which covered an entry group of some 3,200 men and 5,900 women.[2]

There were considerable variations in the proportions of students naming colleges in their own regions as first choices. In London and the South-East nearly 60 per cent of both men

[1] Hebden, R. 'Colleges of Education—Local Colleges?', *Education for Teaching*, February 1966.

[2] The regions are as follows: NORTHERN (Cumberland, Durham, Northumberland, Westmorland, N. Riding of Yorkshire), YORKSHIRE (E. and W. Ridings), NORTH-WESTERN (Cheshire and Lancashire), NORTH MIDLAND (Derbys, Leics, Lincs, Northants, Notts and Rutland), MIDLAND (Herefords, Shrops, Staffs, Warks, Worcs), EASTERN (Beds, Cambs, Essex, Herts, Hunts, Ely, Norfolk, Suffolk), LONDON AND SOUTH-EASTERN (London, Kent, Surrey, Sussex), SOUTHERN (Berks, Bucks, Hants, Isle of Wight, Oxfordshire), SOUTH-WESTERN (Cornwall, Devon, Dorset, Gloucs, Soms, Wilts) and WALES.

and women chose colleges within the region, whilst in East Anglia only 12 per cent of the men and 20 per cent of the women made such first choices, no doubt reflecting the small number of colleges in this area.

A substantial majority of candidates were accepted by the college of their first choice. In several areas a larger proportion eventually obtained places in their home regions than had originally applied for them–in the Northern region, for example, where only 14 per cent named local colleges as first choice, over 20 per cent obtained places within the area. But a more accurate picture than that provided by regional comparisons can be gained by examining the actual distance of students' homes from the colleges where they were accepted.

Overall, more than a fifth of both men and women were accepted by colleges less than fifteen miles from their homes, a third lived within thirty miles of their college, and over a half within sixty miles. At the other end of the scale, a quarter were in colleges more than a hundred miles from home. But once again there were differences between the regions. In London and the South-East, over 40 per cent of the men and 34 per cent of the women were in colleges within fifteen miles of their homes. In the following summary, students in colleges *less* than thirty miles from their homes are shown for each region. The significance of thirty miles clearly varies from one part of the country to another–it can be the distance between a student's home in a remote Northern village, with a weekly bus service, and his college in Newcastle or Durham, or the distance between, say, a suburban street in Chatham and a college in the centre of London. Such distances are in a very real sense non-comparable. But it may nevertheless be of interest to show the proportion of 'local' students by this definition. (See Table VIII.)

These figures take on particular significance in relation to the way in which colleges of education have developed as residential institutions. This has not simply been a matter of attracting students from other than the local area, although the national basis of recruitment of the earlier denominational colleges undoubtedly provided a spur for the new local authority colleges to provide residential accommodation in the years after 1904. The tradition of residence is very strong in English higher education and is seen by many as an important constituent of the all-round education as opposed to specialized training, that universities and colleges provide. Nearly 90 per cent of English undergraduates are resident in college, hall of residence or lodgings. Only 19 per cent live within thirty miles of their university. The situation is very different in Scotland, where over half of all undergraduates attend universities within thirty miles of their homes.[1]

TABLE VIII

Students with Homes within Thirty Miles of their College,
by region of College

Region	Percentage of students with homes within 30 miles	
	Men	Women
Northern	20·2	43·4
Yorkshire	41·9	26·2
North West	35·2	28·4
North Midland	34·8	26·6
Midland	21·6	32·4
Eastern	26·1	26·5
London and South-Eastern	51·5	43·0
Southern	31·9	40·9
South-Western	17·3	19·2

It is not possible to say with any exactness how many of the 'local' college of education students are resident and how many are attending on a day basis. But an estimate of the overall proportions within the sample colleges in each region who occupy different types of accommodation was made available by the University of London Student Residence Research project, and in the following table these proportions are compared with the numbers of local students referred to in Table VIII.

The capital and maintenance costs of permitting students to apply for university and college places in any part of the country are high, but there are many good educational reasons why such a free market in places should exist. It appears

[1] University Grants Committee, *Returns from Universities and University Colleges in receipt of Exchequer Grant*, Academic Year 1964–5. London: H.M.S.O. Cmnd. 3106, Table 1, p. 12.

from the figures in this section, that at least some of the students who occupy colleges of education accommodation or lodgings have homes that are close enough to their colleges to permit daily travel – in London and the South-East, for example, only 14 per cent or so of students appear to be living at home, but over half the men come from homes that are within thirty miles of their colleges. It can be argued that the social, educational and professional advantages of living away from home are such as to justify this situation, but it would at least seem important that these advantages are weighed against the cost of providing accommodation on a scale sufficient for the needs of a half or more of a total student population of 111,000.

TABLE IX

Types of residence of College of Education Students, by College Region (percentages)

		N	Y	NW	NM	M	E	S	L&SE	SW
'local'	M	20	42	35	35	22	26	32	51	18
students	W	43	26	28	27	32	26	41	43	19
living at home		29	17	16	17	18	12	21	14	20
living in hall		41	58	55	50	50	61	64	51	39
living in digs		29	26	29	32	32	27	14	34	42

Educational background

The Robbins Committee found that 74 per cent of the men and 69 per cent of the women in their sample of 1,085 students in colleges of education in 1961–2 had received their secondary education in maintained grammar schools.[1] Of the 9,000 students who constituted the 1964 entry to the Robbins sample of colleges, surveyed in connection with the study referred to in the previous section, 68·2 per cent of the men and 70·2 per cent of

[1] *Students and their Education, op. cit.*, Part One, Tables 1 and 2; Part Two, Table 79 and 80.

the women had been educated in grammar schools, 3·9 and 8·3 per cent respectively in public and independent schools, 4·3 per cent and 9·5 per cent in direct-grant schools and the remainder in secondary modern, comprehensive and other type of secondary school. There were again marked regional differences. In the sample colleges in the Southern area (Berkshire, Buckinghamshire, Hampshire and Oxfordshire) a quarter of the men and a fifth of the women had been to public and independent schools, whilst in the North-West rather similar proportions held for those with a direct-grant school background.

Analysis of the number of 'A' level subjects candidates intended to take between applying for college places and the following September showed that only 17 per cent of boys and 18 per cent of girls educated in public and independent schools were working for three or more subjects, whilst over 40 per cent of the boys and 37 per cent of the girls who had attended or were attending maintained grammar schools were so engaged.

Recent years have seen a larger recruitment of mature students to colleges of education, some of whom have been 'exceptional admissions', without the normal requirements of five 'O' level passes or their equivalent. A survey of the 1964 entrants to the nine day colleges that existed at that time showed that although the types of schools that had been attended by such students did not differ very much from those characteristic of the younger age groups attending residential colleges, there were substantial differences in the proportions who had never spent time in the sixth form.

Social background

If a certain amount of information on the academic qualifications of entrants to teacher education is now becoming available, there is still very little known about their social background and personality characteristics. Some facts about social origins can be culled from the appendices to the Robbins Report. Table X has been compiled by extracting data from a number of Robbins tables and combining these so as to show differences in the occupational class of the parents of students in different forms of higher education. It can be seen that whereas 71 per

TABLE X

Occupations of Students' Parents, 1961–2

	Non-Manual			Manual			Not known	All
	Higher Prof.	Other Prof. and Manual	Clerical	Skilled	Semi-skilled	Unskilled		
University Undergrads								
MEN	17	40	12	19	6	1	5	100
WOMEN	20	43	11	16	6	1	5	100
Postgraduates	10	37	14	25	7	2	6	100
Training College Students								
MEN	5	27	16	32	13	2	5	100
WOMEN	8	36	14	27	7	2	5	100
Full-time Further Education Students	12	32	14	28	8	2	4	100
Part-time Further Education	6	20	16	39	12	4	3	100

Source: Derived from *Students and their Education* Report of the Committee on Higher Education, Appendix Two (B), 1961, Tables 5, 65, 81, 102, 105.

cent of male and 75 per cent of female university undergraduates came from families where the father is in some non-manual occupation, only 48 per cent of the male and 58 per cent of the female teacher trainees are from non-manual backgrounds, and nearly half the men and over one-third of the women are from homes where the father is employed at some level of manual work.

The social gap between the families of undergraduates and teacher trainees, particularly in the case of men, is clear and important. The educational gap, especially at the post-school level, is even more marked. Taking undergraduates in Great Britain as a whole, 22 per cent came from homes where neither parent had attended a selective school, against 34 per cent for teacher trainees; 29 per cent of undergraduates had one or both parents who held a degree or a teacher certificate, but only 13 per cent of teacher trainees had parents who were so qualified. But, once again, there are significant differences between the backgrounds of men and women in these respects—nearly twice as many women as men in colleges of education had parents who held a degree or teacher certificate, and whilst just under a half of the men came from families where neither parent had been to a selective school, well under a third of the women were in this category. The figures are given in Table XI below.

TABLE XI

Education of Parents of Undergraduates and Teacher Trainees (Percentages)

	Undergraduates		Teacher Trainees	
Parents attending a selective school	Men	Women	Men	Women
Both	46	53	19	35
One	26	24	27	29
Neither	23	19	48	31
Not known	5	4	6	6
One or both parents having a degree or teacher certificate	27	34	8	15

Source: *Higher Education, op cit.*, Appendix Two(B), Tables 1, 2, 79 and 80.

THE BACKGROUND OF STUDENTS

Although these figures do little to throw light upon the functioning of the complex processes of social and educational selection and mobility of which they form part, they are of interest in indicating that the colleges of education, because their students start from a lower base, still provide a relatively more significant social and educational lift than the universities. This is especially true in the case of men. Three-quarters of all male undergraduates already come from the lower middle and middle-class families where one or both parents attended a selective secondary school; a quarter come from homes where one or both parents have a teacher's certificate or university degree. In comparison more than half the male teacher trainees come from a family where the father is a manual worker, one or both parents of about the same proportion went to a selective school, and only one out of every twelve had a father or mother with a teacher's certificate or degree.

The humbler social origins of teacher trainees, and the ambiguity that surrounds the social status and financial rewards of the teacher, may help to account for the resistance that has been noted to the discussion of social class in college of education courses. Although this is gradually disappearing as sociological topics come to occupy a more assured place in the syllabus, there is still the feeling on the part of some tutors, as well as students, that the topic is 'embarrassing' and best avoided. In a review in the *Student Teacher* of a textbook in the Sociology of Education, it is suggested that 'it is a pity that social class is mentioned so frequently as though it were an obsession of sociologists and educationists, let alone statisticians.'[1]

A comparison between teacher trainees and undergraduates in respect of the type of secondary school attended shows trends similar to those that have already been noted in this section. A higher proportion of students in colleges of education (72 per cent) had attended maintained grammar schools than their university counterparts (61 per cent) and a lower proportion had been pupils in direct-grant and independent schools—21 per cent as against 37 per cent for undergraduates.

[1] Review of Musgrave, P. W. *The Sociology of Education* in *The Student Teacher* 2, Spring 1966, p. 30.

188

Personality factors

Very little information is available regarding the personality characteristics of teacher trainees as compared with other groups of young people inside and outside full-time education. There is a similar dearth of hard evidence about the personality of the practising teacher–reviewing several hundred research studies that have been undertaken during recent decades, Getzels and Jackson are obliged to conclude that 'despite the crucial importance of the problem and a half-century of prodigious research effort, very little is known for certain about the nature and measurement of teacher personality, or about the relationship between teacher personality and teaching effectiveness. The regrettable fact is that many of the studies produced so far have not produced significant results. Many others have produced only pedestrian findings. . . .'[1]

An example of work done by psychologists in this country is a study by E. G. S. Evans which compares reasoning ability and personality differences among student teachers in a university department of education and in four colleges of education. Using a sample of 131 men and 158 women Evans applied reasoning ability schedules, the Maudsley personality inventory and the revised Bernreuter inventory, the latter having been designed to differentiate 'between individuals who are self-assured and those who tend to be handicapped by self-consciousness and feelings of inferiority . . . on the sociability scale, low scores are associated with good sociability, high scores with solitariness and independence.'[2] Having shown certain differences to exist between the scores of department of education students and those in the colleges, Evans then goes on to draw a wide variety of conclusions–the italics are added.

'The personality test showed that, while university graduates were just as stable as training college students, they were inclined to be more introverted. Furthermore, in spite of differences in age and intelligence between the two groups, university

[1] Getzels, J. W. and Jackson, P. W. 'The Teacher's Personality and Characteristics' in Gage, N. L. (ed.), *Handbook of Research on Teaching*. Chicago: Rand McNally, 1963, p. 574.
[2] Evans, E. G. S. 'Reasoning Ability and Personality Differences among Student Teachers', *British Journal of Educational Psychology*, XXXIV.

men were less sociable than training college women and university women less confident than training college men. Again, *one cannot help wondering whether these differences are induced by the different experiences the students have in university and training College.* One would expect a greater social maturity and confidence to develop and, indeed, be accelerated as a function of a university education, but this does not seem to happen. On the contrary, the present findings suggest that many students go through a university and gain a fair level of academic success and competence in their special subject fields, *they do not appear to achieve much in terms of their personal development.* For example, 30·88 per cent of the graduates came within the category of neurotic introvert as compared with 17·12 per cent of training college students. This fact, together with the poor scores obtained by many graduates on the confidence and sociability tests suggest that *universities could learn a thing or two from training colleges* in their approach to students' needs and problems and by so doing, bring about a radical change of attitude towards the purpose of "reading for a degree" and towards the purpose of education in general.'[1]

The lack of any pre-university or pre-college testing that might show the points from which the students began their experience of higher education in terms of the personality dimensions concerned would seem seriously to limit the usefulness of the final comparisons made. We have already noted how psychological studies of this kind lack a comparative dimension in terms of the groups that need to be contrasted; they also lack the time dimension that would enable the effect of the experiences concerned to be gauged.

However scanty may be the evidence regarding the personality characteristics of the successful student and the effective teacher—and the equation of the two is itself without much empirical backing, as the recent studies of Wiseman and others have shown[2]—those concerned with the selection of students are

[1] *Ibid.* p 313
[2] Wiseman, S. 'Measuring Success in the Teaching Profession', *Proceedings of the International Congress of Psychology*, Washington, D.C., 1963. Wiseman, S. and Start, K. B. 'A Follow-up of Teachers Five Years after completing their Training', *British Journal of Educational Psychology*, XXXV, November 1965.

continually engaged in making assumptions in this field. K. M. Evans has argued that the inevitable differences between interviewers as to what characteristics are important provide somesomething of a cancelling out effect.

'It is noticeable that there are considerable differences between the students selected by different training colleges, although the basic qualifications for entry are the same for all. Selection is made in accordance with the assumptions of the selectors about what is desirable teaching. Some emphasize one aspect of the work, some emphasize others, and they choose their students accordingly. The difference of emphasis is sometimes made because of differences in the age groups or of the specialized subjects to be taught. It is arguable that, since all teachers are not going to be employed on exactly the same work, then they should not all be the same kind of person. Training is based upon the same kind of assumption that governs selection, and the results are equally good for different colleges.'[1]

Even if a wide spread of assumptions about what makes a good teacher does exist, it seems unlikely that the assumptions made by a particular college will be sufficiently well known to enable sixth-form teachers, parents and intending students to match personality with college in drawing up their list of preferences. In fact it seems likely that interviewers and selection panels are responding to certain fairly standard sets of assumptions regarding the relationship of certain personality traits to subsequent performance. As long ago as 1931 Cattell carried out a survey of those concerned with selecting and interviewing teachers and intending teachers and reviewed the existing literature on the subject, producing a final list of qualities which were regarded as fairly permanent and not susceptible to training. In order of importance these were: intelligence, personality and will; sympathy and tact; open-mindedness; sense of humour; idealism; kindness; enthusiasm; perseverance; selfcontrol. Of this list, Cattell noted that only intelligence was capable of objective assessment.[2]

Nearly twenty years later the A.T.C.D.E. carried out an investigation among principals of training colleges regarding the

---

[1] Evans, K. M. 'Research on Teaching Ability', *Educational Research*, 1:3, June 1959, p. 22.
[2] Cattell, R. B. *British Journal of Educational Psychology*, I:1, 1931.

qualities that they looked for in intending teachers. In order of frequency of mention the following list resulted: good speech and voice; sense of vocation; interest in children; social poise and confidence; good appearance; wide interests; good manners; alertness; vitality; humour; personality; sincerity. A subcommittee of the Association subsequently produced a list of the chief qualities that appear to make for success in teaching, without reference to the possibility of assessing them at the time of selection. The committee went farther in suggesting that there were also certain qualities, 'which, if present in any marked degree, should cause candidates to be rejected'. These were, firstly, cynicism – 'an attitude implying no convictions or belief in values, and that nothing is worth while' – unfriendliness, neurotic instability, acute nervous mannarisms, lack of vitality, general dullness of personality, slick superficiality, and physical abnormality or irremediable defects of speech.[1]

Given the difficulty of making anything more than a very impressionistic assessment of the long list of positive characteristics that investigators have noted, it seems likely that at the point of entry to teacher training such negative factors as those mentioned above will be taken as more important than anything else in determining acceptance or rejection. It is at point of entry that assessment of this kind plays its most important role in the process of becoming a teacher. Although a number of students drop out from courses each year because they find themselves, or are found to be, temperamentally unsuited to teaching, there is little by way of systematic personality assessment as the course proceeds. As Vernon has noted 'teachers are as diverse in their psychological traits as any other occupational group, and ... it is fallacious to talk of the teaching personality as something distinct and constant.'[2]

[1] *Selection for Teaching*. London: Association of Teachers in Colleges and Departments of Education, 1950; 'Picking out the Teachers; Training College Interviews', *Times Educational Supplement*, 22 October 1954.

[2] Quoted Allen, E. A. 'Professional Training of Teachers: A Review of Research', *Educational Research*, V:3, 1963, p. 200. For other reviews of the literature on the teacher's characteristics see Getzels and Jackson, *op. cit.*; Evans, K. M. 'An annotated bibliography of British research on teaching and teaching ability', *Educational Research*, IV, 1961; Westwood, L. J. 'The Role of the Teacher', *Educational Research*, IX:2, 1967.

The selection of students

A boy or girl who wishes to train for teaching in England or Wales has first to decide, or have decided for him, whether he will undertake a three-year degree course in a university or a three-year course in a college of education. As far as men are concerned, it appears from the figures given in earlier parts of this chapter that the vast majority who are likely to be academically qualified to enter a university will attempt to do so. At the same time they may apply for places in colleges of education or other institutions of higher education as an insurance against failure either to secure a place, or the appropriate number of 'A' level passes at the necessary grades to enable the provisional offer of a place to be confirmed. Information about the courses available in each college is obtainable from the *Handbook of Training for Teaching*, a compendious book of reference which, enquiries suggest, many grammar schools do not have available for their pupils. The more easily handled *Compendium of Teacher Training courses in England and Wales*, now issued free of charge to all schools by the Department of Education and Science, provides information on the basis of which the intending student can send to the colleges of his choice for prospectuses and application forms.

The college prospectuses vary a great deal in the information that they provide and the manner in which the academic and residential life of the college is presented.[1] A standard pattern is for the range of courses available to be set out fairly briefly, with choices and options, and for something to be said about the history of the college, its student life, the nature of the accommodation available and the amenities of the surrounding area. Photographs are usually included, nearly always showing some or all of the following scenes; a study bedroom (usually in a modern block); a general view of the college; the library; a laboratory; a group of men and/or women involved in modern dance or gymnastics; the dining hall or refectory; specialist rooms and facilities; a common room. Some of the least attractive prospectuses are those of colleges known to have a large proportion

[1] For a survey of prospectuses current in 1965 see *From Sixth Form to Classroom*, Special Supplement No. 3 to *Where*. Cambridge: Advisory Centre for Education, 1965.

THE BACKGROUND OF STUDENTS

of well-qualified students and a considerable oversupply of applicants. Some prospectuses of local authority colleges give a good deal of prominence to the names and awards held by the councillors and aldermen who make up the governing body, but provide little detail of the academic qualifications of the staff. On the basis of his examination of the factors affecting choice of college, Simons concluded that prospectuses have a relatively small influence, especially since they are sent for by the candidate after a 'short list' of colleges in which he or she is interested has already been decided upon.[1]

The Central Registry sends to each college all the forms naming it as a first choice. Some colleges can afford to reject five out of every six first-choice applications they receive; these are then passed on to the second college in each applicant's list. If this happens to be another popular college it is likely to be already filled by candidates giving it a first choice, so the application is passed on again. There are a number of colleges that receive very few first-choice applications, and are obliged to 'select' their students from those naming them as a second, third or reserve choice, or on the basis of a 'second round' whereby the forms of candidates who have failed to obtain a place in any of the colleges of their choice are circulated to those colleges where places are still available. The process is complicated by the candidate's choice of subject and/or age group—some 'first-choice' colleges will accept less well qualified and second- and third-choice candidates for certain courses for which there does not exist such a strong demand, even at the price of turning away better-qualified applicants who have chosen heavily over-subscribed options.

Few students are accepted without interview. These are usually conducted at the college, although in some cases the principal or members of staff spend short periods at other centres seeing applicants from the local area. Interviewing procedures vary widely. At the one extreme the candidates spend a quarter of an hour or less talking with the principal, vice-principal or head of a subject department, who is responsible in the light of the impression created and the candidate's references and qualifications, for deciding whether or not a place can be offered. At the other extreme some colleges have complex batteries of tests

[1] Simons, op. cit., p. 184.

and structured interview procedures on which recommendations are based. In one college, interviews are held on a number of mornings and afternoons during which all lectures and other teaching are cancelled, and the whole staff takes part in the process. Every candidate takes a verbal reasoning test and objective tests in English and Arithmetic, and is then interviewed independently by two members of staff, one of whom teaches the subject of the candidate's choice, for two periods of thirty minutes. Each interviewer works from a standardized interview schedule, drawn up in accordance with the best available knowledge regarding interviewing procedure. Clearing House Form 3, which normally accompanies 'passed on' applications, includes the interview comments and grade suggested by each of the colleges of the candidate's previous choice. It is of interest that this form is not available to interviewers in this particular college, thus avoiding any 'halo' effect. The decision as to the offer of a place is taken by the vice-principal or principal on the basis of the two independent interview reports, the test results, references, head teacher's report and school record. Whether or not the complex procedure results in a more 'efficient' selection—whatever the criteria for this may be—it does have the advantage of involving the whole staff, ensuring that all the available information is taken into account, and satisfying the candidate that his application has received a due measure of attention.

The factors that cause certain colleges to be preferred to others have been fully investigated by Simons.[1] A large proportion of students were influenced by the accessibility of the college in relation to their home, but rather few wanted to be close to home. The numbers preferring single-sex colleges were small, except in the case of specialized courses of various kinds and particular institutions that had built up national reputations for certain types of work. The availability of particular subject courses is of very great importance in determining the candidate's preferences—'no other question on the form elicited such a uniformly high number of responses from all the groups, and only on the question of co-education was there such a strong bias . . . there is an almost overwhelming number of verbal contributions on the question of subject. These range from

[1] *Op. cit.*

expressions of dismay at the lack of courses in modern languages and the sciences from students who have been compelled to enter colleges they did not want, to fairly frequent statements that students had heard the subject department in the first-choice college was particularly good.'[1]

Shipman found the advice of friends and acquaintances who have had experience of a particular college plays a substantial part in the choice made by candidates, and this is confirmed by Simons, who suggests that it is influential in about a quarter to a third of the cases.[2] The candidate's school also provided a good deal of advice, which was 'detailed' in about a quarter of the cases surveyed. Such advice sometimes amounted to telling the boy or girl which colleges they should apply to, and some schools draw up a list of colleges as 'A', 'B' and 'C', 'first-choice', 'second-choice' and 'reserve' categories. Students coming up to college have been found to believe that such lists have some form of official status. With a growing sophistication regarding the selection process, schools now frequently advise candidates to choose a second college that is less popular than their first preference, in order to ensure that the second choice is not already full if their forms have to be passed on. But with access to some of the lists prepared by students, Simons was obliged to conclude that the information given was often wildly inaccurate. Some of the weaker candidates were advised to apply to what the school took to be a 'C' college in order that they should stand a better chance of success. This, coupled with the fact that many candidates appear to have a fairly clear impression of their own abilities and limitations, tends to increase the proportion of candidates accepted by their first-choice college.

Mature Students

Of the students entering colleges of education for the first time in 1965, just over seventy per cent were eighteen or nineteen years of age, fourteen per cent were between twenty and twenty-five, and a similar percentage over twenty-five.[3] The

[1] *Ibid.*, p. 157.
[2] *Ibid.* See also Shipman, M. D., *op. cit.*
[3] Calculated from *Statistics of Education*, 1965, Part II, Table 48, London: H.M.S.O. 1966.

number of mature students in colleges has been increasing a good deal in recent years as government policies to exploit every available source of teachers have taken effect. Many older students attend three-year residential colleges alongside boys and girls straight from school; others are involved in one-year or two-year shortened courses on the basis of possessing certain educational qualifications or experience. Colleges have been encouraged to recruit older candidates from their local areas as day students, and the Secretary of State announced his intention in April 1966 of 'blanketing the country' with courses in colleges of education, technical colleges, college annexes in large towns, and by setting up additional day colleges, so that no city or town with a population of one hundred thousand or more would be without a college or 'outpost'.[1]

The largest number of mature students can be found in day colleges, which have been set up in large centres of population since 1961. Information on the students in these colleges is not given separately in the official statistics or the reports of the Central Registry and Clearing House, but a certain amount of data are available from two 'one-college' surveys and an analysis of the application form of candidates successful in obtaining places in the nine day colleges open in October 1964.[2] Seventy per cent of the men and 62·2 of the women students in these colleges were above the age of twenty-five – 14 per cent of the men and 17 per cent of the women were over forty. Over half the women were married. Although the types of schools attended by the day college students did not differ very much from those characteristic of the younger groups entering the residential colleges, there were substantial differences in the proportions who had spent time in the sixth form. Nearly all the eighteen- to twenty-year-olds admitted to courses of initial training in recent years have undertaken sixth-form studies, and this is equally true for the proportion of men in this age group who enter the day colleges – 37 out of 46 had two years or more of

[1] Speech at 1966 National Union of Teachers' Conference, reported in the *Guardian*, 13 April 1966.

[2] Pickering, S. 'The Late Starters', *New Society*, 20 January 1966; Porter, J. F. 'New Horizons for Mature Students', *Education for Teaching*, May 1962, p. 38. Taylor, W. 'Regional and Educational origins of Students in Colleges of Education'. Bristol: University of Bristol Institute of Education 1967 (mimeographed).

sixth-form work behind them. Rather fewer women in this age range in the day college entry had a full sixth-form course – 118 out of 248. Far fewer of the older groups had any experience of sixth-form study. Taking all the age groups together, 71·5 per cent of men and 61·2 per cent of women had not spent any time in the sixth form, and only 22 per cent and 20 per cent respectively had followed a full sixth-form course. Since the vast majority of the day college students – 70 per cent of the men and 83 per cent of the women – had been pupils in selective secondary schools, it appears that the groups that the day colleges are chiefly drawing from are the sixteen-year-old leavers from grammar schools of an earlier period. Under a fifth of the men and only 7 per cent of the women had received their secondary education in non-selective schools, and there is little sign that the day colleges are tapping different social and educational sources from those of the residential colleges for the bulk of their students, who come from the same selective groups as the general entry to teacher training.

A large proportion of both men and women had been in employment of some kind prior to applying to enter college; some 43 per cent of the men had been working for at least fifteen years. Most of the jobs held fitted into the routine non-manual and skilled manual categories, although there was also a sprinkling of professionals, army officers, managers and unskilled workers.

The problems of the mature student tend to be very different from those of the straight-from-school entry, and impose different sets of demands upon the college staff. The college day is inevitably affected by the time taken by students to reach college from their homes – although three-quarters of the 1964 entry lived within fifteen miles. Pickering refers to the fact that some of the women at James Graham College, Leeds, spend two or three hours a day in cars, buses and trains; the average travelling time was forty-two minutes, and 80 per cent of the students lived within twenty miles and half had cars available.[1]

Other sources of strain are legion. Pickering refers briefly to some of the less customary backgrounds.

'One student, who became a widow during the course, had embarked on it knowing that her husband was dying and that

[1] Pickering, *op. cit.*

198

her children would soon be entirely dependent on her. Another has a schizophrenic husband who is in and out of a mental home. Another has an alcoholic husband. Several deserted wives with children have at times been destitute and on national assistance. One was evicted for not paying the rent. Another had married an Italian who attacked her with a knife and was subsequently deported. Several women had to bring up handicapped, spastic, intellectually sub-normal or deaf children. One or two had children or husbands in trouble with the law. But all these women successfully completed the course.'[1]

The contribution of the day college to the total output of colleges of education has grown rapidly, and the numbers of mature students from such sources will do something to offset the growing youthfulness of the teaching profession as a whole. The mature student, however, brings into the colleges and into the schools a contact with the outside world and its work that may be missing from the experience of many teachers who have followed more conventional paths from the back to the front of the classroom. The influence that such teachers will have upon the work of the schools is difficult to predict. One headmaster who recruited a well-qualified graduate physicist from industry, believing that he might get across to boys a greater understanding of the industrial world and what it offered, found that the man concerned was having a precisely opposite effect. The fact that he had himself relinquished industry for the classroom did not pass unnoticed by the pupils, and did little to encourage them to examine the prospects of this type of employment.

There is a tendency for the largest numbers of potential mature students to be found in areas where the shortage of teachers is least acute. Most of the women candidates are married and 'immobile'; when trained, they expect to obtain an appointment close to their homes. If these students are to represent an increment to the total teaching force, schools must appoint them in preference to younger and more mobile teachers, who are presumably then available for work in a shortage area. But many local authorities, and especially those in areas where it happens that larger numbers of immobile teachers are available, have within recent years given heads of schools independent powers of appointment, and no longer

[1] *Ibid.*

maintain a general list or 'pool', to which teachers are appointed for service in any school within the authority's area. It is sometimes difficult to persuade a head that, in the national interest, he should appoint the immobile Mrs. X, recently qualified with a D teaching mark from the local day college or outpost, rather than the lively Miss Z, with an excellent recommendation from her college in the North of England. The clash here between the freedom of the individual head and the interests of a national policy of teacher supply is very real.

Choice and Selection

From all this it is clear that a great variety of factors enter into the process whereby students are selected for teacher education. Much of the selection is effectively in the hands of the candidate himself and his advisers, and affected by his previous educational and social history, rather than under the direct control of the colleges. Out of a total of 52,892 applicants for places in 1967–8 only 4,911 were eventually unplaced, and 3,795 of these were either unqualified or graded as 'unacceptable'.[1] The extent to which colleges themselves can be selective is governed by the numbers of applications they receive. Looked at as a whole, the process operates in such a way as to create a hidden pecking order of colleges, which may be based on no very justifiable criterion. The college with six times the number of first choices than it can accommodate is responsible for determining the groups from which the less fortunate colleges will make their selection, and so on down the line. This hierarchy of reputation is complicated by location and the availability of specialist courses, together with the tendency for some candidates to choose less popular colleges because they stand a better chance of getting into these or because there is some other feature that appeals to them.

In all this there is scant opportunity to assess the factors of 'personality' that receive the lion's share of attention in much that is written and spoken about the selection of teachers and teaching proficiency. Only at the college level, where selection takes place according to the various criteria that individual

[1] *Report on Entry to Colleges of Education, 1967–8.* London: Central Registry and Clearing House Ltd., 1968.

interviewers or the academic board have determined as relevant, and to the extent that the numbers coming forward permit, can such personality factors play much part.

Little is known about the assumptions that are made about these factors, except that they are complex and are likely to be based upon inadequate information. The process of selection at the college level is represented on the diagram below. The interviewer is being asked to make a decision (A) about the relationship of certain qualifications and personality attributes (B), to subsequent behaviour and performance as a student (C) and as a teacher (D). It is unlikely that he has much information about the crucial relationships between B and C, B and D and C and D on which a decision could reasonably be based. In this situation it is inevitable that experience and hunches should play the greatest part.

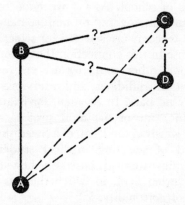

Turner has distinguished between what he calls *sponsored* and *contest* mobility, the former being represented by early selection on the part of an élite group, followed by controlled induction into this group, the latter by a more open, competitive system whereby membership is available to all those who can display the appropriate credentials.[1] The English educational system has tended to be characterized by strong elements of sponsorship, whilst the Americans have been influenced more by the

[1] Turner, R. H. 'Modes of Social Ascent through Education' in Halsey, A. H., Floud, J. E. and Anderson, C. A. *Education, Economy and Society.* New York: Free Press, 1961. See also Hopper, E. I. 'Educational Systems' *Sociology* 2:1, 1968.

organizing norms of a contest system. Discussions of educational selection in this country tend to be dominated by the norms of sponsorship, with considerable attention being given to personal qualities, suitability for the course, motivation and commitment. The ideology of the selection of students for training as teachers reflects these emphases, but in fact the selection processes themselves are conducted more in accordance with contest than sponsored norms. There is a place, somewhere, for nearly all the qualified individuals who apply. Apart from a handful of candidates who prove unacceptable to all the colleges that receive their applications or interview them, questions of personality and suitability are largely irrelevant. The really important thing is not an individual's suitability for teaching, but his possession of certain minimum qualifications, which can be freely obtained in a variety of ways, not just by attending particular kinds of school. As yet we have not accepted this situation into our thinking and pronouncements about the way in which future teachers are selected, or select themselves. It is interesting to note in this connection that admissions to higher education in some other countries are entirely based on the academic record of candidates, and interviews and personality assessments play no part. In Sweden, for example, this is true even of medicine, one of the most professionalized types of training. In the words of the Dean of a Swedish medical faculty:

'This method of selecting medical students [using only objective academic criteria] is based on the view that medicine is a wide and varied field, in which there is scope for many different types of personality.'[1]

---

[1] Quoted by Tomasson, R. F. 'From Elitism to Egalitarianism in Swedish Education', *Sociology of Education*, 38:3, 1965, p. 212.

8

THE STAFF OF THE COLLEGES AND DEPARTMENTS OF EDUCATION

The number of men and women teaching in the colleges of education more than doubled between 1938 and 1948 and doubled again in the period up to 1962. Before the Second World War there were only 181 men and 515 women working in the colleges. By 1966 the figures were 4,027 and 2,665 respectively. The proportions of men and women have varied a great deal during the period in question. The ratio of one man to just under three women that held pre-war was affected by the setting up of a large number of emergency colleges after 1944 and the demand for men teachers in secondary schools. For a brief period after the war men exceeded women by a small margin (919 to 813 in 1948) but then the proportion of women rose steadily. In 1954 out of a total of 2,296 lecturers, only 671 were men, practically the same ratio as pre-war. Within the next ten years, however, the numbers of men recruited went ahead by leaps and bounds, and today they exceed women by 1·5 : 1. Not only are there a larger number of mixed colleges which require men staff; many of the women's colleges have recruited men lecturers, particularly in subjects such as Mathematics and Science for which it is difficult to obtain suitably qualified women candidates, but also for Education, English and the whole range of Arts and professional subjects. There are now several women's colleges in which the headships of the physical education department and/or the department of modern dance are held by men. It seems likely that the proportion of men staff will increase. The principal of a large mixed college of the North of England reported in March 1966 that the posts advertised so far that year had attracted 370 applications from men and only thirty-four from women.[1] The advertisement early in 1968 of the principalship of a local authority mixed college, in which women students outnumber men by three to one, attracted 115 applications, only 4 of which were from women.

It is clear from the numbers of those involved and the age of entrants that this field now offers career possibilities that hardly existed twenty years ago. In their evidence to the McNair Committee, the Training College Association drew attention to the fact that

'It was not promotion for a secondary school teacher to be appointed to a training college; and, moreover, the prospects of further promotion were reduced. Lecturers on the staff of training colleges were seldom appointed to headships of secondary schools and women lecturers were seldom selected for high administrative posts.'[2]

To some extent, the colleges were still suffering in this period from the poverty that had been associated with their earlier development. The staff of the colleges in the nineteenth century were not distinguished by their qualifications or accomplishments. Instructing the under-privileged instructors of the under-privileged did not attract many of high academic standing. It was the general practice to recruit staffs from the ranks of former students, some of whom had no practical experience in schools before taking up their appointments. Even those who had experience had usually obtained it in an elementary school, with the result that 'the avowed secondary education of the college took the colour and form of that of the primary school at its worst period of sterility.'[3] These words were written in 1898; in this context, the fact that by 1928 over 70 per cent of the college staffs were university graduates must be seen as representing a very substantial improvement in academic quality. But employment in the training college continued to carry little by way of prestige and status. The salary scale was the same as that for secondary schools, and there were certain disadvantages in serving in a college, to which the McNair Report drew attention.

[1] Letter in the *Guardian*, 2 March 1966.
[2] Training Colleges Association evidence to the McNair Committee, 1943 (A.T.C.D.E. Archives).
[3] *Report of the Committee of Council on Education*, 1898.

'There are not many men and women who are qualified to teach their subject at post-secondary level and who also appreciate the part it should play in the education of children and have had substantial experience of teaching it to them. Where such men and women exist they may be reluctant to join the staff of a training college under present conditions. The small size of many colleges means that one lecturer must play many roles and many specialists are naturally unwilling to do this or learn to do it. Moreover, in many cases the isolation of a college, particularly when combined with small size, results in lecturers losing touch with others who profess the same subject and in their falling behind current thought and practice.'[1]

Isolation was not limited to academic life. The well-worn stereotype of the college of this period, in which a diluted form of gracious living was engaged in by a largely spinster staff, in an impressive if educationally unsuitable and draughty building at the end of a mile-long drive, ten miles from the nearest town, implied isolation of a different kind. Whatever relation this stereotype may or may not have had to the reality, it added to the apparent hazards of leaving a well-established and flourishing grammar school to engage in preparing the less able sixth-formers to teach largely non-academic children. Something of this feeling has survived, both in the colleges (although the number grows smaller as their size increases) and in the schools, where, until recently, a head of a department in a grammar school found little to attract him, either professionally or financially, in a lectureship or senior lectureship in a college. But the steadily improving level of qualifications of college students, the differentia that exist, at the highest levels at least, between the Burnham and the Pelham scales, the greater scope of the work undertaken by colleges and their increasing size, are all serving to create a recognizable career structure within the colleges, particularly for younger and well-qualified teachers. There has been concern in official circles that the possibilities and attractions of work in teacher training should be more widely known; to this end the Ministry of Education issued in 1963 a pamphlet entitled *The Work of the Training Colleges*, containing a number of

[1] *Teachers and Youth Leaders* (McNair Report). London: H.M.S.O., 1944, p. 71.

verbatim extracts from lecturers' statements about the satisfactions obtained from college work, and the Department of Education and Science also runs courses for suitably qualified school teachers which involve a programme of visits to the colleges and discussions with college staff.

Structure and Grades

The vast majority of lecturers in colleges of education come direct from their schools; their ages on entry to college vary from the early twenties to the late fifties, although most entrants today are in their thirties and early forties. The main recruitment grade is lecturer, which accounts for some 35 per cent of all staff, but substantial numbers of men and women with advanced qualifications or previous responsible experience are appointed at senior lecturer or principal lecturer level. Promotion has been rapid during the period of expansion, and a large number of those appointed as lecturers have attained senior-lecturer status within one or two years.

It appears that a substantial number of those who eventually obtain appointments in colleges give some thought to the possibilities of work in this field at an early stage in their teaching careers. Nearly a third of a sample of staff who provided information on this point had considered entering college work during their first three years after qualifying. A similar proportion of the sample had been seeking other forms of promotion at the same time as applying for college posts.

Respondents to the survey—undertaken in 1964 with the aid of a grant from the Nuffield Foundation—were asked why they were attracted to work in the colleges. Whilst there is considerable variety in the statements made, the frequency of mention of certain features of college work is of interest in terms of the task of the colleges and their relation to the schools. The sample of newly appointed lecturers making these statements was a small one (one in four of those entering college work in 1963–4), and not necessarily representative of all those entering teacher training at that time. The table opposite shows the results of a content analysis of the questionnaire replies.

In many respects, the reasons given for the attractiveness of college work are common-sense ones—more variety and flexibility than in schools, improved salary, promotion prospects and status, the opportunity to work with volunteer students rather than a captive audience of schoolchildren, the chance to teach the discipline in which one has been trained and with which one identifies to a higher level, and the likelihood of a better response than might be forthcoming from some children.

TABLE XII

Attractions of work in teacher education, by number of times mentioned by newly recruited lecturers

	Men	Women
Interest in subject and possibility of teaching it to a higher level	25	11
Possibilities of working with more mature students	20	9
Variety and scope of the work as compared with teaching in schools	20	9
Improved salary and/or promotion prospects	11	2
Desire to propagate new ideas, interest in work and greater variety of children contacted	9	6
Opportunity to pass on experience to teachers in training	8	8
Improved opportunities for research, writing and private study	7	6
Opportunities for pastoral work with young people, residential possibilities	5	2
Exhausted possibilities of the classroom	4	4
Improved work conditions, freedom from administrative responsibilities	3	3
Contraction of opportunity in previous post (e.g., in art education, adult education, etc.)	2	0

However commonplace these reasons may be felt to be, they leave an impression of an approach to educational process which is somewhat at odds with the prevailing progressive ideology and image of teacher education. This may be made clearer by first quoting some statements by new entrants which it can be suggested do match this ideology.

'Concern at lack of spontaneous expression afforded to children in primary and secondary schools. Children treated as "sitting brains" carrying out cerebral processes from early age. Need for development of character through spontaneous expression and some training of the senses and emotions. Best place to achieve this is where new teachers can be brought to an understanding of the child's emotional needs. Hence training college.'

'I believe education to be the most effective instrument of social change in a democracy. I believe I can be most effective in the training of teachers for schools in general education. I am attracted by the variety of work to be done, the contact with students and the contact with schools and the children in them.'

'Possibly having transformed an old-fashioned school into a modern Infant school, as one of a team including all my staff, having many visitors, having given lectures at LEA courses and eventually recommended by an H.M.I. to do the work. But, more than all this, my love of children, their welfare, and the hope that I can influence many more people to give everything they have to give to these all important infants. (May I add that I miss these children very much?)'

'I believe that children, all children, ordinary children, are capable of much more interest in life and a higher standard of performance than they are credited with by the average schoolmaster. Especially the recent developments towards bringing mathematics to life have increasingly fascinated me and made me want to play my part in them.'

But, as the table shows, a much larger share of attention is given in respondents' replies to rather less child-centred reasons for being attracted to college work. For some, a lectureship represented a way of escaping from a situation that, for various reasons, was becoming uncongenial.

1. 'I think I had exhausted the possibilities of the classroom, and had come to the point where I needed larger scope for research, *and* opportunities of improving my professional and social status.'

2. 'A new lease of life, new interest in a different field. At the end of fourteen years' teaching, and approaching forty, felt the pressure of another twenty-five years of mixture as before. . . .'

3. 'An immense fear of becoming typed as an "old teacher"–

a revulsion at the rapidity with which senior members of grammar school common rooms (especially single sexed) tended to become senile. I felt I wanted to escape from teaching before I reached their age and state. I still feel that at that level it is a young man's game.'

4. 'It seemed aloof from the promotion rat race in which successful junior schoolmasters have to compete because of their low level of salaries. . . .'

5. 'Means of utilizing experience in secondary modern schools, without being involved in the more tedious side of continued work in this field.'

6. 'Conversion of my grammar school of 750 into a comprehensive school of 1,750 with the resultant inability to make satisfactory personal contacts. Danger of becoming an administrator even as head of department in such a large school.'

For many the chief attractions were to be found in the opportunity to teach a subject at a higher level, and to work with more mature students.

1. 'Work with mature students in my own subject—as an extension of the sixth-form work I was already doing. . . .'

2. 'In order to enjoy the privilege of having classes who really wanted to attend and were not simply "day release".'

3. 'I enjoy teaching my subject to a high standard and I thought training college work might give me further scope. . . .'

4. 'This field of work offered the opportunities to do advanced work in my subject. Teaching offered a frustrating life where inadequate facilities restrict this advanced work.'

5. 'Training young musicians—i.e. those with basic knowledge and skills and real interest in music.'

6. 'As a means of earning one's bread and butter, I prefer teaching students to children as they are old enough and intelligent enough to understand the type of work for which I was trained.'

7. 'Enjoy the age group, working with forthcoming teachers, and the more advanced and varied work that is possible.'

8. 'More scope for individualism than in the teaching of schoolchildren. Work should be more stimulating and interesting with students who have chosen this kind of work.'

9. 'More mature age range—less necessary to impose discipline and therefore a more relaxed atmosphere.'

It must be emphasized again that the sample whose statements are given here is small and not necessarily representative. These statements, however, are useful in pointing up some of the problems that are involved in any process of training for a type of work that trainers themselves are no longer performing. This is the source of a good deal of cynical, and often uninformed comment on the part of teachers in training and teachers in the schools–twenty years ago Sir Walter Moberley drew attention to the way in which the remark 'Those who can, do, those who can't, teach' is invoked *a fortiori* when teaching is the form of doing in question.[1]

Such criticism is frequently brushed aside on the grounds that the vast majority of lecturers have in fact enjoyed a highly successful career, and that in the colleges they have opportunities–through school practice, experimental work in the classroom, group practices and so on–to maintain close contact with teachers and children. Whilst all this may be true, the fact remains that the trainers have explicitly turned aside from the career for which they are preparing their students, and to an increasing extent as the size of the teacher-training enterprise grows, and the average age of staff recruited falls, are in process of building a career in an educational environment in which schoolchildren only feature to a very limited extent. It is no doubt inevitable that this should be so. No one would want the colleges to return to their pre-war status, and there are many advantages in the fact that a career in teaching Education has now become both respectable and worth while in terms of both salary and status. But the effect upon communication between lecturers and students of the diverse career orientations of the two groups needs due attention. The demand for higher academic and intellectual standards in the colleges, the growth of departmental and professional rather than institutional groupings and loyalties among staff, are the necessary concomitants of the inclusion of teacher training within the corpus of higher education, but they carry with them the danger that the college staffs will lose touch with the realities of the everyday classroom situation.

Such loss of direct contact need not necessarily reduce the

[1] Moberly, W. *The Crisis in the University.* London: S.C.M. Press, 1949, p. 252.

effectiveness of staff in preparing students for work in the schools. If success as a classroom teacher does not guarantee success as a lecturer or tutor in a college of education, it is probably equally true that there are some very successful members of college staffs who would perform a good deal less well in a school. Frances Chase has stated:

'There is no evidence to support the notion that only those who continue teaching in the lower schools can offer effective guidance to prospective teachers. Trainees need not just one model of excellent teaching, but many kinds of models. The person who is tied to his own teaching assignments cannot observe enough different models of teaching to help his students analyse the elements of effective teaching.'[1]

It seems reasonable to suggest that educators of teachers do require some experience of the kind of work for which they are preparing students if they are to be fully aware of these students' needs and the teaching problems that they will encounter. Existing evidence does not, however, enable any final judgement to be made regarding either the type or amount of such experience that is most valuable.

Qualifications and Experience of College Staff

At first glance the position regarding academic qualifications is worse than it was forty years ago—in 1928, 88 per cent of the men and 67 per cent of the women had university degrees, whilst now the proportions are only 61·2 per cent and 40·8 per cent respectively. But a large proportion of the non-graduates today are lecturers in Primary and Infant Education, Art and Craft, Home Economics, Physical Education and so on—fields in which it has been very difficult to obtain degree qualifications. A 1964 survey of college staff showed that the proportion of graduates with honours degrees (77 per cent of men and 84 per cent of women) was close to the figure for university teachers given in the report of the Robbins Committee. Amongst those so qualified, between a quarter and a half, according to subject,

[1] Chase, F. S. 'On "The Education of American Teachers" ' in *Freedom with Responsibility in Teacher Education*, Seventeenth Yearbook of the American Association of Colleges for Teacher Education. Chicago: The Association, 1964, p. 41.

had higher degrees of some kind or another. If all college teachers are taken into account, not just the graduates, the comparison with the universities is less favourable–only 20 per cent of the men and 12 per cent of the women in the colleges held a master's degree or doctorate, against 40 per cent of university teachers. London University accounts for over a third of the higher degrees possessed by college lecturers, and relatively few of those with first degrees from Oxford and Cambridge had acquired any form of further qualification. A similar finding emerged from parallel studies of university teachers of education and college principals–it seems that the Oxbridge graduate feels less need to enhance his qualifications than a graduate from London or a redbrick university.[1]

A quarter of all the men and 12 per cent of the women in the colleges were found to be working for additional diplomas and degrees in their spare time, and it is clear from the analysis of qualifications by age that large numbers of staff obtained their higher qualifications only after having taken up college appointments.

As far as classroom teaching is concerned, women tended to have more experience at each grade than men and the senior staff had more than their junior colleagues. Well over a third of the men who were principal lecturers, and 40 per cent of the women, had spent thirteen years or more in school teaching, against 17 per cent of men and 27 per cent of women at lecturer grade. Overall, about one in eleven of the men and one in twelve of the women had no experience in the classroom, a third of the men and a quarter of the women had between one and six years' teaching experience, 53 per cent of both sexes had between seven and eighteen years, and 5 per cent of the men and 10 per cent of the women had taught for more than nineteen years. The largest proportion of staff with less than six years of school teaching was found among the scientists, some 16 per cent of whom had never taught in schools at all. In contrast, of the lecturers responsible for professional courses in Education, only

[1] Fuller details of the University Teacher of Education Survey are given in Taylor, W. 'The University Teacher of Education' in *Comparative Education*, 1:3, July 1965. See also 'The Training College Principal', *Sociological Review*, 12:2, June 1964, and 'Who Teaches Education?', *Universities Quarterly*, 20:1, December 1965.

4 per cent—presumably specialists in Sociology, Psychology and other disciplines—were without school experience, and over a third had taught for thirteen years or more.

As yet, comparatively few college teachers have first-hand experience of comprehensive schools, in which many of the students now being trained will work, and it is mainly among the education staff that experience in primary schools is common.[1] Nearly a fifth of both men and women had experience of work in educational institutions other than schools and colleges—mainly in colleges of further education, universities, technical colleges and overseas.

Given the rapid rise in the number of posts available, it is inevitable that few lecturers have previously taught in other colleges of education. Over 80 per cent of the men and 60 per cent of the women were in their first appointments. Staff were asked to state whether or not they intended to remain in college of education work—the choice was a forced one, providing only for 'yes' or 'no' responses, but many respondents added an 'undecided' category. The analysis of intention by age showed that a substantial number of young staff were firm in their intention *not* to remain in college work; of those born after 1930, less than half stated that they wished to continue in such teaching for the remainder of their careers, against 80 per cent in the fifty to fifty-five-year age group. A further analysis by grade and age showed that there were few differences between the intentions of staff in a given age group who were still lecturers and those who had already reached principal lecturer level.

Higher salaries, a better status, more scope for experiment, research and personal study, the promise of more liberal college government, and a place in the centre of the country's educational efforts, have had the effect of making posts in colleges of education more attractive to well-qualified people, and have provided an incentive for many teachers to undertake advanced studies in Education. There has been the beginning of a two-way flow between universities and colleges, particularly of well-qualified young lecturers into university appointments and of more senior university staff into principalships. The relative

[1] For a discussion of this point see Taylor, W. 'The impact of secondary reorganization on the Education and Training of Teachers', *British Journal of Educational Studies*, June 1967.

ease of promotion in the colleges, coupled with a slowing down of university expansion, seems likely to hinder some forms of this movement during the next decade. It is now by no means unknown for a man with good academic qualifications to secure a principal lectureship in a college when he is still in his early thirties. With senior appointments in universities restricted in number, it becomes very difficult for such an individual to transfer to a university post without a serious loss of income, and this may well limit the opportunities of the Departments and Institutes of Education to recruit staff experienced in teacher education.

Student Quality and Staff Qualifications

In all the discussion and publication that has gone on during the past twenty-five years about recruitment to teaching, comparatively little attention has been given to the very real differences that exist between colleges of education in the quality of their intake. Within the past two or three years these differences have been highlighted by the creation of the B.Ed. degree. In the words of the Robbins Report.

'. . . not all colleges will have the staff and facilities to offer courses leading to degrees, and students in those that do not will have to transfer to other colleges if they wish to study for a degree and are capable of the work entailed.'[1]

The fact that some kind of pecking order exists between the colleges as far as student entry qualifications are concerned, and that this has something to do with the reputation of the colleges and their attractiveness to potential students and their advisers, raises interesting questions about the relationship of this order to the quality of staff. It seems to be generally accepted in the education world that high-quality students and high-quality staff go together–however ambiguous and confused the definition of what constitutes 'quality' may turn out to be when this equation is examined in detail. Halsey has shown that there is a tendency for particularly well-qualified and productive university staff to cluster together in certain institutions, which have the reputation of attracting equally well-qualified students.

[1] *Report of the Committee on Higher Education* (Robbins Committee). London, H.M.S.O., 1963.

In the United States there is a fairly close correspondence between the selectivity that colleges or universities are able to show in their admission procedures and the academic strength and reputation of their faculties.[1] In order to examine the extent to which a similar pattern holds for colleges of educaton, eight colleges with the best-qualified and eight with the least well qualified students during the academic year 1962–3 were selected from Simons' list, and the qualifications and experience of the staff of these colleges, obtained in the 1964 survey of educators of teachers were analysed and compared.

It is important that the limitations of the comparisons made should be clear. Just as 'A' and 'O' entry qualifications do not necessarily tell us very much about admissions policies, the quality of the work subsequently undertaken, or the academic and classroom potential and performance of students, so class of degree, length of teaching experience and number of publications are uncertain guides to the quality of staff. The really important variables may turn out to be of a kind that cannot readily be measured, but which nonetheless have a powerful effect on the life and work of a college. All that the figures provided here permit us to say is that there does or does not appear to be a difference between the staff of one group of colleges and that of another in respect of the variables concerned for the year in question.

The colleges with best-qualified students are referred to here as the 'high' group and those with least well qualified as the 'low' group. The response rate of staff to the 1963–4 questionnaire in the two groups of colleges was virtually identical – 81·9 per cent for the 'high' group and 82·0 per cent for the 'low'.

One of the criteria to which universities tend to give attention when evaluating academic standing is the proportion of staff with degrees and advanced qualifications; these are particularly important where the status of recognized teacher within the university is given to lecturers in the colleges. In the 'high' colleges 30·6 per cent of the men and 38·4 per cent of the women were non-graduates, compared with 28·4 per cent and 43·4 per cent respectively in the 'low' group. The differences in respect

[1] Reisman, D. *Constraint and Variety in American Education*, University of Nebraska Press, 1958. Halsey, A. H. 'Halsey on Dons', *Oxford Magazine*, Michaelmas 2 1965.

of the class of first degree held were small, and only one of these–that between the women with first-class honours in 'high' and 'low' colleges respectively–was statistically significant.

A more detailed analysis by subject group–Arts, Science and Mathematics, Education, and Practical and Aesthetic–showed few significant differences between high and low colleges in any of these categories.

As might be expected, the proportions of graduate staff varied sharply between the various subject groups. In Arts and Science subjects only a small proportion of lecturers in both high and low colleges were non-graduates, and between a quarter and a third had a higher degree of some kind. In Education nearly half the women lecturers in both college groups held no degree, but there was a substantial and significant inter-group difference between the proportions of non-graduate men Education staff–19·0 per cent in the high colleges, 47·6 in the low. In Practical and Aesthetic subjects over three-quarters of the staff surveyed had no degree.

A considerably larger proportion of staff recruited since 1960 were engaged in some sort of study for further qualifications than lecturers entering college work before that date. In the low colleges men were significantly more active in this respect than women, although the sub-sample numbers are small and too much reliance should not be placed on these figures.

Other criteria that are of importance in determining academic standing in the field of higher education are publication and research. Staff were asked to state if they were pursuing individual or group research other than for further qualifications. No attempt was made to define 'research' with any precision, and it is clear that some work was included under this heading that would be only marginally acceptable as research as against private study. The colleges of education have no formal research function, although recently efforts have been made to place greater emphasis upon such work, and research projects are being placed in some colleges, timetable concessions being sometimes made to members of staff who are involved in research activity. There were hardly any differences in the proportions of staff who claimed to be involved in research in high and low colleges–for the men the percentages were 23 and 22·2 respectively, for the women 13·2 and 19·6.

As far as articles in journals were concerned, although there was no difference between the men in the two groups, a significantly greater proportion of women in the high compared with the low colleges had published at least one article during the preceding five years; the differences with respect to other forms of publication in this period, for both men and women, were slight and non-significant.

Further analyses were made to see if any differences could be found in the universities that graduate lecturers in the two groups of colleges had attended. The only significant differences were in respect of the numbers of men who had been at Oxford and Cambridge, such graduates being more numerous (33·2 per cent) in the high than the low (22·9 per cent) colleges, and in the larger numbers of men (13·2 per cent) in the low colleges with degrees from overseas universities.

The general pattern of small and mainly non-significant differences between the staff of the high and low colleges was repeated in the analyses made of duration and type of teaching experience. Of the men in the colleges with academically superior students, 34·8 per cent had less than five years' teaching experience, against 27·2 per cent of the men in colleges of which students were less well qualified; 33·4 per cent of the men in the high colleges had taught in schools for more than ten years, compared with 46·2 per cent of those in the low group; this last difference was significant at the 5 per cent level. There was also a significantly larger number of women in the high colleges without school experience – 13·3 per cent as compared with 3·1 per cent.

Rather more of the staff in the low colleges had taught in secondary modern, senior elementary and primary schools than their colleagues elsewhere (significant at the 5 per cent level for women in secondary schools and men in primary schools), but there were few other differences in types of teaching experience. The lecturers in the low colleges had more *varied* teaching experience – when the numbers in the sample were compared with the total of types of school mentioned the ratio was 1·61 for men and 1·45 for women in the high colleges, 1·80 and 1·84 respectively for the low group.

Colleges recruiting well-qualified students tend to be larger than those at the other end of the qualification scale. A final analysis was made to determine the extent to which staff teach in more than one subject area in the two groups of colleges, on the assumption that the larger college permits a greater degree of specialization. The subject areas used – Arts, Maths. and Science, Education, Practical and Aesthetic – are too broad to show some of the important differences that may exist, e.g. whether the lecturer who teaches History also undertakes work in English or Geography, how far the Science teaching is broken down into Physics, Chemistry, Biology and so on – but even so the differences between the two groups of colleges are not large and are not always in the expected direction. Some 14·7 per cent of the men and 11 per cent of the women in the high colleges teach in more than one subject area, compared with 13·7 per cent and 17·9 per cent respectively in the other group of colleges. None of the men in the low group combined Education and an Arts subject, whilst 18 of those in the high colleges did so; the same trend held for women in the two college groups. These figures indicate that specialized teaching is just as common in the small as in the large colleges; the differences probably reside in the size and internal organization of departments; in the smaller colleges the one-man department has been commonplace until recently. The Education lecturer in a large college may undertake specialized teaching in Psychology, Sociology or Philosophy in a way that it is not possible in the smaller institution.

There is little evidence at present that the undoubted differences between the quality of students' initial qualifications on entry to college are related in any systematic way to the qualifications, experience and background of staff in the colleges concerned. Whether this situation will persist seems doubtful. With the introduction of the B.Ed. there has been a move on the part of many colleges to recruit highly qualified staff who will be acceptable to the university department responsible for validating courses in the colleges. Within the next decade it seems likely that there will be some colleges that are able to enter a quarter to a half of their intake for the B.Ed., while others will be fortunate if they reach a figure as high as 10 per cent. If this happens, there may well be a tendency for the better-qualified staff to gravitate towards those colleges that offer better opportunities for work with degree students.

AND DEPARTMENTS OF EDUCATION

The University Teacher of Education

The men and women who teach full time in Departments and Institutes of Education in English and Welsh universities form only a small proportion of the twelve thousand university teachers of all subjects. Small though this group may be, it is involved in educational activity in this country at several crucial points. A substantial proportion of the graduates of our universities pass through the Departments and Institutes en route to a teaching career–25 per cent of men and 37 per cent of women graduating in Arts in 1964–5 continued their studies in Education departments.[1] Education staff are responsible for most of the limited but expanding range of educational research. They are concerned in the initial training and subsequent guidance of a large proportion of the lecturers who train the 90,000 intending teachers in colleges of education. Many of the lecturers and teachers whom they do not reach through their certificate, diploma or higher-degree courses, they influence by means of a multitude of in-service conferences, short courses and workshops.

The volume and importance of all this activity, however, has not been reflected in the position and status of Education as a field of study in universities; Departments and Institutes of Education have tended to be small, inadequately staffed, badly housed and held in poor regard within the university and in the schools. The Director of our largest Institute has admitted that until recently Education has been barely tolerated.[2] Student opinion of the post-graduate year of teacher training has also tended to be critical. In a generally sympathetic appraisal, an experienced teacher who returned to the university for his professional year stated that, among his colleagues,

'. . . the general feeling was that the Upper Fourth had at last succeeded in driving me irrevocably round the bend. Those who had taken a similar course had little to say in its favour except that it promised two terms of idleness in the untroubled atmosphere of a university.'[3]

[1] *First Employment of University Graduates, 1964–5*. London: H.M.S.O., 1966.
[2] Lionel Elvin, reported in *Universities Quarterly*, 17:2, March 1963, p. 179.
[3] 'A Correspondent', 'A Teacher Taught', *Universities Quarterly*, 15, 1961, p. 252.

Among the other indications of lack of status is the poor staffing ratio that holds for many departments–one to seventeen at Oxford, for example, as compared with one to nine for the university as a whole.

Historical factors have undoubtedly contributed to the lowly status of the Departments of Education. Armytage has drawn attention to the baleful effects of the 'pledge' in this connection, whereby students were required, as a condition of receiving grant-aid, to commit themselves to train for teaching.

'The Departments . . . suffered severely from this conscript draft which was annually precipitated before their doors. Students, who might have discovered another vocation in the previous three years as undergraduates, began complaining before they began the course. And during the course they often vented their own frustrations on the hard-working and alas, often too earnest, members of the department. . . . The Departments were also blamed by professors for swallowing promising pupils, as well as by head-masters of every kind for being "impractical".'[1]

Indeed, from the earliest days of the Departments of Education, their professional orientation, their inevitable need for modifying the highly specialist outlook of the majority of their students, their concern with communication rather than content, had made them suspect in the eyes of academic purists. Sometimes these factors were combined with more practical difficulties. Wolters relates how in the early days of the University of Reading Day Training College, '. . . the staff consisted of M. J. H. Gettins, who, harassed but cheerful, worked from morn to night, giving lectures and supervising school practice, knowing all the time that by reason of the training being concurrent with academic studies his Department was a nuisance. So all through two terms we were drafted by batches into school, leaving disgruntled lecturers with depleted classes, and disgruntled students with three weeks' lectures missed'.[2]

Such attitudes have persisted in some quarters despite the efforts of educationists to improve the image of the study of

[1] Armytage, W. H. G. *The Role of an Education Department in a Modern University*, Sheffield, 1954.
[2] Wolters, A. W. 'Early Days' in *The Education Department through Fifty Years*. Reading: The University, 1949, pp. 18–19.

Education in the university. As recently as 1960 the then Vice-Chancellor of Leeds University stated:

'I do not know of any authoritative piece of research which seeks to determine and analyse the state of opinion about the value of the work of [Education] departments; but I suppose some facts are fairly clear. Many headmasters and other senior schoolmasters – although not so many headmistresses – positively speak ill of them; the public schools, and perhaps the direct-grant schools, do not, to say the very least of it, give them any encouragement; the morale of students during their year of graduate training is commonly accepted as being rather low ... and ... finally the professors and other university teachers in the primary university subjects have not themselves come to believe in the value of graduate training. ...'[1]

As far as those who teach Education in the university are concerned, it seems that many teachers of academic subjects echo Koerner's summing up of American Education faculties – 'a sincere, humanitarian, well-intentioned, hard-working, poorly informed, badly educated and ineffectual group of men and women'.[2] Sir Walter Moberly pointed out twenty years ago that 'to teach teaching, seems doubly removed from any practical grappling with reality. There is in the university a good deal of scarcely concealed doubt as to whether the credentials of the staff of training departments and the quality of their work have the university hall-mark.'[3]

University teachers of Education differ from their colleagues in other subjects in certain respects that may help to account for their comparative lack of status. The basis of recruitment of Education staff places them somewhat outside the university career structure, which, especially in the Arts and Social studies, is typically based upon entry soon after graduation or assimilation from an outside institution of university status. Education lecturers are a good deal older when recruited to university work and they include a larger proportion of women. A recent career analysis showed that their prospects of promotion to senior grades were much poorer. They have a lower proportion

[1] Morris, Sir Charles *The Universities and the Teaching Profession*. London: National Union of Teachers, 1960, p. 7.
[2] Koerner, J. D. *The Miseducation of American Teachers*. Boston: Houghton Mifflin, 1963, p. 37.   [3] Moberly, W. *op. cit.*, p. 252.

or men and women with first-class honours degrees than the staff of most other faculties, and a smaller percentage of Ph.D.s. They do more teaching, and less research. Data on these points can be quantified; less susceptible to measurement are the opinions that are held regarding the quality of a good deal of educational research and publication and the doubts that are expressed regarding the status of Education as a university subject. These opinions and doubts seem to be subscribed to and voiced by Education staff themselves as frequently as by their colleagues in other subjects. Membership of a Department or Institute of Education appears to create little sense of disciplinary solidarity, for reasons that are perhaps connected with the nature of educational studies and the basis of recruitment of staff. The ambiguity that surrounds the status of educational studies highlights the importance of the reference models that staff employ. Some lecturers, particularly those responsible for teaching post-graduate students in courses of initial training, retain many of their former links with the classroom, tend to identify with the schools and the teaching of particular subjects, and are not infrequently engaged in the preparation of books for school use and the utilization and development of teaching aids.

A second group maintain their identification with the subject field in which they originally graduated, undertake 'hard' research in this field and publish in specialized journals.

Finally, there is a third group of staff who concern themselves more directly with educational processes and institutions as such; although not usually possessing initial qualifications in Psychology, Sociology or Philosophy, they may research in and write about the educational applications of these underlying social sciences. But 'pedagogism' is regarded with some suspicion in other quarters of the university.[1] As Strother has suggested, 'Even within the framework of inter-disciplinary activities, there is a strong urge to preserve the basic subject-matter identifications. The academic system does not reward diffuse activity'.[2] Furthermore, those members of Department and

[1] Carmichael, P. S. 'Troubles in the Pedagogical Closed Shop', *Journal of Higher Education*, 31, 1960, p. 143.

[2] Strother, G. B. 'Development of a Social Science of Organizations' in *The Social Science of Organizations*, edited by H. J. Leavitt. Englewood Cliffs, N.J.: Prentice Hall, 1963.

Institute staff who do not possess some form of qualification in the social sciences that underlie educational study may themselves be concerned with maintaining disciplinary affiliations, and be critical of a good deal of the amateur effort that they see as characteristic of Educational Psychology, the Philosophy of Education and so on.

There are several other reasons that can be adduced to explain the lack of status of Education staff. Except in a very few places, teachers of Education work only with post-graduates and with serving teachers, and in a country where undergraduate teaching still constitutes a major rationale for an academic existence, this again serves to place them on the edge of the academic community. The quality and methodology of a good deal of educational enquiry has been subject to criticism by specialists in other departments, and such work is often regarded as 'soft' research when compared with original work in other disciplines. The academic standards required of students by Education staff are also regarded with some suspicion, the attention being given by Departments of Education to the 'development of the whole man' being viewed as potentially anti-intellectual in its effects.[1] Furthermore, although many types of professional training are now represented in the programmes of universities, and the training of teachers has been established a good deal longer than most other professional courses, there is still a certain ambivalence in the attitudes of many university teachers to the presence of directly vocational training within the university.[2] There are signs, however, that some of the old attitudes may today be changing. As Jean Floud has put it:

'The universities [are] dependent today as they have never been hitherto on the disposition and quality of the *whole* school population, and it is difficult to conceive of a case against the adoption of teaching that does not rest on false grounds of misunderstanding and snobbery about Education as a subject of study at university level, or mistaken grounds of expediency and temporary convenience of administration.'[3]

[1] Weiss, R. M. and Rasmussen, G. R. 'Grading Practices in Undergraduate Education Courses', *Journal of Higher Education*, 31, 1960, p. 143.
[2] Carmichael, *op. cit.*
[3] Floud, J. E. 'Teaching in the Affluent Society', *British Journal of Sociology* XIII, 1962 December.

The generally favourable response of the universities to the Robbins proposals for the education of teachers and the recent expansion of Education staff–there were only thirty-one Professors of Education in England and Wales in 1964; three years later there were nearly sixty–offer hopeful auguries for the future. At the same time, attempts are being made within the Departments and Institutes to improve the quality of educational studies; the need for specialists in Psychology, Philosophy, Sociology and History, rather than practitioners of 'general method' is finding increasing acceptance. There is growing agreement that 'Education' as such does not constitute a unitary discipline, but a practical field of activity within which the contributions of the more fundamental forms of thought can be made and pedagogic applications sought.[1] The growth in the research activities of the Departments and Institutes is emphasizing the importance of precision and high standards of scholarship. If, as seems possible, a course of training is made compulsory within the next few years for all graduates entering teaching, the scale and importance of the work undertaken by the Departments and Institutes will be further enhanced. Changes are also taking place in the structure of the Departments. In an increasing number of universities steps are being taken to create unitary 'Schools' of Education, frequently within an independent faculty. Within these new bodies the post-graduate training work and research of the Departments of Education is brought closer to the initial and in-service training activities of the Institutes and their associated colleges. At a national level, these changes have been recognized by the disappearance of the Conference of Institute Directors and the Conference of the Heads of University Departments of Education as separate organizations, and the creation of a new Universities Council for the Education of Teachers (U.C.E.T.).

All these developments underline the importance of the way in which schools, Departments and Institutes of Education are staffed; the status and growth of educational studies within the

[1] See Tibble, J. W. (ed.) *The Study of Education*. London: Routledge and Kegan Paul, 1966; Peters, R. S. (ed.) *The Concept of Education*. London: Routledge, 1967; Walton, J. and Kuethe, J. L. (eds.) *The Discipline of Education*. University of Wisconsin Press, 1963; Taylor, W. 'The Organization of Educational Studies', *Education for Teaching*, 1964, November.

next few years will depend at least as much on the ability of the new schools to attract and hold members of staff with appropriate qualifications, experience and ability as on any other factor. In the United States, Koerner has suggested that the 'inferior intellectual quality of Education faculties is *the* fundamental limitation of the field, and will remain so . . . for some time to come. Although a number of able men are to be found . . . in Education, particularly among the younger people, their number is minute in relation to the whole. . . . Until the question of the preparation and the intellectual qualifications of faculty members is faced head on in Education, the prospects for basic reform are not bright.'[1]

For the next few years at least, graduates who a short time ago might have become school teachers and potential lecturers in Education will be finding it easier to go straight into university work in their degree subject or some closely related field. In terms of the current staffing needs of many Departments and Institutes, Education cannot compete with other faculties for newly qualified graduates, and it is almost inevitable that any general shortage of highly qualified people will be felt even more acutely here than elsewhere. Ths is particularly regettable at a time when the study of Education, viewed as a multi-disciplinary field of enquiry within the applied social sciences rather than as a unitary discipline in its own right, is in process of establishing itself as something more than a by-product of the training of teachers. There are signs that in the larger institutions a certain number of men and women with specialist qualifications are being recruited soon after graduation. Such lecturers do not have the teaching experience that enables them to undertake 'method' work in the post-graduate courses—this may increasingly become the responsibility of 'teacher tutors', such as those employed by the Leicester, Oxford and Bristol Departments of Education—but they can express what Conant calls a 'commitment to the public schools and their improvement' through their studies and researches in educational processes.[2]

Another possibility is the creation of centres for advanced

[1] Koerner, *op. cit.*, p. 18.
[2] Conant, J. B. *The Education of American Teachers.* New York: McGraw-Hill, 1964.

study and research in Education, attached to but not forming part of existing Departments and schools, where teachers and research workers in other subjects could undertake educational research without relinquishing their existing disciplinary affiliations.[1] The implementation of compulsory training for graduate teachers may present an opportunity for colleges of education to take over a larger share of the work for initial qualifications, leaving the schools of education free to initiate more research and to provide more advanced courses.[2] In view of the small output of those with higher qualifications in Education at present, and the growing shortage of suitably qualified lecturers in colleges of education and elsewhere, some regional concentration of higher degree work would seem to have advantages–although, on the other hand, the part-time character of most advanced study makes it important that some facilities should be available within reasonable travelling distance of the teacher's home.

Twenty years ago, Sir Walter Moberly suggested that the only short-term way in which the mediocrity and low status of Education in the universities could be broken was by a willingness of 'a substantial proportion of our very best graduates and younger teachers (university as well as school)' to join the staffs of Education departments. Such action, he admitted, required 'risk and sacrifice, because the prospects of high promotion are poor'.[3] There is little sign that such sacrifice was ever made by more than a handful, and, despite recent improvements, the prospects of promotion are still poor. In the long run, Moberly argued, recruitment must be on the basis of a 'reasonable prospect of a career such as will appeal to normal motives'. It is important that developments in the universities should enable such prospects to be created, and that Education, as one of the central activities of a modern industrialized society, comes to occupy a more central place in the structure of the higher

[1] See Peterson, A. D. C. 'The Future of Education at Oxford', *The Oxford Magazine*, 5:3, p. 46.
[2] For a discussion of the functions of a professional school within a university see Hutchins, R. M. *The Conflict in Education in a Democratic Society*. New York: Harper, 1953; *The Graduate Study of Education*, Report of the Harvard Committee. Cambridge, Mass: Harvard University Press, 1965.
[3] Moberly, *op. cit.*, p. 253.

learning. This will not only require radical thinking on the part of the universities as a whole; it will also demand that the existing defects of a good deal of educational study and research are recognized by university teachers of Education themselves.

PART FOUR
SOCIAL PROCESS

9

SOCIAL STRUCTURE AND SOCIAL CONTROL IN THE COLLEGE OF EDUCATION

Colleges of education are physically and administratively distinct from the other educational institutions to which their work is related, although several are sited close to and sometimes within the campus of a university – Hull and Coventry, for example – and one or two, such as Bulmershe College, Reading, are on the same site as a primary or secondary school. The older colleges still occupy the sites on which they were founded in the first half of the nineteenth century, although the original buildings now form a small part of a mixture of structures in every style from Victorian Gothic through Edwardian redbrick to contemporary concrete and curtain walling. The denominational and independent colleges founded during the last century usually had the residential and teaching accommodation included in the same building – there was no sharp separation between living quarters and teaching rooms. In this respect the colleges reflected both their links with the tradition of clerical training and with the Oxford and Cambridge colleges – the only models of higher education available at that time. In contrast, the local education authority colleges founded after 1904 took as their model the civic university, with its hostels and halls of residence in separate buildings, at varying distances from the main teaching block. In some cases, in an attempt to reproduce some of the conditions of the autonomous college, each hall was provided with its own dining rooms, kitchen and common rooms, but to an increasing extent the halls on the main college site came to provide sleeping and common room accommodation only, with all meals being taken in a central refectory or cafeteria. Many colleges now use detached halls or hostels some considerable distance from the college itself; within recent years a great variety of accommodation has been taken over for this purpose, including seaside hotels and hutted camps previously occupied by the army.

Teaching accommodation has been similarly diversified. The single lecture room for each year-group of students of a former era has become a complex pattern of lecture theatres, seminar and classrooms, laboratories, gymnasia, art studios, television and visual-aid centres and workshops for practical activities. Where tutorial groups are small enough they sometimes meet in the tutor's study or flat. This provides one of the few remaining links between the provision made for residential and for academic and professional work.

In the various sections of this chapter the social structure of the colleges of education will be discussed, a broad distinction being made between the teaching organization and the residential pattern. First, however, the processes of leadership and decision-making in the colleges will be considered, with special reference to the role of the college principal.

Leadership in the College of Education

There have been few studies in this country of school, college and university administrators and educational leaders and the ways in which they perform their tasks. The headmaster and the school inspector have received some attention, but the focus of interest has been historical rather than sociological.[1] The education officer and the deputy head have recently been subjects for research.[2] In the United States there have been a number of analyses in recent years of college professors, superintendents of school systems and school principals and the nature of their work. Such studies vary considerably in scope, complexity and theoretical orientation. Some are straightforward fact-finding surveys. Others are simple 'position-descriptions',

[1] Baron, G. 'Aspects of the "Headmaster" tradition', *Researches and Studies*, 14, 1956, June; Edmonds, E. L. *The School Inspector*. London: Routledge, 1962.
[2] Burnham, P. S. *The Role of the Deputy Head*. Unpublished M.Ed. thesis, University of Leicester, 1964.

which set out, usually in a normative fashion, the elements of a person's responsibilities at a given level within the educational organization.[1] At the opposite extreme are highly conceptualized task and action analyses, sometimes based upon large-scale empirical investigations and often owing a good deal to industrial studies and small-group research.[2]

However complex and conceptually differentiated a model for the study of a particular educational leader's work may be, it always rests upon certain assumptions regarding the nature of the organization in respect of which administrative and leadership functions are exercised. The commonplace line/staff, formal/informal dichotomies, familiar in the study of industrial organizations, are frequently used, although the viability of these in educational contexts has been questioned.[3] In his study of university administration, for example, Millett has emphasized the danger of an uncritical adoption of models derived from other fields, and stresses the community basis of academic life, where 'the power of administration is conceived as a constituent element of a community of power' rather than the fount of authority within the institution.[4]

A conceptual distinction between the organizational attributes of schools, colleges and universities on the one hand, and other commercial and industrial institutions on the other has been suggested by Etzioni, who bases his classification of complex organizations on types of *compliance*.[5] In the prison and the custodial mental institution compliance is based upon coercion;

[1] See Eckert, R. E. and Stecklein, J. *Job Satisfactions and Motivations of College Teachers*. Washington, D.C.: Office of Education, Comparative Research Monographs No. 7, 1961; Ayers, A. V. and Hollis, E. V. 'Differentiating the function of administrative officers in colleges and universities', *Higher Education*. Washington, D.C.: U.S. Department of Health, Education and Welfare, Office of Education, 1963 December.

[2] Hemphill, J. K., Griffiths, D. E. and Frederiksen, N. *Administrative Performance and Personality*. New York: Bureau of Publications, Teachers' College, Columbia University, 1962.

[3] See Burns, T. 'The Sociology of Industry' in *Society—Problems and Methods of Study*, edited by A. T. Welford. London: Routledge, 1962.

[4] Millett, J. D. *The Academic Community*. New York: McGraw-Hill, 1962, p. 180. See also Ashby, E. *Technology and the Academics*. London: Macmillan, 1958, and Brook, G. L. *The Modern University*. London: Deutsch, 1965.

[5] Etzioni, A. *A Comparative Analysis of Complex Organizations*. New York: Free Press, 1961.

factories and other industrial concerns rely upon utilitarian compliance, where remuneration is the major means of control over lower participants; in the third, or normative type of organization compliance rests mainly upon the internalization of directives that are accepted as legitimate.[1]

Within this classification educational institutions fall mainly into the normative category, although other patterns have secondary importance, such as coercion in some schools. The type of leadership style appropriate to such organizations is charismatic, which Etzioni defines as 'the ability of the actor to exercise diffuse influence over the normative orientations of other actors'.[2] Between educational institutions there are differences, however, in the extent to which the leader can exercise charisma.

'... principals in grammar and high schools appear to acquire more charisma over students than do university presidents over their students or heads of hospitals over patients. This difference may be explained in part by differences in function, background and power. In terms of function, the average principal is less of an administrator and more of an educator than the average university president, and less of an administrator than the head of an average hospital. Unlike the others, he can delegate many of his administrative duties to control agents outside the school, such as the parents, the police, the PTA and the superintendent. The principal is ordinarily less concerned with fund raising and construction than the usual average university president, and has far fewer instrumental services to direct than a hospital administrator, who is running a "hotel" in addition to a professional service. Thus the role structure of the school principal is the most expressive and the least instrumental of the three. Charisma is again found to be most common in expressive positions.'[3]

The effects upon role performance of combining academic and administrative leadership within the single office have also been commented upon by Merton.[4] 'The academic who accepts

[1] See Wingate, M. *Purpose in Teacher Training*. London: S.C.M. Press, 1959, for an illustration of normative approaches.
[2] Etzioni, *op. cit.*, p. 40.   [3] *Ibid.*, p. 227.
[4] Merton, R. K. *Social Theory and Social Structure*. New York: Free Press, 1957.

administrative responsibilities finds himself subject to a different range of pressures from those characteristic of his previously free-ranging position on the staff of a college or university. These pressures, operating over a period of time, shape the general perspective of the bureaucratic intellectual; he comes increasingly to think in technical and instrumental terms of ways of implementing policies within a given situation.'[1]

In the smaller, community-based colleges of former times there was a good deal of opportunity for the principal to devote time to personal contacts with students and staff, to take an interest in the personal development of students and to participate in tutorial work.[2] The increasing size and complexity of the colleges has brought about a growing emphasis upon the instrumental rather than the more expressive aspects of the principal's role, with comcomitant effects upon the authority structure of the colleges.[3]

The 1964 study of the qualification and background of educators of teachers in England and Wales, to which reference has already been made in this volume, included a section devoted to the college principal. A final section of the questionnaire used asked for brief statements about the types of work to which respondents would like to give less or more time or attention, and their major sources of satisfaction and dissatisfaction. Not all the principals who completed the questionnaire filled in these items, and no attempt was made to carry out a statistical analysis of the statements made by those who did. There was, however, an impressive degree of unanimity on several issues.

References to 'administration' and 'clerical work' were outstanding among items in the less time and attention category. It is clear that a distinction must be made between what some principals call 'real administration' and the administrative trivia with which they often find themselves involved. One respondent states that he would like to give less time and attention to 'signing invoices and orders for bottles of milk, packets of

---

[1] *Ibid.*, p. 218.
[2] See statement by Sephton, A. G. *Education for Teaching*, February 1964, p. 13.
[3] For a discussion of instrumental and expressive roles in leadership see Parsons, T. and Bales, R. F. *Family Socialization and Interaction Process.* London: Routledge, 1956, pp. 46 ff.

tea, biscuits, etc., etc., etc.' Others complain of the time that must be given to electricians, plumbers and minor aspects of organization that derive from rapid expansion, inadequate space and lack of money. It is clear that not all local authorities are sympathetic to requests for additional clerical help–statements refer explicitly to 'obstruction' by salaries and establishments officers.

Local authorities feature largely in principals' remarks regarding the administrative difficulties under which they labour. There are references to '. . . the vast amount of energy absorbed in getting the pennies to fall in a bureaucratic machine that daily gets clogged with detail' and to the way in which the 'cumbersome structure of training college administration under Ministry, university and local authority' multiplies administrative duties. Principals comment on the 'dogmatic attitude of the local authority on matters of educational policy of which they are ignorant or uninterested', and express their dissatisfaction with the authority's 'many committees, especially for tenders, power seekers and petty tyrants'. The slow pace of administrative action is criticized, where 'obvious needs take so long to get satisfied and need the approval of so many minor officials'. One principal refers to his desire to spend less time and attention on the task of 'shepherding the requisition–an L.E.A. game played with rules similar to snakes and ladders'. Throughout the comments there runs a thread of dissatisfaction with what one principal calls the 'struggle with local authorities and Ministry over administrative matters' and another 'the frustrations and difficulties caused by local authority control'.[1] The

[1] 'In theory, at least, the L.E.A. only administers the college for the Ministry of Education, but in practice it is difficult for departments of local authorities, let alone county councillors, to make nice distinctions between their responsibilities to their schools and to their colleges. Contributions to the financing of all training colleges are made to the Treasury by each county council in proportion to its school population and irrespective of whether it is itself responsible for administering a college. But here again the same officials and sub-committees prepare and prune, accept or reject estimates for all types of educational establishment in the county and it is difficult to remember, let alone apply, these subtle differences, especially when as a rule that have only one or two colleges to administer and may have many hundreds of schools. Furthermore, an institution devoted to the training of teachers can be involved through its governing body and its finances in the party-political winds that blow these days through local

principals of voluntary colleges do not experience the difficulties of their local authority colleagues in this area, but their greater freedom of action imposes a somewhat heavier load of administrative responsibility. One such respondent states 'Seven-day week – the Principal of a Church college is educator, clerk of works and lay equivalent of a rural dean; no let up'.

Three points stand out among the satisfactions reported by principals – variety, contact with young people and with colleagues, and the constant challenge that the work provides. The following is typical of many of the comments made:

'(1) The satisfaction of working with people and knowing all the students personally. This is still a relatively small college so it is still possible to do this.

'(2) The satisfaction of watching the students mature and develop as people.

'(3) The challenge which the problems of expansion have brought. The chance to play a part in the planning of new buildings, and the opportunity to develop and experiment with new courses.'

Some principals contrast the variety of the work with the conditions previously experienced in schools and other employment. Many make clear that their greatest satisfactions are essentially from their personal relationships with students and staff. One emphasizes this in the following terms:

'(1) To see students change and develop during the three years and leave as poised, mature, independent beings.

'(2) To see success come to a student who has had to struggle – particularly in teaching.

'(3) To hear both verbally and from letters how very much the majority of students enjoy teaching.

'(4) To help a student who has personal difficulties, or, rather, to see her emerge as an integrated young woman.'

The special position of the principal in being able to create the conditions for the academic and personal development of students is an important source of satisfaction to many.

There is considerable agreement among principals about the types of work to which they would like to give more time and

councils. This is a particularly undesirable possibility, and one which officials do their best to guard against. But it remains, despite their best endeavours.' Wingate, M. *op. cit.*, pp. 30–1.

attention. Teaching, tutorial work, lecturing, research, personal study, 'thinking about education', writing, reading—all these receive frequent mention. Principals are, in fact, the best academically qualified group in the teachers' colleges, including a higher proportion of graduates, more first-class degrees and more higher degrees than any other level of staff, and it is not surprising that they wish to maintain their contacts with the academic world and their own disciplines and to contribute to these through lecturing and writing. But the principal's task is not conducive to the maintenance of a high level of academic effort—one respondent notes how in the seven years prior to his appointment as principal he 'wrote and published a dozen school books and books of poetry, etc., and have had no time to write one since'.

There is a certain contradiction in the fact that the activity which did much to obtain the principal his job is the one for which there is no time when he has secured it. It seems possible that this may place limitations on the extent to which principals can supply academic leadership within the college, and have some influence on the standard of work maintained by students and the quality of teaching forthcoming from staff.

Although the replies to the questionnaire gave no evidence to show that training-college principals, as a group, are dissatisfied with their lot or unhappy in their work, it is of some significance that the particular difficulties which do cause dissatisfaction are those which are likely to be exacerbated as the size of the colleges increases, and this at the expense of those activities which are currently the chief sources of satisfaction.

A Model for the Analysis of the Principal's Role

The work of the college principal would appear to have four major aspects. Firstly, it is academic in that the principal is concerned with maintaining and developing the work of the college as an institution of higher education. In this part of his work he is in direct contact with the university Institute of Education through the academic committee, boards of studies and other groups of which he is a member. Within the college he is concerned with the recruitment of adequately qualified and experienced staff and with the overall pattern of departmental organization and teaching. He probably undertakes a limited amount of teaching himself, and, according to his own report, would like to do more. In addition to academic responsibilities, however, he is also in charge of a residential institution; the provision of buildings, catering, the hiring and firing of domestic staff, the morale and welfare of the residential community are all under his purview. In this area his main external contacts will be with the local authority, or, in the case of a direct-grant college, with the Department of Education and the providing body. In a local authority college some of the institutional administration will be handled by the County or Borough Education officers, but the principal will still have overall responsibility for the community life of the college. The academic and the institutional functions can be regarded as the opposite ends of a task dimension, particularly so because the major external authorities to which the principal relates are fairly clearly divided between these two areas of interest and activity. Within these areas, however, a cross-classification of functions may be suggested. Some of the academic tasks with which the principal is concerned are clearly instrumental in character; Institute regulations, the fulfilling of examination requirements, the selection and admission of students are all relatively bureaucratized procedures, subject to more or less formally stated and generally understood procedural rubrics. Other forms of work in the academic sphere are of a more expressive kind less subject to rational calculation, involving a more flexible relationship between persons and groups, having a greater effective content than the largely cognitive instrumental type of activity. Tutorial work with students, personal study, research and teaching, the principal's own professional and disciplinary concerns and interests feature in this academic/ expressive category. A similar division of instrumental and expressive functions can be suggested with respect to the institutional aspects of the principal's work; relationships with the local authority, negotiations on buildings and equipment, the organization of residential and domestic provision and property management are principally instrumental in character.[1] The

[1] Although not, of course, entirely. There is no doubt that the personal relationships existing between a principal and the 'office' can play a significant part in the way in which a college is run.

morale of the community, the maintenance of good staff/student relationships, the welfare of students and so on are largely expressive. If the academic/institutional and the instrumental/ expressive dimensions are placed at right angles to one another, as in the following diagram, most of the principal's tasks can be placed within the four cells that are produced.

INSTRUMENTAL
(task-centred)

Buildings and Equipment	Relationships with ATO, university
Relationships with local authority	Examinations and assessment
Domestic staff organization	Admissions

— INSTITUTIONAL ——————— ACADEMIC —

	Educational Policy
Community relationships	Research and teaching
Staff/student welfare	Tutorial work
Relationships with local community	Personal development of students

EXPRESSIVE
(person- and group-centred)

The background and previous career of principals shows that the majority of their experience has been in areas that we have labelled as academic/expressive and, to a more limited extent, institutional/expressive. Only one in five has had experience as vice-principal of a college such as would provide opportunities for skills in the upper two segments of the diagram to be acquired and displayed. Nearly half have very limited experience of college work in any capacity; of those who came to principalships direct from other work a few have held administrative appointments—such as deputy director of Education—but most have been employed in university teaching or as heads or senior staff in grammar schools, where what has been referred to as earlier as 'charismatic' styles of leadership are appropriate. With qualifications and experience in the areas below the horizontal axes of the diagram, the principal would like to give more of his time and attention to work in these areas, where his major satisfactions are to be found. It seems that a large number of principals feel that their 'real' work, that which gives them a *legitimized identity* as head of the college, is concerned with the maintenance of group relationships, the personal development of students, tutorial work, research, study and the determination of academic policy.[1] Yet, at the present time, internal and external pressures are combining to shift the principal's attention to matters in the upper segments of the diagram. The need for rapid expansion, the pressure of numbers of the available space, the difficulties of recruiting and retaining effective domestic staff, the problem of admissions when applications far exceed the number of places available, the task of negotiating for finance and facilities with the local authority and the Department of Education—all these conspire to take up the greatest part of the principal's time and attention, yet provide only limited satisfactions. In sum, the present situation involves a progressive bureaucratization of the principal's role, and a limitation of his opportunities to provide academic leadership within the college. If the existing administrative structure is taken as given, by the time that most colleges have 750 students it seems possible that the gap between the principal's own conception of his role and the demands that will be made upon him will widen still further.

[1] In the terms suggested by Getzels and Guba, the leadership style that seems to be appropriate to the existing concept of the training college principal's role is *idiographic* rather than *nomothetic*. See Getzels, J. W. 'A Psycho-Sociological Framework for the Study of Educational Administration', *Harvard Educational Review* XXII, 1952.

Delegation and the Academic Board

In the nineteenth century the Inspectors' reports on the training colleges were included in the volume of Minutes of the Committee of Council on Education that dealt with elementary education; up until the Second World War the salaries of their staff were based upon those for teachers in secondary schools; during the decades after that war, despite the link with the universities through the Institutes of Education, there were frequent references to the 'post-secondary' nature of the college courses; only with the publication of the Robbins Report and the introduction of degree studies can the colleges be said to have attained full stature as institutions of higher education. Nothing illustrates the slow climb more clearly than the way in which policy and decision-making have been carried out in teacher education. As earlier chapters have made clear, full autonomy has by no means yet been obtained in the external sphere; the central government, working through the local authority, is still responsible for the basic decisions on questions of size, the balance of courses and staffing. Within the colleges the pattern of administration has had until recently more in common with that of a school than that of a university. Principals have sometimes ruled their colleges along lines similar to those adopted by traditional authoritarian headmasters. The measure of consultation and delegation allowed has varied from college to college; in those where the principal was disposed to operate in a democratic manner the smallness of the staff and the close day-by-day contact that they have had with one another has made the creation of specialized machinery for discussion of policy and for decision-making largely unnecessary.

As colleges have become larger so the complexity of internal administration has increased, and it has become necessary for some delegation of responsibility to take place. In most, regular staff meetings have been held, but these have lacked any formal advisory or executive function. The A.T.C.D.E. has from the beginning taken a considerable interest in the internal government of colleges, and in 1958 Council passed the following resolution:

'That this Council considers that the time has long passed when the academic policy of a college could properly be determined by a governing body or by a principal without the fullest consultation with members of the college's academic staff, and urges that each college should have a properly constituted Academic Board with rules of procedure determined by that Board and with provision for democratic discussion and decision, including the right to vote, on academic matters.'

Official support for this policy was made public in 1960, when in a circular to the colleges it was stated that the Minister wished to commend the value of academic boards and also of boards of studies in individual subjects, to act as a counterpart to the boards of the Institutes of Education. More and more colleges began to set up such academic boards, with a variety of constitutions, some of which gave the staff considerably more influence over the conduct of academic affairs than others.

When the Robbins Committee's proposals for the cessation of local authority control and the inclusion of the colleges in reconstituted University Schools of Education were rejected by the government at the end of 1964, the pill was sugared by a statement of intent regarding the reconsideration of local administrative arrangements. The study group on the government of the colleges that was subsequently set up and which reported in March 1966 ('Weaver Report'–see Chapter 3) stated that it was 'essential that every college should have a properly constituted academic board',[1] and that this, rather than being a body comprising the whole staff, should number some twelve to twenty-five members, including the heads of departments, lecturers in charge of subjects, and some representatives elected by the staff as a whole.

The A.T.C.D.E. set up a sub-committee to consider the implications of the Weaver Report, and issued a memorandum in September 1966. This supported the view that academic boards should not be a committee of the whole staff–'[The] concept of an academic board as an executive body, under the chairmanship of the principal, should be extended to all colleges. This type of responsibility cannot be carried by a full staff.'[2] The memorandum envisaged that, in accordance with the study group's report, governing bodies would in due course

---

[1] *Report of the Study Group on the Government of Colleges of Education.* London: H.M.S.O., 1966, p. 21 (Weaver Report).

[2] *Academic Boards*, Memorandum of the Working Party set up by the A.T.C.D.E. Executive Committee. London: The Association, 1966.

assign executive responsibility for the academic work of the colleges to the academic board. Thus, as now conceived, the academic board plays a role in both the external and internal administration of the colleges.

If and when local authorities show themselves willing to accept the full implications of the Weaver Report, and academic boards begin to function universally along the lines now agreed upon, it is clear that the former powers of the principal, and, *inter alia*, of the local education authority, will be considerably attenuated. Colleges of education will begin to be run along lines that are closer to those of a university, the academic board coming to resemble the senate in its functions, and the principal assuming a role similar to that of a vice-chancellor. But a change of this kind requires more than formal constitutions and official approval if it is to be fully operative, and it seems likely that a residual element of the earlier pattern will continue to characterize the attitudes and behaviour of some principals and members of staff for many years to come.

Organization for Teaching

The major vertical divisions within the college as far as its teaching work is concerned are between the subject departments; the main horizontal split is between year-groups of students. The organization of distinct subject departments is a fairly recent innovation. The early colleges had few staff, and these performed a great variety of functions.[1] Most recruited their staff from the ranks of former students, with all the limitations of outlook and intellectual horizons that this entailed, although by the end of the nineteenth century the inspectors were able to report a steady improvement in the quality of men and

[1] The Wesleyan College for Schoolmistresses had a staff of six, comprising the Reverend C. Stubbs, Chaplain and General Superintendent, Mr. and Mrs. Baker—the former lecturing on school management, Arithmetic and Geography and supervising school practice, his wife being in charge of domestic affairs— and three certificated governesses, plus visiting teachers for Drawing and Music. (Dimond, D. *Colleges of Education for Teaching.* London: A.T.C.D.E., 1961, p. 18.) The early women's colleges all had clerical principals. Policy later became that of always having a woman principal for a women's college, but in recent years a number of men have been appointed to these positions.

women lecturers. But the size of colleges was still small, and many members of staff had to lecture in at least two and sometimes as many as four different subjects. There were few opportunities to recruit specialists, who could concentrate solely upon their particular subject interest; even where this was possible, only one such person could be employed for each subject taught, which provided scant base for any real departmentalization. Only with the considerable growth in the size of the colleges during the past twenty years has it been possible for distinct departments to emerge. Such developments are clearly of great importance to the institutional life and social cohesion of the colleges, and departmentalizing has sometimes been resisted by the principals and members of staff who are mindful of the effects it might have.

In a sense departmentalization is part of the inevitable process of differentiation into sub-groups that occurs when an institution becomes too large for all its members to have regular face-to-face contact with one another. But the basis for this differentiation is important in assessing its effect upon the organization as a whole. A series of sub-groups based upon halls of residence or hostels is less likely to represent a threat to the institutional identification of staff and students than structuring along departmental lines. Social cohesion within the department tends to be based upon a commitment to the disciplines of study rather than to the institution; contact with the teaching, research and writing undertaken by teachers in other colleges and universities encourages the growth of professional, extra-institutional loyalties. The academic system rewards the individual entrepreneur rather than the loyal college man; this is less of a problem in the university, where academic excellence and intellectual pioneering are highly valued, than in the colleges of education, where too exclusive a devotion to the pursuit of interests in narrowly defined subject areas is believed by many to limit rather than enhance the effectiveness of a lecturer's work.[1]

The grounds for this view are twofold—first, that a strong subject commitment on the part of a lecturer encourages the same attitude on the part of the student, who is in any case

[1] See Knapp, R. 'Changing Functions of the College Professor' in Sanford, N. (ed.) *The American College.* New York: Wiley, 1962.

already disposed in this direction as a result of his experience in the grammar school. Such an attitude is held to be inappropriate to the teacher of younger and less academic children, who should be concerned with broader aspects of personal and social development than mere subject competence. Second, and less frequently discussed, the lecturer whose reference group is professional or extra-institutional is much less amenable to influences from within the college, less willing to undertake tasks that distract him from his central interest, less subject to the sort of interpersonal social control that staff and students exercise upon one another. A recognition of the existence of this situation within the colleges, and the absence of any generally accepted research function, has in the past limited the number of first-class scholars who have been willing to work in teacher education and reduced the opportunities of the college to attain high standards of excellence in the work that they undertake. The development of the large subject departments–some now have up to a dozen members–has made specialization easier, and this, together with improved conditions and salary scales, may attract a larger number of men and women who are more deeply committed to scholarship and disciplinary interests. It is clear, however, that for some time to come there are likely to be strains involved in the strengthening of departmental forms of organization.

More rapid mobility of staff as a consequence of increased opportunities may exacerbate these problems. In the United States it has been suggested that as a result of '. . . the prevalent opinion that the professional growth and reward depend primarily on the attitude of one's peers in an academic area, universities are having more and more difficulty in finding faculty members who are really interested in the institution in which they teach'.[1]

As a result of the operation of the Pelham scale, which, in line with its Burnham counterpart for teachers in schools, has tended to become more differentiated and hierarchical in recent years,[2] the internal organization of departments usually

[1] Weeks, I. D. 'Teaching and Institutional Service versus Research and Professional Writing', *Journal of Higher Education*, December 1963, p. 45.

[2] Taylor, W. *The Secondary Modern School*. London: Faber, 1963, Chapter VI and Appendix IV.

reflects the overall structure of grades and authority in the colleges, the head of department receiving an allowance on top of his principal lecturer's salary, and being responsible for directing the work of a mixed staff of lecturers, senior lecturers and principal lecturers. The extent to which staff interaction is along departmental lines varies a great deal from college to college. Those departments that have sole use of a particular group of rooms or teaching facilities, especially if these are concentrated in a particular building ('science block', 'gym block', and so on) tend to develop a more exclusive network of personal relationships than those where no special claim can be made upon a particular physical space. The grouping of lecturers' studies can have a similar effect, encouraging greater informal contact and interchange of ideas and consultation than when a more arbitrary distribution exists. In some colleges a sense of departmental identity is fostered by a weekly department meeting; sometimes these are used to thrash out the unified policy with which to confront a full staff meeting or academic board.

The co-existence of strong departmental allegiance alongside older and less functionally specific types of relationship within the college can sometimes bring about severe clashes of loyalties and a good deal of inter-personal conflict. Should the lecturer in one department who is personally friendly with the head of another convey to the latter his misgivings regarding the competence or decisions of his own head of department? Should the group of resident tutors feel free to discuss departmental matters? Should the proceedings of the recent department meeting be regarded as common property among an inter-departmental friendship group of junior colleagues, or should the decisions arrived at remain confidential until the head of department reveals them at Monday's academic board? Within a fully bureaucratic structure questions such as these are covered by established protocol, and give rise to little conflict and personal anxiety; within an organization that is still in a state of transition such confusion and anxiety tend to be a good deal stronger.

A strong sense of social cohesion within departments and a willingness on the part of a college principal to consult with his staff on policy matters can also produce competition between departments for the scarce resources of the college – teaching space and equipment, timetable hours, new staff, library allowances and so on. Such departmental rivalry has been seen by some as having beneficial effects upon the overall work of the colleges and as fostering a willingness to respond positively to innovation and change. Within the context of medical education Merton suggests that competition between departments serves many of the same functions as competition in the market economy, but has the advantage of involving a common commitment to certain overall goals–the production of better teachers, the improvement of quality of medical practice–rather than self-aggrandisement. Such rivalry, whatever its other outcomes, serves 'to keep many medical educators alerted to new problems and potentialities of medical education. It is difficult for them, even if they were so inclined, to rest comfortably on their oars.'[1]

In some colleges departmental conflict is a permanent feature of the social organization. A split between the Education department and those responsible for the academic subjects has been common; the child-centred orientation of the former, the fact that it contains fewer graduate members, that it is often larger, and has control over a number of aspects of college work such as school practice organization that affect the whole staff, all help to emphasize this split. Where practical subjects–Physical Education, Handicraft, Domestic Subjects–play an important part in the college programme there may also be some strains involved between these and the academic departments. In some cases the attitude of the local university towards the inclusion of such subjects within the new B.Ed. degree has increased the insecurity of lecturers in these departments.

It is clear that the bureaucratization of the teaching organization within the college, the tendency for staff relationships to become functionally specific and the rise in the number of non-residential lecturers, limited to working hours, has not been altogether welcomed by a substantial number of lecturers and senior staff. Such a process is very much against the grain of what may be called the 'culture' of teacher education, with its stress upon personal relationships, small groups, individual attention and diffuseness rather than specificity of inter-personal obligation. The identification of teacher education as a process

[1] Merton, R. K. *The Student Physician.* Cambridge: Harvard University Press, 1957.

248

more acute to the preparation of a social worker than to the personal education of a historian, scientist or specialist in physical education suggests that the social structure of the college should reproduce the characteristics of what has been called a 'therapeutic' rather than a 'bureaucratic' milieu. In the latter persons are held responsible for the performance of distinctly different tasks, and are subject to well-defined relationships of power, authority and prestige. Formal lines of communication are laid down, and members are not expected to encroach upon the responsibilities of others. In contrast, the therapeutic milieu is characterized by the overlapping responsibilities, minimal emphasis upon the definition of relationships in terms of ascribed power, authority and prestige, and informal patterns of communication.[1]

Teaching Units

The division of the academic and professional studies of the college among departments is reflected in the workgroups that exist among the student body. In some subjects that are taken by all students, attendance at lectures is still on a 'year' basis, but for most purposes work is undertaken in smaller groups. The Robbins Committee found that of the 16·2 hours of timetable study per week that was the average for general and specialist students in England and Wales, half were spent in lectures, just under two hours in 'large seminars' (with ten or more students), half an hour in 'small seminars' (5 to 9 students), only six minutes in tutorials of one to four students–against thirty minutes for undergraduates–4·3 hours in practicals and thirty-six minutes in 'other periods'.[2] Just over half the lectures were attended by between ten and nineteen students, a fifth by between five and nine and another fifth by between twenty and 100. Overall, three-quarters of all lectures were given to twenty students or less.[3] In some colleges main-subject groupings are retained for curriculum courses and Education; in others there are separate groups for each of the types of work

[1] Rosengren, W. R. 'Communication, Organization and Constraint in the Therapeutic Milieu', *Administrative Science Quarterly*, 9:1, June 1964.
[2] *Higher Education*, Appendix Two (B), Table 45, p. 296.
[3] *Ibid.*, Table 99, p. 343.

undertaken. Where the main subject is the principal basis for student grouping it facilitates a departmental identification – 'he's a third-year biologist', 'she's a second-year historian' – that may be only partially functional as far as the other work that makes up the course is concerned. Especially among students preparing for secondary teaching there is sometimes a resistance to Education and curriculum courses, a feeling that these are taking time or attention away from the real meat of the course; main-subject-based groups may provide mutual reinforcement for this attitude. Against this must be placed the opportunity that such homogeneous subject groups provide for educational studies to be oriented around the broader educational implications of the subject concerned, thus helping to liberalize the student's attitudes in his central area of interest.

Some ideas as to the importance that students attach to various parts of the course and methods of study can be obtained from the enquiry made by the Robbins Committee. Students in universities, colleges and further education were asked if they would like to have changes made in the amount of time they spent in receiving various types of teaching. In all cases the proportion favouring change of some kind was high, but teacher-trainees emerged as the least satisfied with existing arrangements. Sixty-six per cent of undergraduates, 60 per cent of full-time students in further education and no less than 78 per cent of students in training colleges (83 per cent of the men, 74 per cent of the women) wanted changes made.[1] Over half the sample wanted more time to be given to tutorials, 39 per cent more time to seminars, 31 per cent more time to practicals and 11 per cent more time to lectures; the last was the only type of teaching of which any significant number of students (22 per cent) wanted less. The Robbins Committee also sought the views of teacher trainees regarding the balance of work between main subjects, curriculum courses, education courses and teaching practice. No fewer than 90 per cent of the men and 82 per

[1] *Ibid.*, Table 8, p. 262, Table 53, p. 301, Table 74, p. 321. It is interesting in this connection to note that in their study of the satisfactions and dissatisfactions of teachers, Rudd and Wiseman found that non-graduate men in junior schools were the most dissatisfied group, not simply in terms of salaries, but also in connection with other aspects of their tasks. Rudd, W. G. A. and Wiseman, S. 'Sources of Dissatisfaction among a Group of Teachers', *British Journal of Educational Psychology*, XXXII:3, 1962.

cent of the women on general courses wanted changes of some kind; 43 per cent wanted more time on main subjects and only 11 per cent less; 70 per cent wanted more teaching practice and only 4 per cent less; on curriculum courses, 21 per cent wanted more time, 26 per cent less and 51 per cent were satisfied with the existing distribution. The proportion of students wanting more time on Education was 26 per cent, less time 17 per cent and no change 55 per cent.[1]

It is clear that a large proportion of the time that teacher-education students spend receiving instruction is within the face-to-face situation, in groups small enough to permit the lecturer to know each member of his class individually. Apart from the value of group-based teaching procedures as a way of improving the quality of academic instruction and ensuring that attention can be given to the needs of individuals, they also serve as part of the process whereby the college brings influence to bear upon its students in the direction of commitment to 'professional' values. Although created initially for instrumental purposes, teaching groups provide a good deal of 'unused affective potential', and there is much interest among educators of teachers as to how this might be used as part of the educational programme. Although students normally appear to welcome the opportunity for more discussion and seminar work rather than attendance at the more impersonal formal lectures, there is sometimes a degree of suspicion of the way in which the small group settings are used to manipulate values. The literature of teacher education gives ample evidence of how 'the group' is seen as a way in which *gemeinschaft* relationships may, in Wilson's terms, 'be cultivated within, or grafted on to, the *gesellschaft* society, so that the latter may achieve its ends.'[2]

Within the small teaching units of the college it is easier for informal relationships to exist between staff and students than in the universities. Of particular interest is the fact that these relationships are likely to be more readily facilitated in the student's main subject studies rather than in Education courses. In the latter, which are taken by all students, the staff/student ratio may be as high as 75 : 1, against only 12 : 1 in the main

[1] *Higher Education*, Appendix Two (B) Para 100, p. 230
[2] Wilson, B. 'A Sociologist's Footnote' in Phillips, M. *Small Social Groups in England*. London: Methuen, 1962.

subjects. It can be suggested–and the available evidence permits no more than this–that the informal influence of subject tutors is greater than that of Education staff, although it is the latter who are usually most concerned with developing child-centred and professional attitudes in the student body.

Teaching is essentially a privatized activity, and we know very little of what actually goes on in classroom, tutorial room or lecture hall. Everett Hughes has drawn attention to some of the major issues about which information is at present lacking.

'Obviously no [college] teacher delivers ten or twelve or fifteen prepared and organized lectures a week, or even five. Teachers are not supermen. But probably most American college teachers do something in the classrooms for twelve or more hours a week. What is it that they do? Do they mumble in their beards? Do they engage in chit-chat? Do they really discuss subject matter and ideas with their students? In what combinations do they do these or other things? And how, for their part, do the students take part in what goes on? What skills have they developed for controlling what goes on in the classroom? And how is all of this affected by the teacher's conception of his job, and by what he considers to be the contingencies of his survival and advancement?

'I am convinced that many American college teachers have learned how to restrict production, their own and that of their students. . . . Most of our studies are based on the assumption that the teachers–and the administrators of the institutions in which they work–have as their goal an ever higher level of effort on the part of the students. If we were to study the interaction among administrators, teachers, pupils and students, we might very well discover whole systems of checks upon the efforts of all concerned, a knot of fetters made tighter by the movements of all.'[1]

Informal staff/student relationships in small-group settings take on a particular importance in relation to the process of continuous assessment that has been adopted in lieu of traditional examinations in some colleges and institutes. In secondary schools, where external examinations play an important part in structuring courses and determining norms of effort, teacher and

[1] Hughes, E. C. 'Is Education a Discipline?' in Walton, J. and Kuethe, J. L. *The Discipline of Education*. Wisconsin, 1963, pp. 157–8.

pupils share a common task in beating the examiner, and this facilitates social cohesion and the absence of conflict in the classroom. Where a teacher combines the role of counsellor, guide and assessor, the inter-personal situation is more complex, but in so far as the assessor function can be partially externalized, in the form of an end-of-course examination, role conflict is not likely to be too serious. Students recognize that the area in which they can influence the assessment process is limited – they may try to 'spot' a question the lecturer will ask, or to pressure him by a variety of subtle devices into revealing them, but they assume the marking of the final scripts will be carried out objectively, in terms of a rank order of excellence and in accordance with standards that are outside the staff/student relationship itself. Continuous assessment produces a new set of problems for both lecturer and students; there is little claim that this is objective – Shipman found that 'in all the discussions on weak students, raised because of poor examination results in course work, the final decision was always made on tutors' views of particular characteristics of students, never on the results alone'.[1]

As we have seen in an earlier section, general qualities also receive attention when students are assessed by more conventional methods, and procedures also exist whereby students who do not exhibit satisfactory forms of character development may be cooled out prior to taking the final examination.[2]

The combination of small group teaching with continuous assessment provides many opportunities for the tutor to bring influence to bear upon the students' intellectual and personal development. But it also complicates the interpersonal relationships of tutor and student and encourages the latter's efforts to make the relationship reciprocally influential. The tutor has a stake in the group performance of his students, as he has in any assessment situation. Where formal examinations are used, however, this involvement is mediated through academic

[1] Shipman, M. D. *Personal and Social Influences on the Work of a Teachers' Training College.* Unpublished Ph.D. thesis, University of London, 1966, p. 263.
[2] Clark, B. R. 'The Cooling-out Function in Higher Education' in Halsey, A. H., Floud, J. E. and Anderson, C. A. *Education, Economy and Society.* New York: Free Press, 1961.

standards in a more direct and straightforward way than in the case of continuous assessment, whereby the partial dependence of the tutor on student performance is a function of his own relatively unstructured and subjective perceptions of quality. The task of the student is not only that of obtaining power over the subject matter of his studies, but also of obtaining power over the lecturer concerned in assessing them; attempts may be made to involve the tutor in student activities; he will be invited to coffee brews in student rooms, and there may be a tendency to value any opportunity of catching him out, especially in small administrative errors.[1] Where a member of the college staff refuses, partly perhaps as an act of self-protection, to become involved in this way he may be subjected to sustained criticism by the students, to whom his behaviour constitutes a threat in respect of both assessment and the amount of work likely to be required of them. The tensions generated in this way are much less than they might be, because of the very low failure rate in the colleges. But in so far as there is a drive to achieve 'good grades', however meaningless these may be in determining job chances, some such tensions do affect staff/student relations.[2]

Socialization and the Organization of Student Life

In the early colleges, as we have seen, the residential and the academic life of students could hardly be distinguished. The régime was an onerous one, as befitted the future teachers of the poor. At St. Mark's College, Chelsea, the daily schedule in 1844 was as follows:

5.30 Rise. Half an hour allowed for washing and dressing.
6.00 Housework, etc., for three-quarters of an hour.
6.45 Study, commencing with prayer, an hour and a half.
8.15 Breakfast, 25 minutes.
8.40 Prepare for chapel, 20 minutes.
9.00 Morning service, one hour.

[1] See Mechanic, D. 'Sources of Power of lower Participants in Complex Organizations', *Administrative Science Quarterly*, VII:3, December 1962, p. 349.
[2] For an extended theoretical analysis of relationships of this kind, see Blau, P. M. *Exchange and Power in Social Life*. New York: Wiley, 1965.

10.00 Study, two hours.
12.00 Industrial occupations, 50 minutes.
12.50 Prepare for dinner.
 1.00 Dinner, half an hour.
 1.30 Leisure, half an hour.
 2.00 Study, two hours. On Wednesday and Saturday, draw-
        ing.
 4.00 Industrial occupations.
 5.30 Prepare for music, 10 minutes.
 5.40 Music, an hour and five minutes, more or less.
 6.45 Prepare for tea, a quarter of an hour.
 7.00 Tea, 20 minutes.
 7.20 Prepare for study.
 7.30 Evening study.
 9.00 Evening prayers and a short lecture, from half an hour to
        forty minutes.
 9.35 Put up books, etc., and retire to bed.
10.00 Gas lights extinguished.

This arrangement assigned to ordinary days eight hours five minutes study, three and a quarter hours of industrial occupations and very little leisure.[1] But students were well aware of the type of life they were letting themselves in for when they came to St. Mark's. Among the information they had to provide when applying for a place were answers to the following questions:

'. . . Are you sincerely desirous of becoming a schoolmaster, and do you seek admission into the National Society's training college expressly to be fitted for that difficult and responsible office? Are you prepared to lead in the college a simple and laborious life; working with your hands as well as acquiring book knowledge, and rendering an exact obedience to the discipline of the place? Are you aware that your path of duty on leaving the college will be principally, if not entirely, among the poor? And are you willing to apprentice yourself to the Society on that understanding?'[2]

Such a pattern of life contrasted sharply with that of the university student of the time. The Royal Commission on the

[1] *Minutes of the Committee of Council*, 1844. Report of the Revd. Moseley on St. Mark's College, Chelsea, p. 583.
[2] Rich, *op. cit.*

University of Oxford of 1852 found that, although a great advance had been made in standards, 'the grosser exhibitions of vice, such as drunkenness and riot, [having] in Oxford, as in the higher classes generally, become rare', an improvement in relationship between senior and junior members having taken place and a religious student no longer being regarded as an object of persecution or scorn, there was still much to criticize. A large proportion of the students were found to be under-employed, without adequate incentive to study and not subject to sufficient guidance and control on the part of their colleges.

'Thus the whole time, from 2.00 in the afternoon until midnight, is every day left at the disposal of the undergraduate; and he often has two whole days in the week unoccupied by college duties beyond attendance one in the day at chapel. Many students live in the town in lodgings of their own selection, to which they may return as late as they please; and they may even pass the night away from their lodging, with little risk of detection.'[1]

The tight control exercised over the lives of students by the training colleges was slow to change—in Rich's terms, the life of the average student was 'narrow, strenuous and rather drab'. Common rooms hardly existed until the nineties, bathrooms were considered luxuries, and students slept in dormitories and curtained-off cubicles. Life outside the college was rigidly supervised, particularly for the women; walks were taken in supervised 'crocodiles', the unsupervised walk being strictly forbidden. Even as late as 1912, students entering training colleges had to subscribe to such rules as those set out for the Lincoln Diocesan College, which required that no new acquaintance be made in the city, that the names and addresses of relations and friends who might live in Lincoln be given to the head governess ('No visit must ever be paid without leave having previously been given'), and that no student might leave the college unaccompanied without special leave.[2] Writing in 1924, Jones refers to the fact that the disciplinary arrangements

[1] *Report of Her Majesty's Commissioners appointed to enquire into the state, discipline, studies and revenues of the University and Colleges of Oxford.* London: H.M.S.O. 1852, p. 28.

[2] Zebedee, D. H. J. *Lincoln Diocesan Training College.* Lincoln: The College, 1962, p. 142.

IN THE COLLEGE OF EDUCATION

of the colleges were based on those of the secondary school, with a well-established prefect system in operation in the majority, such prefects being elected by the staff and assuming responsibility for the 'general discipline of their fellows in all but the formal lecture and private study periods'.[1] The timetable continued to exercise considerable demands as compared with the situation today, but hardly bore comparison with the pattern of eighty years earlier. The structure of the day in the early twenties was one of lectures and classes in the morning, and games, demonstration lessons and practical subjects in the afternoon, more lectures and/or private study between tea and supper, and a little free time available before lights out at eight or nine o'clock. The weekends were free, apart from Saturday morning, and a compulsory roll call together with a chapel service on Sundays.

During the early post Second World War years the impossibility of imposing these formal restrictions upon mature men and women returning from the forces, changes in the status of the young and the modification of the value climate of society all combined to alter the type of social control exercised upon students.

The majority of college places are still residential, although a larger number of students than heretofore now spend some part of the college course in approved lodgings or commute daily from their homes. Importance is attached to the beneficial effects of residence on the development of professional attitudes and competences. In this respect the colleges have modelled themselves upon the collegiate ideals of the ancient universities. In providing halls of residence and other living accomodation they have been inspired by the same ideals that were referred to by a former president of Columbia University.

'Halls of residence were provided precisely as libraries, laboratories and teachers themselves are provided, in order to exert educational influence and to offer educational opportunity. These halls were built, not as an educational convenience, but as an educational necessity. It is not merely by individual attendance upon lectures or recitations or by individual work in laboratories or in libraries that one can gain the full benefit of university membership. That comes, and can only

[1] Jones, *op. cit.*, p. 78.

come, when the individual student regards himself and treats himself as a member of the academic family to which he owes companionship and loyal allegiance. . . .'[1]

Claims made for the benefit of residence in the nineteenth-century colleges stressed the superiority of institutional boarding and feeding over that found in the homes of the majority of students as much as they emphasized the effects upon character.[2] A minority statement included in the final report of the Cross Commission on Elementary Education, 1888, suggested that whilst residential colleges were probably desirable at a time when students were drawn from 'uneducated' homes, 'in proportion as the colleges are brought within reach of the homes of the students, and these are drawn from families of wider education, we consider that the preservation and extension of the home influence, side by side with that of the training college, will be a great advantage.'[3]

Within the residential community of the college, recent years have seen a shift from a directive, supervisory emphasis towards a pattern intended to facilitate the internalization of 'professional' standards without giving rise to antagonism or negative feeling. The tendency today is to stress the positive role residence can play in the education of students, and of the contribution of the staff to this informal education. 'Let us rid ourselves once and for all of the mistaken conception that staff are resident solely or even largely for disciplinary reasons. Communication between persons is so difficult and so precious that planning must provide conditions of every kind to encourage it, and nowhere nearly as well as in good halls of residence.'[4] Anxiety is sometimes shown lest the beneficial effects of group participation, both in residential settings and in the arrangements made for teaching, should be diminished by the impact of the autho-

---

[1] Butler, N. B. President of Columbia University, Annual Report for 1932, quoted Childs, W. M. *Making a University.* London: 1932, p. 167.

[2] *Final Report* of the Commissioners appointed to enquire into the Elementary Education Acts, England and Wales. London: H.M.S.O., C-5485, 1888. See in particular the evidence of Canon Daniel, Principal of Battersea Training College, and Mr. Maniford, Vice-Principal of the Wesleyan Training College, Westminster, referred to on pp. 99–100 of the *Final Report.* [3] *Ibid.,* p. 291.

[4] Malloch, E. 'Communication and Commitment', *Education for Teaching,* February 1960, p. 8.

rity of the tutor, which is seen as having a potentially deadening effect upon the spontaneity and responsiveness of the group.[1]

In some colleges the residential pattern is still strongly middle class, as is illustrated by the times and names of the major meals; dinner is eaten at 7, high tea only on Saturdays and, sometimes, Wednesdays, lunch is at 1 or 1.15 and afternoon tea is provided at 4 p.m. Latin graces precede and follow all main meals, certain types of informal dress are proscribed, and the student body stands for the entry and exit of the principal and academic staff. Elsewhere the greater convenience and economy of a cafeteria system have been adopted, and the familiar 'chow line' of the union refectory or the American university has begun to assert itself. It is interesting in this connection to note that the sub-committee of the University Grants Committee that reported on halls of residence in 1957 was emphatic regarding the importance of a formal dinner on each night of the week.

'. . . Formal, that is, in the sense that it happens at a given time, and that the students and senior residents are present, waited on either by a rota of students, or by domestic helpers. Pressure of numbers will in many cases no doubt make it necessary to hold two sittings, but this is much to be preferred to a supper served on a cafeteria system.'[2]

There appears to be only minority support amongst students themselves for the type of residential régime that such arrangements imply, particularly when the fare offered is out of keeping with the manner of its presentation.

Despite recent changes, the colleges still accept a greater direct responsibility for students conduct than is usually the case in the university; the need for a training in professional values is cited as the chief justification for this emphasis. In practice, such a concern shows itself in a variety of regulations regarding the hours during which students may be absent from the college, the entertainment of visitors in students' rooms, the consumption of alcohol, the driving and parking of motor cars and so on; the variety of such regulations is very great. In a

[1] See Gibson, E. M. 'The Development of Personality–a Conference Report', *Education for Teaching*, February 1960.
[2] *Halls of Residence*, Report of a sub-committee of the University Grants Committee, 1957, p. 15.

large number of colleges they are a good deal less stringent than in some university halls of residence; a *de facto* open-door policy exists, members of the opposite sex may be entertained in study bedrooms during substantial parts of the day and evening, and weekend leave is freely available. Elsewhere, particularly in the smaller women's colleges, regulations are a good deal more restricting. Most colleges have student unions or similar organizations, although it is clear that the extent of staff involvement in the work of the unions is in some cases considerable. Delegates of the Ninth Annual Conference of Colleges of Education organized by the National Union of Students in 1965 complained that some principals prevented the development of student union autonomy, most wanted to approve all alterations in the union constitution, some demanded that all minutes of union meetings should receive their approval, and a few even appointed themselves as chairmen of union meetings.[1]

But it cannot be assumed that the views expressed by the more militant students who attend such gatherings are necessarily representative of the colleges as a whole. Shipman has shown that, in one college at least, there was considerable pressure upon the staff to participate in student affairs; staff had the right to vote as members of the Student Council, and were criticized by student opinion when they failed to do so. Nor do the existence of regulations regarding evening or weekend leave necessarily seem onerous to students. Shipman found that first-year students left the colleges only on an average of once each week, and that there was pressure within the student body against going home for the weekend; some delegates of the 1965 Conference already referred to thought that a student who went away for most weekends would lose the advantage of mixing at leisure with his fellow students. The existence of a strong 'college spirit', the availability of a large number of leisure activities within the college, the absence of attractions in the local area, and, especially in a mixed college, the opportunities to meet the opposite sex on the premises can all serve to minimize the amount of time that the student spends or desires to spend outside the gates. All this helps to increase the impact of college life upon the development of attitudes and values,

[1] *Ninth Annual Conference of College of Education.* London: National Union of Students, 1965, p. 23 (mimeographed).

to enhance the socializing effect that the college culture has upon its members. The inclusive organization, within which the individual finds most of his needs satisfied, is more likely to be influential in this respect than the one which provides merely instrumental skills and knowledge through its courses and formal teaching.

It is clear that interpersonal relationships among students in the future, when most colleges will have at least 750 students, will be very different from those characteristic of the smaller, self-contained, intimate colleges of the past. Shipman observed changes taking place in the pattern of these relationships in a mixed college that grew considerably in size during the period of his study.

'Whilst traditions persisted, increases in size were leading to a new basis for social life based on student rooms rather than on hall, stage or sports field. Meanwhile an active minority, roughly the size of the active group in the old college, carried on a level of activity similar to the old pattern, whilst increasing numbers adopted the new, passive role, based on small groups. These groups tended to remain outside communal activity and felt less tied to the college in the evenings and at weekends.'[1]

In her Chairman's address to the A.T.C.D.E. for 1966, the principal of Homerton College, Cambridge, referred to the lack of desire of the contemporary student to participate in community affairs and a tendency to concentrate exclusively on her private relationships with her boyfriend and a few intimate friends. She saw this as inimical to the development of the 'concerned open relationship' which provides the context within which staff 'try to communicate a sense of purpose and commitment'.[2]

Student Sub-cultures

Student cultures are not autonomous. The patterns that we encounter in a college are the product of many influences. The history and traditions of the institution, the type of courses that it provides and the students for which they cater, the positions

[1] Shipman, *op. cit.*, p. 151.
[2] Paston Brown, B. 'A Time for Revaluation', *Education for Teaching*, February 1966, p. 10.

attained by its alumni, the qualifications, standing, competence and attitude of its staff, its physical facilities and the pattern of its internal organization all play their part. One of the most obviously important factors is the amount of direct contact that students have with one another. A day college is much less likely to develop a recognizable culture than one in which a high proportion of students are in residence. Despite the impressively large number of studies that have been made of student cultures, all too few of these have been directly concerned with the colleges of education. Much of the work so far undertaken has been American in origin, and such of it as has been done in this country has been concerned with universities rather than colleges.[1]

Among the most useful American efforts in this field have been the attempts to create typologies and analytical frameworks that might act as heuristic devices for the study of college culture. Among the best known is that of Clark and Trow, who distinguish between collegiate, vocational, academic and nonconformist sub-cultures. The term collegiate tends to be used in a somewhat derogatory sense in the United States, where it has come to be associated with fraternity hazings, anti-intellectualism and a tendency to devote time and money to those three great enemies of an effective higher education, cars, women and alcohol. More seriously from the point of view of the goals of higher education, the collegiate culture has been shown by Goldsen and others to be a powerful conservative influence, tending to insulate students from the liberalizing effects their studies might have.[2] In Clark and Trow's terms, this system of values and activities is not hostile to the college, to which, in fact, it generates strong loyalties and attachments. It is, however, indifferent and resistant to *serious* demands emanating from the faculty, or parts of it, for an involvement with ideas and issues over and above that required to gain the diploma.[3]

[1] For a general review of work in this field see Jacob, P. E. *Changing Values in College.* New York: Harper, 1957, and Barton, A. H. *Studying the Effects of College Education.* New Haven: E.W. Hazen Foundation, 1959.

[2] Goldsen, R. K. *et al, What College Students Think.* Englewood Cliffs, N.J.: Prentice Hall, 1960.

[3] Clark, B. R. and Trow, M. *Determinants of College Student Sub-Cultures.* Berkeley, Calif.: Centre for the Study of Higher Education, 1961, p. 5 (mimeographed).

IN THE COLLEGE OF EDUCATION

There is evidence that the colleges of education have traditionally secured a substantial loyalty and institutional commitment from their students, to which the continuing attendance at college reunions of large numbers of former students provides testimony.[1] Shipman refers to the culture of the college of education as 'relatively homogeneous and very pervasive', characterized by a substantial consensus between staff and students – 'staff perceptions of college life and their evaluations of it were very similar to those of students. Further, they obtained similar pleasure from communal activity. The net result was an integration satisfying the needs of the majority, but possibly delaying adaptation to external forces. High satisfaction could make change unwelcome.'[2]

A second sub-cultural type has been referred to as the vocational, where the value of the college experience in occupational terms is the overriding consideration. This instrumentalism can take two contrasting forms. If the course provides access to a valuable qualification of universal currency, valued in its own terms rather than representing a particular educational content or set of skills, then students will be less concerned with the 'relevance' of the subjects they study to the jobs they will later perform, more concerned with the ease or difficulty with which satisfactory grades in these subjects can be obtained towards the final certificate. Where the latter does not in itself carry status, where the pass rate is high, there will be more interest in the course as providing a saleable set of skills and knowledge, and subjects not seen as relevant to the occupational destination may be devalued. The latter type of instrumentalism seems to be common in the college, where the theoretical part of the Education course is often seen as having little value for the future teacher, and those who teach it are criticized for being 'out of touch' with the real problems of the classroom.[3]

[1] Jones, *op. cit.*, Report of the Board of Education 1912–13, *op. cit.*

[2] Shipman, *op. cit.*, p. 89.

[3] Such opinions are not limited to institutions for the training of teachers. Dornbusch, analysing the induction processes of the Military Academy, refers to the way in which rumours helped to prepare the cadets for their jobs as officers. 'Several of the instructors at the Academy were supposed to have been transferred from sea duty because of their incompetence. . . . In addition, many stories were told about a junior officer whose career at the Academy had been singularly brilliant. He had completely failed in his

The vocational sub-culture involves the availability of suitable role models for the students, and these are provided by the teachers in the schools in which school practice takes place and by the expectations regarding the type of demand that will be made in the subsequent teacher role.[1] Shipman indicates that some elements of this role are anticipated while the student is still himself a pupil in school, and that socialization into the teaching role is in many respects 'too efficient', guaranteeing that students would 'mesh smoothly into teaching as it is today and was yesterday. The price seemed to be an unwillingness to face what it will be tomorrow'.[2]

The strength of the vocational commitment may also help to account for the college of education students' lack of interest in political issues on a national level, including student politics. To take a single example, when the campaign for nuclear disarmament was at its height a number of ex-sixth-formers would arrive each year at a men's college of education in the North of England wearing C.N.D. badges; within the first six months of the course these had completely disappeared; general political activity or interest among the student body was virtually nonexistent. Shipman notes the same phenomena; despite encouragement from the staff, attempts to organize a political society were opposed by the student body as 'inappropriate' in a college for teachers.[3] Pinner has suggested that a high level of political activity on the part of students can be seen as 'role seeking' behaviour; it follows that where no such search is seen as necessary the level of such activity will be low.[4]

The third type of sub-culture delimited by Clark and Trow is 'academic' in its orientations, identified with the intellectual concerns of the serious faculty members. 'The students involved work hard, get the best grades, talk about the course work

handling of enlisted men because he had carried over the high standards of the Academy. The cadets were thus oriented to a different conception of discipline when dealing with enlisted personnel.' Dornbusch, S. M. 'The Military Academy as an Assimilating Institution', *Social Forces*, 33, 1954, p. 316.

[1] 'Can We Really Teach Teaching?', *New Education*, March 1967.

[2] Shipman, *op. cit.*, p. 285.

[3] *Ibid.*, p. 291.

[4] Pinner, F. A. 'Student Trade Unionism in France, Belgium and Holland', *Sociology of Education*, 37:3, Spring 1964.

outside of class, and let the world of ideas and knowledge reach them in ways that neither of the foregoing types do.'[1] There has been concern that in some institutions of higher education there will be a tendency on the part of student bodies to insulate students from these various academic purposes, to denigrate the rate buster, the 'damned average raiser' who hands in 4,000 words when the norm has been set at half that amount. In an account of the social structure of a men's hall of residence in the University of Hull Gittens describes the common attitude to work as one of 'general disparagement and disapprobation'.

'When students return from a vacation the question they usually ask others is: "How much work did you do over the vacation?" The invariable reply is: "I just didn't seem to get round to doing any", or the question is laughingly dismissed– "Work? I don't work while I'm on holiday!" In term time, when a student appears to be working harder than most, he becomes the butt of some such semi-jocular statements as, "I see we've got a serious student here", or, more contemptuously, "Keen, isn't he?" The intention, whether conscious or not, seems to be to enforce a certain norm of amount of work against amount of leisure over a minority who wish to work harder.'[2]

By such means pressures are created against the enlargement of the academic sub-culture, which exists in some form or another almost everywhere. But such pressures need not be so direct as is implied in Gittens' account. In the non-competitive climate of the college of education, where only a very small percentage of students either terminate the course prematurely or fail their final examinations, the efforts of a small group of academically active individuals represents much less of a threat to the general student body than in other circumstances. Hence such a group is more likely to be tolerated, albeit referred to disparagingly as 'greasy grinds', 'grey men', 'swots' or 'cloggers'. Furthermore, it is perfectly possible that there are some colleges of education where the academic sub-culture is dominant or plays a larger part than elsewhere, although there are so many

[1] Clark and Trow, *op. cit.*, p. 6.
[2] Gittins, J. 'The Social Structure of a Men's Hall of Residence', *Sociological Review*, 9, 1962.

other influences in the work of all the colleges–for example the professional orientation, the child-centred nature of the curriculum, the previous educational history of the students–that the numbers of such may be small. With the introduction of the B.Ed. it is possible that the academic sub-culture will be strengthened, but since only a minority of students will be involved this may mean that the backwash effects of higher standards and expectations on the work of those who will not be receiving recognition of their efforts in the shape of a degree may be resented and opposed. It is clear from the figures given in Chapter 5 for the pre-course qualifications of students in various colleges that there may already be a tendency for the more academically oriented students to choose particular institutions. Stern remarks that:

'The differential representation of [intellectually oriented] students among schools at different levels of academic quality has led Reisman . . . to attribute the distinctive ethos of the more productive, high-potency colleges to characteristics of their students rather than the institutions or their faculties. The Centre for the Study of Higher Education at Berkeley has also espoused this provision, and marshalled considerable evidence in its support. . . . Their findings demonstrate that the highly productive colleges attract highly motivated students who are more inner directed, socially independent, receptive to learning, non-authoritarian, theoretical, unconventional and creative. They conclude that "the merit of certain institutions lies less in what they do to students that it does in the students to whom they do it".'[1]

The final sub-culture in Clark and Trow's scheme is the non-conformist, involving a substantial commitment to ideas and intellectual pursuits, but on a cosmopolitan rather than a local basis. 'The distinctive quality of this student's style is a rather aggressive non-conformism, a critical detachment from the college attended and its faculty . . . and a generalized hostility to the college administration'.[2] It is this non-conformist sub-culture that has come into prominence on a number of American campuses in recent years, associated with political

[1] Stern, G. G. 'Characteristics of the Intellectual Climate in College Environments', *Harvard Educational Review*, 33:1, 1963, p. 5.
[2] Clark and Trow, *op. cit.*, p. 6.

radicalism at both the student and the national level.[1] There are few indications of such orientation on the part of students in the colleges of education in this country. The pressures are almost all in the opposite direction, encouraging a degree of conformity to the role expectations set by experienced teachers, encountered as pupils in school, and formed by practical teaching during the college course and by the climate of attitudes among the student body as a whole.

The Impact of the College Course

The evaluation of the impact of the college course on students, the consideration of the degree to which the colleges are successfully fulfilling their goals of producing competent teachers for the schools, is central to any study of the process of teacher education. Yet the questions involved are beset with definitional and methodological difficulties of bewildering complexity. Is there any such thing as a 'good teacher', independent of the particular situation in which he finds himself working? What are the qualities in the graduating student that are predictive of subsequent success, and by which criteria should this success be measured? How can we control the psychological and social variables that are associated with the educational process in college? These difficulties help to explain why there have so far been few attempts to evaluate the way in which the colleges influence their students and the relationship of this influence to subsequent occupational and social performance. Much more has been done in the United States in this direction, but with little significant effect. Howard comments that 'with all the attention being given to decision-making about the training of teachers, few research findings appear to be pertinent to the basic problem. All discussion about teacher-training seems to assume that something happens to people in the course of such training, that they change in the direction of becoming good teachers; but there is little empirical support for such an assumption.'[2]

[1] Lipset, S. M. and Wolin, S. S. *The Berkeley Student Revolt*. New York: Doubleday, 1965; Miller, M. V. and Gilmore, S. *Revolution at Berkeley*. New York: Dell, 1965.
[2] See Howard, E. Z. 'Needed: A Conceptual Scheme for Teacher Education', *School Review*, 71:1, 1963, p. 12.

At the time of writing there are a number of studies of this kind under way–all students entering colleges in the Manchester area training organization have been tested by means of Stern's college characteristics index, activities index and teacher preference schedules, Oliver's survey of opinions and Allport and Vernon's study of values.[1] The University of Manchester's school of education have also undertaken a number of follow-up studies of college students.[2] The University of Toledo cross-country study of teacher education students in England and the United States provided a limited amount of information about changes in student performance, attitudes and values across the years of the course, but the interpretation of some of these findings is complicated by the inclusion of graduate teachers in the 'final-year' samples.[3] There are several unpublished theses which examine the effects of the college experience among which those of Chambers, Steel and Shipman may be particularly mentioned.[4]

In the United States there have been a very large number of studies of the effects of university education on student competences and values. In part this has been a reflection of the desire to obtain value for money, and in part a concern with the integrating function that American educational institutions must serve in a vast and diverse society. The university experience has also begun to receive attention in this country through the work of Malleson, Marris and others, and interest in this field of research will be stimulated by the current expansion of higher education.[5]

A weakness that affects almost all the studies that have been made of the impact of college on values, both in this country

---

[1] Personal communication.

[2] Rudd and Wiseman, *op. cit.*

[3] Dickson, G. E. *et al*, *The Characteristics of Teacher Education Students in the British Isles and the United States*, U.S. Office of Education Co-operative Research Project No. 2518. Toledo: Research Foundation of the University of Toledo, 1965.

[4] Shipman, *op. cit.*; Steele, P. M. *Changes in Attitude amongst College Students towards Education in Junior Schools*. Unpublished M. Ed. thesis, University of Manchester, 1958; Chambers, P. M. *Changes in Attitude towards Teacher Training*, M.Ed., University of Leicester, 1962.

[5] See the bibliography, abstracts and Register of Research issued by the Society for Research in Higher Education

and the United States, is the absence of comparison with non-college populations. Whatever changes may or may not be shown to take place in college students between the ages of eighteen and twenty-one need to be compared, not simply across the years of the course, but also with other groups of young people who have not been exposed to the environment in question, but whose values and attitudes may be assumed to have matured and changed as part of the process of growing up in an industrial society.

We have already seen how the college of education student is involved in a process of *anticipatory socialization* towards the teaching groups of which he is likely to become a member, and the influence in this respect of his experience of school practice and contact with what goes on in the schools. Where there appears to be a gap between the 'reality' of the latter and the content of the courses and advice provided by the college there is a tendency to identify with the schools; Shipman has referred to the way in which the 'role conflict potential in a situation where two parts of the role set held conflicting attitudes was solved by holding a dual set of values, one for "on stage" work in examinations, seminars, tutorials, questionnaires and so on and the other set for use "backstage" in college and in school where actual performance was necessary'.[1]

Student responses of this kind can be seen as functional behaviour in terms of the need to avoid what Merton calls *trained incapacity*—'that state of affairs in which one's abilities function as inadequacies or blind spots. Actions based upon training and skills which have been successfully applied in the past may result in inappropriate responses under changed conditions. An inadequate flexibility in the application of skills, will, in a changing milieu, result in more or less serious maladjustments.'[2] The perceptual load for the beginning teacher is a heavy one, and it is to be expected that students will favour methods that 'work', and are relatively uncomplicated, over those that demand a greater range of teaching skills and a sensitivity to class and individual feedback that they may not yet possess. In the words of another observer, 'From the second-year practice onwards,

[1] Shipman, *op. cit.*, p. 268.
[2] Merton, R. K. *Social Theory and Social Structure*. New York: Free Press, 1957, p. 198.

the processes of anticipatory socialization to the norms of the local teacher is accelerating, and it becomes easier and easier to treat the "nonsense" talked in college as merely something to satisfy an examiner'.[1]

[1] Watts, G. Unpublished term paper, college of education staff course in Sociology of Education, University of Oxford Institute of Education, 1966.

THE VALUES OF TEACHER
EDUCATION

It is clear that any attempt to describe and analyse the values to which educators of teachers subscribe, and which permeate the culture of the colleges and the types of influence which they bring to bear upon students, must do less than justice to the views and attitudes of the 5,000 men and women who teach in the colleges and those outside who administer and help to determine teacher-training policy. For example, it is doubtful if the articles published in *Education for Teaching* are representative in this sense—or that, if a referendum were held, there would be 100 per cent or even sometimes majority support for the resolutions and decisions of the lecturers' professional bodies. Short of systematic enquiry in depth among large numbers of college teachers it is very difficult to establish what are the dominant values; without careful institutional studies it is impossible to state how these values are represented in action; and without much more thoroughgoing and sophisticated follow-up studies than have been undertaken to date it is difficult to say what effects the value systems of the colleges have upon the development of students and the manner in which they work in the schools. On all these issues we have sometimes to be content with insights, hunches, impressions and partial bits of evidence. But as Boulding and others have pointed out, an image does not need to be empirically based to function effectively in terms of its influence on behaviour.[1] The stimulus 'college of education' and 'teacher training' call up certain images in our minds that

[1] Boulding, K. *The Image*. New York: Harper, 1962.

are only partially empirical, but which are none the less effective in providing a fact-and-value context for our perceptions and decision-making. That this is so provides the rationale for going ahead in this chapter with a discussion that at best can only claim to map out certain areas within which subsequent study might be undertaken and to indicate some of the historical and social foundations for some of the value orientations of those concerned with teacher education.

As a basis for this discussion we can propose following Parsons' three levels of analysis.[1]

At the most general level, teacher education represents a sub-culture within the wider society, characterized by certain complex ways of acting and behaving that owe much to history and to relations with other institutionalized social and educational processes. This sub-culture is characterized by a symbol system in terms of which, at the second level, role behaviour is oriented and, at the third, individual personality is adapted. It is possible, therefore, for purposes of analysis, to discuss the values of teacher education at the levels of culture, social system, and individual personality, although in practice these are related in a complex pattern of interaction, whereby changes at any one level can bring about substantial shifts at the other two. For example, we can expect that a substantial increase in the number of students recruited with good grades in two or three 'A' levels, or in the proportion of staff with high-level academic qualifications, could bring about changes in the culture and the symbol system of teacher education which would then act as a means of control for the value orientations of other participants. The lack of emprical information is particularly noticeable at the social system and personality levels; the culture is easier to discuss, for we have available books, prospectuses, course requirements and policy statements, but we do not have much to go on when it comes to examining the extent to which the symbol system that these reflect is important in influencing action systems within individual colleges, or in shaping the individual student's value orientations to his future task or the way in which he performs it.

[1] Parsons, T. and Shils E. (eds.) *Toward a Theory of Social Action.* New York: Harper, 1961.

THE VALUES OF TEACHER EDUCATION

Values of the early Colleges

The dominant value systems of the early colleges took their colour from the society which they served and the particular position they occupied within it. A former president of the A.T.C.D.E. summed up the effects of this in the following terms:

'Most English institutions draw strength and inspiration from their history, which speaks to them of fundamental ideas. But the training college must forget its past, if it is to meet the needs of today. It was born in poverty–material poverty, intellectual poverty and social poverty.'[1]

Teacher training was part of the provision for elementary education–the inspectors' reports on the colleges were published in the same volumes that contained their reports on elementary schools; there were few contacts between the colleges and other educational institutions apart from these schools, and little chance of the student experiencing the liberalizing influence of secondary school or university. As we have seen, it was not part of the functions of the colleges to promote or encourage educational or social mobility–their role was limited and utilitarian, and during the era of the revised code and payment by results after 1861 became even more so. Until the beginning of the twentieth century nearly all the colleges were provided by denominational bodies, whose teaching occupied an important place in the content of the courses and strongly influenced the character of the residential life. What Jean Floud has called the 'missionary spirit' was encouraged.[2] As future teachers, charged with the education of the unlettered proletariat, students needed to acquire not only the intellectual knowledge and the class management skills that would enable them to bring about conditions of mass literacy, but also the capacity to gentle the masses, to refine taste, modify excess and strengthen the social controls that would prevent literacy and the perception of better things from spilling over into social discontent and refractoriness. Thus the education of teachers always trod a narrow path between, on the one hand, the demands upon teachers as

[1] Dimond, D. 'The Historical Background' in *Colleges of Education for Teaching*. London: A.T.C.D.E., 1960, p. 15.
[2] Floud, J. E. 'Teaching in the Affluent Society', *op. cit.*

273

agents of social and personal betterment, and on the other, the need to prevent their alienation from their own backgrounds and that of their pupils; unlimited horizons in the colleges might create the same discontent that must be prevented at all costs in the schools. Today the social situation has changed, but the task that the teachers need to perform has still a good deal in common with that of the nineteenth century. In so far as the role of the school includes maintaining some degree of social cohesion, no society, however pluralistic, can afford to remain indifferent to the influence that the teacher exerts, and thus to the training for this task that she receives. From their beginnings, institutions for training teachers have been subjected to the pressures of central authority. As we have seen, the notion of a state normal school foundered on the rocks of denominationalism, but in a society with an established church, where at the time secular and sacerdotal values were virtually indistinguishable, there was no great risk (and considerable financial and administrative advantage) in leaving teacher education in private hands, especially when, through the grant and examination system, close surveillance could be maintained. At the present time, although many of the formal activities of the state in respect of the licensing of the teachers and the approval of courses have been taken over by the universities, the central authority still maintains a substantial reserve of power. This is mainly exercised in quantitative spheres, but the need for the colleges to be responsive to social need, used to justify their remaining in the hands of the local authorities rather than taking their place in the autonomous sphere implies a degree of potential influence, if not of day-to-day control, on the part of the central government that goes beyond the adjustment of demand and supply.

If the teacher is an agent of social cohesion, aiding the process of influence by means of which compliance and commitment to certain fundamental values on the part of the entire population is achieved, it follows that in his training there must be a parallel concern with securing a cognitive and affective identification with appropriate social and educational values rather than a mere intellectual recognition of their legitimacy. In subsequent sections of this chapter an attempt will be made to show how this concern permeates not only the social but also the more strictly educational value orientations of the culture of teacher education. There are signs, however, that it is only partially successful in influencing role behaviour and personality formation.

'Child-Centredness'

One of the major concerns of the colleges is to secure the student's commitment to the task of the teacher, to get him to see his future role as not just a job but as a vocation, demanding more of him than mere compliance with instructions and a willingness to work from nine to four. By these means the teacher can be made to assume responsibility for the socialization of the child rather than simply his instruction. A diffuse commitment of this kind is best secured if the teacher's task is not defined in a functionally specific manner, as the communication of a certain amount of knowledge and skill, but in terms of relationships between teachers and pupils; in the jargon of the trade, as a child-centred rather than as a subject-centred activity. In Parsons categories, the teacher's position is defined towards the right-hand side of the dichotomous pattern variable 'specificity–diffuseness'.[1] This has implications at the level of culture, social system and role behaviour, and personality. Any lack of structure and intellectual weaknesses in the college course can be seen as not so much a consequence of the intellectual limitations of students and the poor quality of staff as a reflection of the way in which the future teacher's task is defined. A child-centred education implies a person-centred training. Langeveld has referred to the way in which

'The teacher from the training college is an active schoolmaster without academic pretentions, and is therefore, to a much greater extent, a professional schoolmaster and much less a graduate in exile. The secondary schoolteacher is often caught out in his own self-evaluation between school and university and not really at home in either. The training college teacher, on the other hand, is anchored from two sides to a double milieu, the elementary school and the training college. It is precisely on account of this firm anchoring that the training

---

[1] Parsons *et al, op. cit.*

college with all its restrictions inevitably gives better training for teaching than a university'.[1]

To invoke the remainder of Parsons' dichotomous pattern variables, the university academic department is characterized by value orientations of affective neutrality, self-orientation, universalism, achievement and specificity. The graduate teacher's role expectations and personality dispositions, influenced to a greater or lesser degree by the culture within which these values are symbolized, are reflected in his subsequent classroom behaviour and attitudes. As Jackson and Marsden, Stevens, Taylor and Musgrove and others have shown, the graduate teacher tends to define his task a good deal more narrowly than his college-trained counterpart.[2] This can cause difficulties for the university department of education, the culture of which may reflect elements of both diffuseness and specificity.

The strength of the values to which we have referred in the culture of teacher education is well illustrated by the decision of the A.T.C.D.E. in its evidence to the Committee on Higher Education not to recommend the creation of liberal arts colleges on the basis of existing training college foundations, but instead to propose the superficially less attractive inter-professional idea. The reasoning behind the proposal was explained by Tibble in oral evidence to the Committee.

'. . . we tried to see the underlying principles in training college work, and how they have developed, particularly in recent years; this brought us to the conclusion that, in general, the training college is providing a liberal education round a vocational core, which has links with other vocations which have to do with human relations, with people whose job is mainly concerned with other people, either children or older people. We felt that if we were able to preserve the character of the colleges, and indeed extend it along its own line of development, it could well include such other people as came into this general vocational category. We also concluded that if the work of the training

[1] Langeveld M. J. 'The Psychology of Teachers and the Teaching Profession', *The Education and Training of Teachers* (The Year Book of Education, 1963). London: Evans, 1963.

[2] Jackson, B. and Marsden, D. *Education and the Working Class.* London: Routledge, 1962.

colleges were put into another kind of institution, with entirely different objectives, it might lose this essential and fundamental character. . . .'[1]

The literature of teacher education is replete with statements that emphasize this value orientation, and it is unnecessary to quote them extensively here.[2] Some evidence of the effect that such an orientation has upon students' need dispositions can be gathered from the comparative study of British and American teacher-education students made by Dickson and associates during 1964–5.[3] Using the Ryans teachers' characteristics index and the Minnesota teacher attitude inventory, Dickson showed that British college of education students preparing for work in primary schools had significantly higher scores than their American counterparts in respect of child-centredness, and that this held good for each of the three-year groups studied. British students preparing for secondary work showed somewhat less child-centred scores than their primary colleagues in this country, but still scored higher than both the elementary and secondary students in the United States. Whereas the child-centredness of college of education primary students changed little during the three years of the course, that of the secondary students declined somewhat between the first and third years, possibly owing to the addition of a graduate group in the third-year sample.[4]

These findings agree with those of Shipman who, using scales of his own devising, found that although 'students held very progressive views while in college, regardless of whether they were primary or secondary', a follow-up study of former students in their first appointments found that 'they had moved in the traditional direction to hold identical views to the staff of the type of school in which they were teaching'.[5]

[1] *Higher Education*, Report of the Committee on Higher Education, Minutes of Evidence, Volume A. London: H.M.S.O., p. 192.

[2] See *The Study of Education in Colleges of Education for Teaching*. London: A.T.C.D.E., 1962, for a succinct statement of this position.

[3] Dickson, G. E. *et al. The Characteristics of Teacher Education Students in the British Isles and in the United States*. Toledo, Ohio: Research Institute of the University of Toledo, 1966 (U.S. Office of Education Comparative Research Project No. 2518).

[4] For an extensive discussion and critique of these measures see the contribution by Getzels and Jackson in Gage, N. *Handbook of Research on Teaching*. Chicago: Rand McNally, 1965.   [5] Shipman, *op. cit.*, p. 77.

The Role of Intellect

The symbol system that supports child-centredness and diffuseness of value orientation and role expectation has implications
for the valuation of intellect and the intellectual. Whilst intellect
is highly valued in the teacher-education culture, it is also
regarded with a certain amount of suspicion. This shows itself
in a variety of ways. Continuing to use Parsons' terminology,
there is a tendency in the college to value expressive rather than
instrumental action, being rather than becoming. Some of the
justification for this attitude stems from the ideology of progress-
sive education, with its emphasis upon the educational process
as a part of life rather than as a preparation for life and its
criticism of the fragmentation that the traditional subject divisions imply. This attitude complex has been well described by
Hofstadter:

'Intellect is pitted against feeling, on the ground that it is
somehow inconsistent with warm emotion. It is pitted against
character, because it is widely believed that intellect stands for
mere cleverness, which transmutes easily into the sly or the
diabolical. It is pitted against practicality, since theory is held
to be opposed to practice, and the "purely" theoretical mind is
so much disesteemed. It is pitted against democracy, since
intellect is thought to be a form of distinction that defies egalitarianism.'[1]

The suspicion of intellect that is part of the culture of teacher
education has led to a high value being put upon attempts to
'integrate' and 'synthesize' subject knowledge into new combinations. Thus a lecturer in Education, discussing the organization of the education course, makes the following points:

'To many tutors who have devoted many years to the task
of helping young people to deserve respect as teachers rather
than as examinees, it is disturbing to hear or read arguments
based on analogies with medical training or specialized university courses . . . it takes the fusion of many kinds of knowledge to
produce the wisdom we want in teachers, and wisdom is not
born at one birth but at many. It is where the 'ologies cross and
recross with each other, and with experience, in the study of

[1] Hofstadter R. *Anti-intellectualism in American Life.* London: Cape, 1964,
p. 46.

Education (where psychology comes to grips with philosophy, or methodology with sociology, in the assessment of a practical situation) that significant learning may take place. For this reason, even at the risk of being labelled as amateurs, Education tutors ought to venture into many fields to attempt a synthesis, rather than parcel out the Education course to a collection of "experts". . . .'[1]

Along with such attitudes as these to intellect and the systematic study of existing disciplines there goes an interest in 'great issues', in the 'fundamental goals of life' that reflects the earlier religious foundation of the colleges and is part of the socializing process whereby students are brought up against their social and moral responsibilities. Only a minority of college staff seem to be deeply concerned about such issues, but they have been influential in the journals and in the counsels of the professional associations. Statements such as the following are illustrative of such concern.

'. . . ways are open for intelligent modern people to achieve levels of insight which give meaning and dynamic to life, and which are integral to the growth of wholeness in persons, and to creative relationships between persons. For the educators of educators who are serious about life, and for whom the old landmarks have disappeared, there is the search for the timeless and living truth, which could enlighten and interpenetrate every aspect of our personal, social, national and international life.'[2]

This element of hortatory transcendentalism is a feature of a good deal of the discussions that go on about teacher education in journals, at conferences, courses and professional meetings and, to a much lesser extent, in staff common rooms. Edwards and Carroll suggest that the effect of such discussions is that 'everything becomes etherealized, the particular becomes general, the real becomes transcendental, the concrete becomes immaterial.'[3]

An awareness of the limitations and potential dangers of a

[1] *Education for Teaching*, November 1960, p. 36. (Correspondence.)
[2] Editorial 'Status, Responsibility and Insight', *Education for Teaching*, 1961 November.
[3] Edwards, P. and Carroll, D. R. 'The Godforsaken Curriculum: A reply to Dr. Henderson', *Education for Teaching*, 1960 February, p. 27.

narrowly intellectual approach easily spills over into a suspicion of the institutions where intellect is most clearly institutionalized —the universities. Relations between the individual colleges and the universities have often been cordial, and there has been general acceptance on the part of the latter for the Robbins Committee proposals regarding the setting up of a Bachelor of Education degree. It is clear, however, that the colleges are by no means uncritical about what they take to be the ethos of university studies, and do not always accept university criteria of scholarship and competence as relevant to the task of the teacher. Although it can be argued that the rational/scientific procedures characteristic of the academic symbol system constitute only one way of perceiving reality, and that aesthetic, affective and intuitive modes of perception are equally valid in this respect, this is not usually the ground for rejection of what is taken to be the university approach. Bibby has suggested that

'...in considering the future relationships between the teachers' colleges and the universities, we should be unwise to look on the former as mere supplicants at the superior feet of the latter. We should be asking ourselves, not only "what can the colleges gain from the universities?", but also "what can the universities gain from the colleges?".'[1]

If certain of the values discussed in this chapter tend to be characteristic of the dominant culture of teacher education, and are not necessarily institutionalized in the role behaviour and personalities of the rank-and-file staff and students, an attitude of wariness towards the claims of the university is probably distributed in reverse proportions. The reasons for this are clear enough. The universities set the scene of higher education in this country, and teacher education has only very recently come to be fully accepted within their sphere. Over half the women staff of the colleges and just over a third of the men are nongraduates and may have a certain sense of inferiority in the face of the status association that university studies possess. Many of the better-qualified staff are university teachers *manqué*, and a substantial proportion of the more able students originally wanted to go to university. Implicit or explicit nonrecognition by the institutions in which they would like to

[1] Bibby, C. 'The Universities and Teachers' Colleges', *Universities Quarterly*, 1960, p. 242.

have worked or studied does little to endear them to the images of these institutions. What Festinger has called *cognitive dissonance*, whereby decisions and choices (in this case forced choices) are legitimized by the devaluation of the previous alternative, may help to explain the attitude sometimes taken by students and staff.[1] On all these grounds it would be right to expect a measure of tension in the relationships between teacher education and the universities. To a certain extent, the colleges stand outside the market of educational and social success and status distribution in which the universities have increasingly come to participate. The demands made upon their alumni to subordinate material prosperity and gain to the interpersonal satisfaction of classroom and school places them in a non-competitive position as far as the fruits of higher education as a whole are concerned; there are many parallels between their situation and that of the secondary modern schools during the early post-war years, which were presumed to 'contract out' from the competitive-sucess system in favour of deeper and more lasting satisfactions.

Culture and Consensus

We have seen that the culture of teacher education incorporates value orientations that stress the role of the teacher as an agent of social cohesion, rather than simply as an instructor, and that this stress is strongest with respect to the preparation of teachers for the youngest children and non-academic adolescents. In addition to orientations towards relational and child-centred concepts of education and affective and expressive rather than intellectual and instrumental modes of interpersonal discourse, this culture also embodies orientations towards social change, the content of which repay examination. In advanced industrialized societies, where universal literacy has already been achieved, the effects of the work of the teacher on social change are much more complex and indirect than elsewhere. The teachers' attitudes may be the least of it. At the one level there are a whole series of questions about demand and supply of teachers of particular subjects, such as Science and Mathematics,

[1] Festinger, L. *A Theory of Cognitive Dissonance.* Evanston, Ill.: Row, Peterson, 1957.

and the extent to which their special knowledge is used to produce larger numbers of computer programmers and technolo-
gists who are the instrumental agents of economic and industrial
growth. At another level there are questions regarding the
effects of teachers' decisions about individual educability or
differing patterns of internal organization on the supply of
talent available in society, or the effect of implicit or explicit
rejection upon social behaviour and deviance.[1] Such questions
are a good deal more manageable than those relating to the
way in which the teacher's values and social attitudes influence
his relationship with pupils and the development of attitudes
towards social change among the population as a whole. Educators of teachers commonly make the assumption that the
teacher exerts a direct influence upon such social attitudes, and
this provides the rationale for a great deal of the overt and
covert moral education that goes on in the colleges and for some
of the work that is done in psychology and social studies.

There is a strong vein of social criticism present in the literature of teacher education, largely apolitical in character and
much affected by moral and religious overtones. Articles in
Education for Teaching abound with references to the 'spiritual
crisis of our age', 'the deterioration of standards in our societies
of the west', the widespread licence and the meagreness and
spurious nature of much of our cultural life. A textbook entitled
Education and Social Purpose provides a predictable list of 'problems'.

'A complete survey of the many problems in contemporary
Britain which concern the educator is impossible. The following,
therefore, have been selected for consideration; mass media,
the dehumanization of man by his own inventions, the decline
of religion, internationalism, the increasing importance of
science and technology, and the welfare state.'[2]

The critical challenge to existing social arrangements that
discussion on these topics arouses is unlikely to threaten the
stability of society or topple the government. The bulk of the

[1] See Holt, J. *Why Children Fail*. London: Pitman, 1964; Hickerson, N.
Education for Alienation. Englewood Cliffs, N.J.: Prentice Hall, 1966;
Fyvel, T. R. *The Insecure Offenders*. London: Penguin Books, 1961.

[2] Garforth, F. W. *Education and Social Purpose*. London: Oldbourne, 1962,
p. 53.

criticism that such value orientations embody is not directed at the major structural and economic features of society—the class system, the effects of the division of labour and industrialization on the distribution of income and such problems, but at the less significant and peripheral aspects of the working of these larger structures—the 'waste makers', the 'hidden persuaders', the 'status seekers', and the 'pyramid climbers', of society. Where such criticism tries to go farther, it becomes even less relevant to the major social issues and lapses into a thorough-going rejection of all the values that 'affluence' is alleged to impose.

The desire for the discovery of 'new social purpose' is one of the minor but important features of the culture of teacher education. Such a purpose, it is hoped, will transcend the vulgar materialism of the present day, replacing the competitive thrust of a modern, industrialized society with co-operative and kindlier impulses, and an opportunity for the worth of an individual to be recognized whatever thē nature of the contribution he makes.[1] This notion is important for the way in which it demonstrates the implicit assumptions of a consensus model of society on the part of many of those participating in teacher education—even when they do not proceed beyond this to the broader implications of 'social purpose'.[2] The assumption of structural/functional interconnections within society places upon the schools the task of securing a commitment to a central core of values for the maintenance of social integration; for those who adopt a conflict model the problem is less important.[3] Madge observes, in terms of the latter position, that in so far as modern industrialized societies have a 'common value system' it is at least as much of a framework of thought within which disagreement can take place.[4]

Associated with the value orientations to which reference has already been made there often goes a nostalgia for the sense of

[1] See Editorial, *Education for Teaching*, 1961 November, *op. cit.*; Martin, P. W. 'Education for What?', *Education for Teaching*, 1962 May, p. 4.

[2] For a discussion of the difference between conflict and consensus models see Rex, J. *Key Problems of Sociological Theory*. London: Routledge, 1961.

[3] Hoyle, E. 'The Elite Concept in Karl Mannheim's Sociology of Education', *Sociological Review*, 12:1, March 1964.

[4] Madge, C. *Society in the Mind*. London: Faber, 1964, p. 104.

community that it is alleged has been lost as a result of industrialization and massification, and which the internal social arrangements of the colleges are often intended to recapture; great emphasis is placed upon the educational effects of residence, as it has been since the early days of the colleges. The Report of the Board of Education for 1913 includes a number of accounts of college life by men and women who had been students during the seventies and eighties of the preceding century; whatever criticisms they have of the intellectual fare or the restrictive regime they are unanimous in approving the opportunities for fellowship and close personal relationships that the residential community provided. A large number of present-day colleges have flourishing old students' associations, which hold annual reunions and continue to attract the allegiance of many of those who qualified half a century or more ago.

Through loyalty to the group and what it represents the student can be inducted into the normative commitments that legitimize his teaching work, and there is thus a need for the residential community to bring together both senior and junior members, staff and students, if these induction processes are to be facilitated. It is claimed that through such interpersonal contacts the student is able to learn the values and forms of behaviour that are appropriate for responsible living in the wider world, and to gain insight into the way in which these may be communicated to his future pupils. Elvin has expressed a caution in this respect that is worth quoting:

'Complete socialization of the young within the norms of one given society may be more dangerous, if other societies will eventually have to be encountered, than perpetual exposure to frictions that enforce reciprocal adaptations. For this reason I should be suspicious of any college community life that brought too much pressure to bear in the direction of *esprit de corps* or college spirit or social conformity or whatever it may be called . . . this may inhibit individual growth rather than promote it and may encourage identification with a small and rather special community at the expense of the development of larger loyalties later on.'[1]

Few colleges now have the type of inclusive and inward-

[1] Elvin, H. L. 'From College to Community', *Education for Teaching*, 1959, p. 56.

looking social life to which Elvin refers, and their increasing size, the diversification of residential provision, crowding up and fuller plant utilization are all making it very difficult to preserve the sense of community that was one of their former strengths. Increasing pluralism and greater variety of groups with widely differing values may, on the other hand, bring compensating advantages that are more relevant to the conditions of the contemporary world than the former arrangements. Some attempt is still being made to preserve the advantages of interpersonal contact through the use of appropriate teaching units. Hanko describes an intergroup technique in which two sets of students are given study tasks that require regular contact between them and a final presentation of their findings to the other set. The tutor does not instruct but observes and acts as a consultant to both groups. The sets establish a variety of modes of communication–delegates to each other's rooms, intergroup meetings, written communications, and so on, and are encouraged to analyse their reactions to the faster or slower progress of the other group, to authority and to 'withheld acknowledgement of goodwill'. The technique has much in common with the intergroup exercises that form part of the courses on interpersonal and intergroup relations originated by the Tavistock Institute of Human Relations.[1] The results of the term's task in the case of the two groups discussed by Hanko were 'a successful presentation on the college stage of a series of five improvised scenes on adolescence to highlight the findings of their term's study' and 'a well-designed tape recording of the group dramatizing relevant excerpts of modern plays, poems and prose passages on adolescent and adult relationships, with connecting taped commentary and cyclostyled notes'.[2] It is claimed that the intergroup exercise permits the study of Education as an intellectual discipline and the exploration of intergroup problems of relationship. Whatever such efforts may accomplish by way of intellectual development and understanding, it is clear that they are of a piece with other features of the work and life of the colleges that derive from dominant value orientations within the culture of teacher education, and which are designed to

[1] Rice, A. K. *Learning for Leadership*. London: Tavistock, 1965.
[2] Hanko, G. 'Intergroup projects in teacher training', *Education for Teaching*, May 1964, p. 43.

create socially appropriate role expectations and need dispositions in the future teacher. The stress upon the interpersonal,
the intuitive and the intangible, the community and the group,
the criticism of 'culture' rather than social structure are all such
as to strengthen the teacher's capacity for socializing the child
within a framework of social attitudes and assumptions that
value cohesion rather than conflict, loyalty rather than dis-
engagement and stability rather than change.

Moral Education and Commitment

Parsons defines morals as 'diffuse patterns of value orientation
[that] define and integrate whole systems of action . . . they are
ways of combining all the other ingredients of action, or recipes
for the arrangement of the elements or aspects that make up
orientations.'[1] Such a definition is appropriate to the emphases
of the memorandum on moral values sent to principals of training colleges in October 1961 by the then Minister of Education,
Sir David Eccles. The Minister suggested that an attitude of
'neutrality towards absolute values' was beginning to be ack-
nowledged as the failure which the churches had predicted it
would be. Large numbers of young people 'whose experience
has been gained among the tensions of the cold war' were
making clear their desire to find firmer moral principles. The
will was growing to define more clearly the ends of life. But,
despite all this, the family, 'the most powerful single influence
on a child's character', found itself without the 'firm convictions
which must be the basis of the protection from evil which the
child needs', thus lending additional importance to the work of
the school in shaping and upholding the ends which society
should pursue. With the coming of the three-year course and
the expansion in the number of college places the Minister was
interested in hearing from principals about 'the extent to which
students will now have more time to hear, read and think about
morals and religion'.[2]

The memorandum underlines the demands that society
makes upon the teacher as an agent of social integration, and
emphasizes the responsibility of the colleges to provide him with

[1] Parsons, T. and Shils, E., *op. cit.*, p. 170.
[2] *Education for Teaching*, November 1961.

appropriate training for this purpose. At the same time it provides an interesting example of the effect of what Merton has called the displacement of goals. This phrase refers to the process whereby rules and procedures designed to achieve certain ends tend to be transferred into ends in themselves. Instrumental values become terminal values.[1] In this case it almost seems as if a reversal of goals has taken place; 'right conduct', hitherto instrumental in terms of wider religious goals, has become the terminal value, towards which the consideration of moral and religious issues is supposed to contribute. The digest of the principals' replies to the Minister's invitation, and the commentary upon these prepared by a member of the inspectorate, provides an interesting series of insights into how the overall educational role of the colleges is perceived.

Writing of the Victorian public schools, Wilkinson refers to the way in which these schools managed to combine intensive loyalty-indoctrination with creative intelligence by keeping these in two quite separate spheres of school life; moral education was largely confined to the extra-curricular sphere, to house life and the playing field. 'The latter was ruled by etiquette; the classroom by reason . . . there was a place for reason and a separate place for loyal emotion.'[2] At the present time this would fit the situation of the universities, in which the disinterested pursuit of truth in the department lecture room or laboratory is complemented by the implicit moral education of college or hall of residence. Wilkinson goes on to suggest that a second method of moral education was to encourage the pupil to associate loyalty-indoctrination and moral education with reason, however unquestioned and irrational the basis of his loyalty remained. It is clear that the interpenetration of moral education and academic study in the colleges of education is intended to go a good deal farther than this, a situation justified by the fact that the task of the college is to provide a professional rather than simply a personal education.

Reference has already been made to the importance of community and group as agents of the type of values that are

[1] Merton, R. K. *Social Theory and Social Structure*. New York: Free Press, 1957.
[2] Wilkinson, R. *The Prefects*. London: Oxford University Press, 1964, p. 200.

stressed within the culture of teacher education. Implicit in a great deal of what has been said about the moral impact of the group is the view that exploration of 'significant' issues in the group setting will somehow provide a substitute for the didactic moral teaching and authoritarianism of an earlier period. This comes out very clearly in an editorial in *Education for Teaching* that was published alongside the Minister's memorandum on moral values.

'Sir David is well aware that the traditional strongholds of morals and religion that were erstwhile didactically taught with conviction and authority have broken down . . . yet authoritarianism in education is slowly but surely being replaced by a quality of relationship which makes joint exploration between tutor and taught a reasonable possibility for those who have the courage to undertake it. This is an aspect of "counselling" which is receiving much attention among groups in our colleges who are exploring the dynamics of human relationships.'[1]

The language of statements in this genre is replete with terms such as synthesis, integration, consensus and wholeness. It is difficult, however, to discover from these sources the particular *content* of the beliefs, attitudes and values in terms of which the lecturer and the student are urged to become committed. Little attention has been paid to the possibly negative effect that group participation may have on an individual's standards, and there is no attempt to examine the extensive, if somewhat contradictory, empirical evidence that is available regarding the impact of college life upon values and attitudes.[2]

Although it is not within the compass of this book to examine the logical and philosophical issues that are raised by the use of a term such as 'counselling' in this context, attention can at least be drawn to the need for a thorough examination of such issues. The heavy stress on 'discussion methods' that is found among educators of teachers is similar in certain respects to the hopeful 'abstractionism' that Dearden has seen as characteristic of some proponents of discovery methods in primary and secondary education. By discussion of problems, concrete instances, per-

[1] Editorial, *Education for Teaching*, November 1961, *op. cit.*
[2] For example, Clark, B. *Educating the Expert Society.* San Fransisco: Chander, 1962; Jacob, P. E. *Changing Values in College.* New York: 1957; Goldsen, R. K. *et al. What College Students Think.* Princeton, 1960.

sonal experiences and the like, it is presumably hoped that students will eventually arrive at an understanding of certain moral concepts and categories. The tutor stands back from this process, carefully avoiding any attempt to influence the outcome. Yet as Dearden states

'. . . without possession of our [i.e. the teachers'] concepts in the first place, it makes no sense to talk of examples or models, because an example, or a model, or an instance, or a feature, is always an example, model, instance or feature *of* something, and unless you know what follows this "of" you logically cannot perceive the things *as* an example, model and so on'.[1]

But in practice, of course, the tutor does not stand back completely from the discussion. Sometimes he quite explicitly guides and directs it, making suggestions here, pointing out consequences there, asking questions and probing responses. What is all-important in evaluating the moral legitimacy of this activity is the spirit and manner in which this guidance and direction is supplied. The worrying feature of some of the techniques that are suggested is that these may be successful in overcoming student resistance, of getting something across, without the student being fully aware of what is happening. As such, these techniques have an element of manipulation within them that is difficult to justify in terms of the requirements of rationality that should permeate the work of institutions of higher education.

Any adequate theory of teaching must reckon with the fact that what the teacher communicates to the student is always more than mere information or technique. In addition to the message, to what is said and what is demonstrated, there is always, in the communication theorist's terms, the background 'noise' of the teacher's values and predispositions and style and of the institutional structure and processes within which teaching and learning take place.[2] Educational institutions vary to the extent to which the relationships between message and noise are recognized and articulated, and this variation can usefully be represented as a continuum between what have

[1] Dearden, R. F. 'Instruction and Learning by Discovery' in Peters, R. S. *The Concept of Education*. London: Routledge, 1967, p. 147.

[2] Henry, J. *Culture Against Man*. New York: Random House, 1963; Cherry, C. *On Human Communication*. Cambridge, Mass.: Massachusetts Institute of Technology Press, 1957.

been called *inducting* and *non-inducting* institutions.[1] At the latter
end of this continuum the emphasis is on the technical aspects of
socialization – on the communication of certain facts and information, skills and techniques, the adequacy of the student's
grasp of which can be tested and certified. Such other effects
that may accrue from these processes are fortuitous, unpredic-
ted and unsupported by any preliminary consensus of goals on
the part of the authorities concerned.

Since the primacy of education of all kinds for the maintenance of social structure tends to receive prominence at times
of rapid social and moral change, and the organizational needs
of educational institutions themselves tend to generate a measure of moral concern, it is difficult to find examples of institutions performing purely technical, non-inducting functions.
Vocationally oriented adult schools and some technical colleges,
which usually have a large, itinerant and instrumentally
minded clientele, are perhaps the clearest cases at the present
time.

At the opposite extreme of the continuum are those institutions that seek to induct the individual into a way of life that
amounts to much more than the ability to exercise a technique
or to display a grasp of a particular range of information. Such
institutions exercise their technical functions within an explicit
framework of moral rules and procedures, for which there exists
systematic ideological support. Doctrinally committed theological colleges and some types of private and preparatory schools
are obvious examples. The ideological basis for the work of such
institutions sometimes comes to affect everything that goes on
within them, even the objective, rational teaching of 'subjects' –
Fichter quotes the case of a teacher in a Catholic school who
gave such problems to her Mathematics classes as 'If it takes
forty thousand priests and a hundred and forty thousand sisters
to care for forty million Catholics in the United States, how many
more priests and sisters will be needed to convert and care for
the hundred million non-Catholics in the United States?'[2]
More generally, however, there is something of a split between

[1] Bidwell, C. E. and Vreeland, R. S. 'College Education and Moral
Orientations', *Administrative Science Quarterly*, 1963, p. 166.

[2] Fichter, J. H. *Parochial School*. Notre Dame Ind.: University of Notre
Dame Press, 1958 (Anchor Books Edition, p. 95).

THE VALUES OF TEACHER EDUCATION

the spirit of critical rationality that permeates much of the actual teaching, and the range of formal and informal influences, pressures and demands that may be exerted outside the classroom and in the general social life of the school. Wilkinson has documented this split with respect to the English public schools in the nineteenth century, and in the university there is ample evidence of the way in which departmental and teaching functions are largely technical and rational, whilst the college and hall of residence combine the provision of living accommodation with both manifest and latent forms of moral influence.[1]

An important aspect of the educational processes that go on within inducting institutions is the pressure towards the non-rational, the tendency to invoke any and every means that may help to bring the individual within the overall framework of expectation and behaviour that constitutes the appropriate way of life. So the individual is not merely taught, but by means of small-group interaction, relationships with staff, the impact of the residential community, and discussions within the Education and Divinity courses, he is brought to a recognition of the importance and the legitimacy of certain moral rules and procedures. Such influences do not qualify for the title of 'teaching', since they are not 'practised in such manner as to respect the student's intellectual integrity and capacity for independent judgement'.[2] Nor do they represent an 'initiation into the rational life, a life in which the critical quest for reasons is a dominant and integrating motive'.[3] Whether or not there is any major dissonance between the teaching activities and the other forms of influence that the institutions brings to bear will depend upon a variety of factors. In institutions where there is a considerable measure of agreement regarding both goals and procedures on the part of both staff and students, where the content and methods of teaching exist within an explicit framework of values, and where the nature of these values is obvious and apparent to both personnel and public, a low level of

[1] Wilkinson, R. *The Prefects, op. cit.*

[2] Scheffler, I. 'Philosophical Models of Teaching' in Peters, R. S. *The Concept of Education, op. cit.*, p. 120. For a critique of Scheffler's position see Cooper, J. 'Criteria for successful Teaching', *Proceedings* of the Annual Conference of the Philosophy of Education Society of Great Britain, 1966.

[3] Scheffler, I. *Conditions of Knowledge.* Chicago: Scott, Foresman, 1965, p. 107.

dissonance can be expected. Where there is a high level of value consensus on the part of the staff alone, but an obligation on the part of students to expose themselves to the socializing processes concerned, authoritarian pressures are likely to be employed to limit dissonance and obtain compliance. Although such methods may be of only short-term effect and may fail to secure the identification and commitment that induction requires, they may reduce the short-term strains that are felt within the institution itself. (An example is a secondary modern school in a 'difficult' area with an authoritarian head and staff.) In the university, the problem of dissonance may be dealt with by the virtual separation of academic and residential functions.

It follows from the argument of this chapter that dissonance within the college of education is likely to be greater than in either school or university due to a number of disparate value orientations within the culture of teacher education. In the first place, the ideological visibility of the colleges is low—except perhaps in some of the doctrinally based voluntary colleges, and in by no means all of these. There is no manifest or acquired commitment on the part of students and staff to a particular set of values or attitudes. Secondly, the functions of the colleges are perceived by students in largely instrumental terms. The course has a vocational purpose and the usefulness of what is provided is evaluated in terms of practical utility rather than as general intellectual preparation.

Thirdly, authoritarian constraint is lacking. The opportunity to exercise control over the lives and behaviour of students by the use of overt sanctions and penalties, made easier in the past by the physical isolation of some colleges, their small size, the residential pattern of staffing, the high proportion of women students and the fact that teacher training acted as an avenue of social mobility for boys and girls of humble origin who were willing to enter into a normative contract in exchange for the utilitarian social advantages of security and status—all this has now largely disappeared.

Fourthly, the content of the subject courses (with the possible exceptions of Divinity and Education in some colleges) respect the integrity of the forms of knowledge on which they are based, and are not structured in accordance with the assumed 'needs' of teachers in the classroom situation.

THE VALUES OF TEACHER EDUCATION

Fifthly, moral rather than technical functions are accorded primacy by the external agencies that legitimize the colleges' goals – the teacher is seen as a moral agent, not simply as a purveyor of knowledge and skill. There is thus a tendency to devalue the intellectual content of the college courses and to overemphasize the need for some form of implicit or explicit moral training – such an emphasis can be found in the Newsom Report, *Half our Future*, and in several of the documents which have been quoted earlier in this chapter.[1]

Finally, recruitment-based consensus on the part of staff cannot be assumed – even in some of the church colleges a substantial number of staff are being appointed who have no particular commitment to the values of the denomination concerned.

What all this amounts to is the likelihood of substantial strains within the colleges as they strive to reconcile the provision of the kinds of knowledge and skill that the student needs, if he is to be initiated into the world of rational intellect, with the kinds of value orientation and attitude that are appropriate to the social, political and moral conditions of a period of rapid change. The value systems of teacher education are likely to alter a good deal as a result of ongoing developments in the structure and organization of the system. Increasing numbers of students and a fall in the proportion in residence; the tendency to build up existing colleges rather than to establish new ones to accommodate the increased numbers, and the accompanying bureaucratization and pluralism; shifts in the production of men and women staff and living-in arrangements; the introduction of closer links with the universities via degree studies; improvements in the intellectual calibre of students; changes in the work of the teacher in the classroom; the carrying on of teacher training in technical colleges and polytechnics – all these are likely to introduce new elements into the role expectations and demands of staff, students and policy-makers, and to bring about a modification of the value system that has been discussed in this chapter.

But if change is to come it needs to be understood and as far as possible controlled, and a recognition of the weaknesses of the

[1] Central Advisory Council for Education, England, *Half our Future*. London: H.M.S.O., 1963.

procedures whereby the moral socialization of the teacher was undertaken in the past should not lead to a neglect of the very real moral function that the teacher will be called upon to exercise in the future. Until very recently there has been a tendency for the intellectual performances of both staff and students to be rated lower than the possession of certain other qualities which are believed to be relevant to the task of the teachers, and the college courses have by no means always adequately extended the more able students; in part this has been a consequence of the scope and emphasis of these courses, but it may also have rested upon the mistaken dichotomy between intellect and character that has affected the whole of educational provision in this country from primary school to university. In the nineteenth century this dichotomy can be seen in the regime of the developing public schools and in the views expressed regarding the dangers of giving the poor an education beyond their station. In the early twentieth century it found support in the widespread misinterpretation and misapplication of the doctrines of the progressive educators. In more recent years it has slowed down attempts to make university education available to larger numbers of the population, provided one of the threads of contemporary social criticism of the effects of affluence and the welfare state, and played some part in limiting the numbers of adequately trained and qualified managers and executives responsible for the promotion of economic activity. The expert and the qualified man represent a threat to traditional structures and practices and to the stability of institutionalized patterns of intergroup relationship; unsocialized, and hence irresponsible, intellect must be controlled if changes in culture and role expectation are to occur in an orderly fashion. A completely open educational system, in which qualifications obtained by correspondence or via the university of the air have equal currency with those obtained by conventional means, provides no guarantee that the qualified individuals possess the needs, dispositions and attitudes that given forms of professional activity are deemed to require, that they are capable of participating in the shared symbol system that legitimizes performances in their roles. The extent to which society exercises control over the education and training provided for the performance of particular tasks is dependent upon the saliency of these tasks within the social structure, and the extent to which socially acceptable norms and values have been internalized within some form of self-governing professional organization. In the case of teachers the saliency of the task is high, the internalization of professional norms comparatively poorly developed. In this situation it is perhaps inevitable that a substantial degree of direct and indirect control should continue to be exercised over the value orientations that are embodied in the culture of teacher education. It seems doubtful, however, if there is much to be gained from a continued emphasis upon the importance of a kind of romanticized value consensus among teachers that, given the size of the group and the pluralism of contemporary society, it must be virtually impossible to achieve. With respect to the attenuation of values that causes such grave anxiety among educators of teachers, Mannheim has stated:

'The economic system is not only far from being liable to immediate disintegration when its ideologies are undermined, but it is even in a certain sense desirable for the elasticity which is becoming a condition of its existence, that individuals should relinquish reactions which are too rigidly determined by tradition and ideological factors, in favour of an ability to adapt themselves to the pressure of socializing factors of a more purely economic kind. The developed economic system functions better when the behaviour necessary within its framework has become emptied of any idealistic motivational content. To the degree, therefore, that economic rationality permeates social life as a whole, we can observe the relaxation of ideological regimentation, documented by the fact that consciences are no longer controlled. This is the social source of the modern idea of tolerance.'[1]

To repudiate the techniques of manipulative socialization that have hitherto characterized some aspects of the training of teachers is not to restrict the teacher's task to the communication of mere facts and information, nor to deny the importance of his moral function and the need for him to be inducted into this during the course of his professional preparation. What such repudiation does imply is the need for a theory of teaching that

[1] Mannhiem, K. *Essays in the Sociology of Knowledge*, edited by P. Kecskemeti. London: Routledge, 1956, p. 246.

no longer makes arbitrary and socially inspired distinctions between intellect and character, that recognizes the moral force that inheres in the organization of academic disciplines, properly taught, and within which can be found means for the formation of appropriate attitudes, habits and dispositions in the same rational spirit of critical enquiry that inspires the whole intellectual enterprise.

BIBLIOGRAPHIES

The following are some of the major British and American bibliographies on the education of teachers.

Allen, E. A. 'Professional Training of Teachers; A review of research', *Educational Research*, V, 3, June 1963.

Cane, B. S. *Research into Teacher Education*, London, National Foundation for Educational Research, 1968.

Ellis, H. C. 'Doctoral Studies in the Education of Teachers and Administrators, 1964–65', *Journal of Teacher Education*, XVII, 3, Fall 1966. (A similar list has appeared annually in the *Journal of Teacher Education* from 1952 – between 1952 and 1957 in the Summer issue, since 1957 in the Fall issue. The list includes Canadian theses.)

Evans, K. M. 'Research on Teaching Ability', *Educational Research*, I, 3, 1959.

Evans, K. M. 'An annotated bibliography of British Research on teaching and teaching ability', *Educational Research*, IV, 1, 1961.

Gage, N. (ed.) *Handbook of Research on Teaching*, Chicago, Rand McNally, 1963.

Harap, H. 'A Review of recent developments in Teacher Education', *Journal of Teacher Education*, XVIII, 1, Spring 1967.

National Foundation for Educational Research. *A Survey of Educational Research in Great Britain – Empirical and Experimental Studies*, London, The Foundation, 1968.

BIBLIOGRAPHIES

Society for Research in Higher Education. *Register of Research into Higher Education*, London, The Society, Annual.

Taylor, W. 'Research on the Education of Teachers' in Taylor W. (ed.), *Toward a Policy for the Education of Teachers*, London, Butterworth, 1969

INDEX

INDEX

INDEX

301

INDEX